Ideology and U.S. Foreign Policy

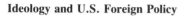

MICHAEL H. HUNT

Ideology and U.S. Foreign Policy

Yale University Press
New Haven and London

Designed by Nancy Ovedovitz and set in Times Roman type by
Rainsford Type. Printed in the United States of America by
Murray Printing Co., Westford, Mass.

Library of Congress Cataloging-in-Publication Data

Hunt, Michael H.
    Ideology and U.S. foreign policy.

    Bibliography: p.
    Includes index.
    1. United States—Foreign relations—Philosophy.
2. United States—Foreign relations. I. Title.
E183.7.H86 1987   327.73   86–15778
ISBN 0–300–03717–1 (cloth)
        0–300–04369–4 (pbk.)

The paper in this book meets the guidelines for permanence and
durability of the Committee on Production Guidelines for Book
Longevity of the Council on Library Resources.

10   9

For Heather and Dee

Contents

Illustrations

Preface

This is a little book about a big and slippery subject: the place of ideology in U.S. foreign policy. It ventures into a complicated realm where conceptual confusion often reigns. Much like imperialism and liberalism, other protean concepts frequently bandied about in serious historical and political discourse, ideology is hard to pin down. I should make clear at the outset that my own efforts to make sense of the intellectual underpinnings of foreign policy have convinced me of the value of a broad and common-sensical working definition of ideology, which I view as an interrelated set of convictions or assumptions that reduces the complexities of a particular slice of reality to easily comprehensible terms and suggests appropriate ways of dealing with that reality.

Readers will no doubt have their own widely varying and sometimes quite pronounced views on what ideology is and how it relates to policy. I have been aware from the start of the difficulties posed by this inherent complexity of my subject and the diverse preconceptions of my readers. At the end I am no less aware of those difficulties and am thoroughly convinced of the truth of Gordon Craig's observation of over a decade ago: "To establish the relationship between ideas and foreign policy is always a difficult task, and it is no accident that it has attracted so few historians."[1] But the subject is too important to be left in a state of neglect like a surly invalid relative whose justified claims to attention we honor only infrequently and even then perfunctorily.

The construction of this broad picture of U.S. foreign relations from its inception down to the present has in large measure involved assembling fragments of historical evidence and interpretation, some of it doubtless familiar to my readers, into a new pattern. The exercise was intended to provide new insights into the past and provoke fresh thinking about the present. It is in terms of those objectives that I would like this volume to be read and judged. I hope at the very least that this work, whatever its shortcomings, will inspire others to take the problem of foreign policy ideology seriously and perhaps even try their own hand at it.

The book begins with an introductory chapter on ideology, especially as it relates to U.S. foreign policy. By formulating the conceptual problem posed by ideology and offering a solution, it leads us across the border into the chaos-prone realm of U.S. foreign policy itself. Once there the reader should look to the following three chapters to impose order. They trace the origins of U.S. foreign-policy ideology, showing how it gained in coherence and appeal in the eighteenth and nineteenth centuries and how by the beginning of our century its elements had coalesced into a powerful, mutually reinforcing body of thought that had gone far toward dominating the thinking of those most concerned with foreign-policy issues. The last two chapters are intended to demonstrate that twentieth-century Americans, even in our day, have carried forward the outlook of their forebears to a much greater degree than is usually conceded. That point, once made, clears the way for some final reflections on the practical policy implications of this ideological persistence. The book concludes with a discussion of the relevant historical literature.

Readers may understand this book better if they know the impulses that inspired it and gave shape to its final form. In some measure this project has been a therapeutic exercise. It has allowed this historian to vent impatience with the characteristic tendency of Americans to ignore the past. The remarkable continuity of our thinking on basic foreign-policy issues is not sufficiently recognized. Even that part of the public most conversant with policy is captivated by the notion that the international problems we face are unprecedented. The past is largely irrelevant, so goes the common wisdom, not only to an understanding of these problems but also to the task of devising appropriately fresh solutions. To the extent that a popular conception of our foreign-policy past exists, it pictures American leaders setting aside the self-limiting and outmoded notions of an earlier era in favor of a mature pragmatism appropriate to the nation's transformed status as a global power. From that popular perspective it is hard to imagine that older attitudes might have hastened, rather than obstructed, the transformation of our international position and that those attitudes might have remained important, even fundamental, to the thinking of policymakers long after that transformation was completed.

Historians of U.S. foreign relations have unwittingly become accessories to the perpetuation of this national foreign-policy myth by reinforcing the public's fixation with the present and neglecting the role of cultural values. Increasingly absorbed in the study of the twentieth-century drama (especially two world wars and a cold war), they too have endorsed and strengthened the popular notion of a contemporary break with previous policy experience. In accounting for the supposedly novel situation the United States has come to occupy, historians have focused their attention—almost invariably in narrowly drawn studies—on changes in strategic thinking, the needs of the economic system, elite interests and influence, the role of the presidency, the workings of bureaucratic politics, and the interaction of foreign policy with domestic politics. It is time that ideology, construed in broad historical terms, received its due.

Writing this book has also allowed me to work out ideas first glimpsed in my work on U.S.–China relations but not easily pursued in that context. I had become increasingly impressed by how powerfully a sense of national mission, stereotypes about "Orientals," and a dedication to a particular path of political and economic development combined to shape the American approach to China. Particularly intriguing, I found, was the way in which the open-door idea, so intimately associated with China policy, "both drew from and fed back into the national fantasies of redemption and dominion."[2] Formulating that phrase confronted me with the fact that I had not properly explored, and was not able adequately to explain, the larger world of policy ideas. By degrees I convinced myself that establishing that general intellectual framework was worth a try.

Finally, writing this book has allowed me to put on paper some notions that my students over the last decade—at Yale, Colgate, and the University of North Carolina at Chapel Hill—have challenged me to develop. Like most Americans interested in foreign policy, they came into the classroom impressed as well as perplexed by the claims the world has made on our attention and resources, eager to understand how Americans have dealt with those claims, but unable to stand back and see how deeply rooted cultural values influenced the way we have interpreted those claims and responded to them. Trying to provide them with some perspective has proven a real education for me.

★ ★ ★

A work of this sort, marked by the breadth and temerity of its argument, is necessarily and peculiarly dependent on the aid, indulgence, and encouragement of others. As the thought of a book on the subject began to insinuate itself into my mind, Charles Grench at Yale University Press came along and provided an enthusiastic push. Since then many friends and colleagues have helped me. Robert Beisner, Dorothy Borg, John Coogan, William Dolbee, James Fetzer, Harry Harding, Thomas Hietala, Don

Higginbotham, Steven Levine, Donald Mathews, Leona and Ellis Simon, and Marilyn Young all deserve thanks for their good-natured response to my appeals for advice and for criticism of this work in one or another of its stages. I am also grateful to Linda Carl and Warren Nord at UNC, Carol Gluck at Columbia University, and Arthur Waldron at Princeton University for creating opportunities for me to try out some of the ideas developed here. Finally, my thanks go to Mary Woodall for invaluable and always patient assistance in translating my scrawl into clear copy; to Linda Stephenson, Laura Edwards, and John Beam for help during the last stages of this project; and to Otto Bohlmann for outstanding editorial guidance. I hope all who have contributed in one way or another find enough here that is fresh, persuasive, or at least provocative to feel partially recompensed.

I also owe an intellectual debt to the many scholars whose works I have drawn on. Since it would be impossible to list them all, I shall have to let my notes and my concluding essay on the historical literature serve as partial and inadequate acknowledgement. There is but one item—a slim volume on Chinese Buddhism by the late Arthur Wright—that compels mention here. Wright's demonstration of the intellectual power and elegance that a crisp synthesis could attain deeply impressed me years ago and came immediately to mind as a model at the outset of this project. Thus do the seeds that teachers sow bear strange fruit.

This work has been in several senses a family affair. Paula Hunt's critical acumen once again did much to clarify my exposition, while my daughters acted as sometime proofreaders. They also served without knowing it as a reminder of my obligations to the world they will inherit, and so this work is dedicated to them. If my efforts here make Americans a bit more self-conscious about their own thinking on international affairs and to that extent more cautious and wise in their use of power, then I shall have partially fulfilled that obligation.

1 Coming to Terms with Ideology

We can best separate appearance from the reality, the transient from the permanent, the significant from the episodic, by looking backward whenever we look forward. There is no great mystery why this should be: . . . the successive generations of men tend to face the same recurrent problems and to react to them in more or less habitual ways. —Walter Lippmann (1943)

The convictions that leaders have formed before reaching high office are the intellectual capital they will consume as long as they continue in office. —Henry Kissinger (1979)

American foreign policy has been in ferment for the past decade or more. The extended conflict in Vietnam proved unsettling for Americans, especially those whose political coming of age coincided with the height of that war. Vietnam loosened the hold of Cold War precepts shaped by Munich and Pearl Harbor, just as involvement in World War I had shaken the crusading faith of an earlier generation. One observer announced in the early 1970s that "Young America" now wanted to "cool it" in foreign policy; another proclaimed a few years later the discovery of "shifting generational paradigms."[1] Though the Reagan administration has tried to end the ferment over foreign policy by reasserting a classic Cold War outlook, academics, journalists, policymakers, and the military continue to debate the lessons of Vietnam and their implications for future U.S. policy.

The critique of U.S. policy that has developed in reaction to Vietnam and Reagan has mounted to impressive proportions. Many of the critics have been foreign-policy analysts with previous on-the-job experience and with interests as diverse as strategic planning, the international economy, the policy process, and the so-called Third World. Collectively, their work constitutes an acute and sometimes devastating attack on a policy based on false assumptions, prone to misguided activism, and plagued by high and some-

1

times hidden costs. The world has so changed in recent decades, the critics tell us, that Cold War policies are no longer appropriate. Some contend that even at the height of the Cold War American leaders profoundly misread the world, to the detriment of their own people as well as others whose destiny they sought to influence. As a group, they argue that a transformation of American policy is urgently needed and that if change is to be significant and durable, it must be accompanied by a fundamental and thorough rethinking of the premises of policy.

Anyone who reads these critics can have no doubt that the conventional wisdom handed down from the early years of the Cold War is in serious trouble, as men who once helped make policy now trumpet its excesses and inadequacies. Richard Barnet has described the consistent, active, and ultimately counterproductive hostility that cold warriors have displayed toward revolutionary nationalism.[2] Barnet's thesis has received further broad development at the hands of Melvin Gurtov and Richard Feinberg, and it has been supplemented by Robert Packenham's account of the failures of an ethnocentric approach to development pursued by the U.S. government in the 1950s and 1960s.[3] Earl Ravenal and David Calleo have examined the lamentable tendency of policymakers to undertake overseas commitments that exceed demonstrable American interests and existing American economic resources.[4] Ravenal offers what might stand as a summary of the critics' case when he calls for a more restrained American policy:

> We must recover a sense of the limits of foreign policy in a world that is no longer malleable. Foreign policy must be seen not as a lance but as a shield. It is not a vehicle for propagating our values or a pretext for projecting our fantasies, but a set of minimum conditions for preserving our vital internal processes. . . . Our primary business is to operate our unique political system, enjoy and enhance our economic activities, and repair and perfect our society.[5]

If these works calling for greater restraint have one flaw in common, it is their inadequate attention to the place of ideology in recent policy. They recognize that American leaders have been caught up in the web of ideology and have in consequence espoused mistaken policies. But they do not consider systematically the dimensions of that ideology, the roots that sustain it and may render it resistant to change, and the precise relationship it bears to policy. The difficulties the critics have had in getting a conceptual handle on this set of issues suggest that they themselves are caught up in an ideological tangle.

Two of the more perceptive recent critics illustrate the problem.[6] Ravenal calls for altering ''our basic strategic 'categories'—the deep cognitive mind-sets imbedded in our decision-making system.'' He recognizes that policy reform will require a direct challenge to the presumption ''that America's actual and proper concerns are universal.'' Reform will also compromise ''the myth of America's uniqueness as a nation and a force in the world'' in a way that may prove ''painful.'' Such national myths serve a purpose, Ravenal notes incidentally but perceptively, for they ''gloss over divisions and bind a society together.'' Moreover, Americans, who are ''used to hearing that their identity depends on a special responsibility for world order,'' may feel diminished by a shift to a policy of prudence and restraint. They may not wish ''to be told that they ought to give up their honorable pretensions and to live modestly, like other nations.''[7]

Like Ravenal, Feinberg grasps the connection between foreign-policy ideology and national morale. He acknowledges that nationalism can be a healthy force that stimulates cultural pride and social cohesion and reinforces democratic values. But for a great power nationalism also ''has a darker, more dangerous side,'' he argues, unleashing ''flashfloods of arrogance and aggressiveness that overflow into chauvinistic and rigid foreign policies.'' Policymakers will find themselves struggling in vain against ''an emotional public clamoring to project their sense of self onto the rest of the world.'' Feinberg, who seems to think of ideology in terms of strong liquor—harmless in small doses but dangerous in large—urges us to bring our ''ideological fervor'' under control. ''It is both unnecessary and often counterproductive for the United States to allow ideology to cloud its perception of events and foreign governments.'' We shall have to give up the grandiose idea that we can ''change the course of history'' and instead ''learn to enjoy our own institutions and values without feeling the need for others to duplicate them.'' Fashioning this ''new self-identity,'' Feinberg concedes, is ''our most difficult task.''[8]

The critics recognize the crucial link ideology provides between American nationalism and an assertive American foreign policy. That they do not grapple with the problem of ideology more fully is understandable. Preoccupied with current policy problems, they are hobbled by the same lack of historical perspective that characterizes the public they address. Understandable though it may be, the failure of the critics in this regard is serious nonetheless, because it minimizes a major obstacle standing in the way of their search for a new policy. Suppose, to begin with, that ideology is central, not incidental, to policymaking. Is it really possible to insulate or divorce one from the other? Suppose, moreover, that some of the central ideas in foreign policy are closely intertwined with domestic political values and arrangements, which continue to sustain them. Can those ideas be eradicated, and can fresh sources of inspiration and guidance appropriate to a policy of abnegation be found? Suppose, finally, that a major assault on those ideas proves successful but in the process shakes national self-confidence and precipitates a prolonged and vituperative debate. How dangerous would such an outcome be, and how likely is it that we would find ourselves better off than we are now?

These suppositions and the questions they raise can give no cheer to advocates of policy change, but there is wisdom (not to mention intellectual honesty) in knowing whether the critics have as their target a flimsy tent city or a great citadel, whether their opponents are a tattered, dispirited band or a formidable host determined to defend the old creed and backed by a sympathetic populace. Though such battlefield intelligence may seem inexpedient insofar as it depresses the enthusiasm of the insurgent forces at the outset, it may be indispensable to the success of the campaign. A reluctance to consider the nature of the struggle ahead—a quick, irresistible thrust or a long and trying siege—may not only diminish the prospect of success but also sow puzzlement, frustration, even defeatism in the ranks if the objective is not carried on the first try.

There is considerable evidence that this is not a hypothetical prospect, that indeed the first foray of the critics has already been turned back. Recent policymakers have proven unexpectedly obtuse. Celebrating familiar Cold War values, they have rejected the notion that the Vietnam commitment was a fundamental mistake, and neo-conservatives have urged that the United States should defend freedom around the world whatever the price. The electorate seems to like the clarion call for the nation to put aside doubts and reassume its proper role as world leader, wanting even less than do the policymakers to be saddled with a policy of caution and restraint appropriate to a complex and politically diverse world. Though many Americans would concede that recent Cold War policy has been too costly and at times ineffectual, they would not agree with the critics that the premises of that policy were flawed.

★ ★ ★

Clearly, to neglect ideology may be to omit a crucial step in setting U.S. foreign policy on a new basis. Critics preoccupied with recent policy have glimpsed the problem but hardly plumbed it. Have historians devoted to the long view on American policy done any better? The answer is an assured yes. Ideology has figured prominently in virtually all attempts to account in broad, interpretive terms for American entry into the thicket of international politics and to explain the conduct of policymakers as they followed the path deeper and deeper into the underbrush. Ideology certainly occupies a central place in what are arguably the two dominant interpretive approaches of the past thirty-five years—one associated with George Kennan and the other with William Appleman Williams.

Neither of these worthy and thoughtful interpreters, however, deals with ideology in a way that would help the policy critics out of their conceptual tangle and provide the fresh insights on the problems of U.S. policy that we seek. It would seem that historians too have become tangled up by ideology— Kennan by a conception that is superficial, even anemic, and Williams by one that is narrow and at times mechanical. Yet their work merits brief consideration, for it may help move us toward a much-needed alternative perspective on foreign-policy ideology.

George Kennan stands as a leading exponent of an approach to foreign-policy ideology that might best be labeled pejorative. His classic articulation of this approach appeared just after he had brought to a close two decades of government service, where he had ultimately distinguished himself as the father of the containment doctrine. In 1950 he took up residence at the Institute for Advanced Studies at his alma mater, Princeton. An invitation to deliver a set of lectures at the University of Chicago provided an almost immediate opportunity to sift through his own experience and apply it to the history of U.S. foreign policy. The lectures, his inaugural performance as a historian, were a great success. Published under the title *American Diplomacy, 1900–1950*,[9] the slim volume served as a bible for a Cold War generation. Frequently reprinted and still widely read and respected, it contributed significantly to shaping the view of past American foreign policy that has dominated in recent decades.

The burden of the work was that errant and inappropriate moralism and legalism defined the American approach to international affairs. By moralism Kennan meant devotion to virtue without the power and will necessary to sustain it. Moralism intruded in policymaking either directly, through the attitude that policymakers themselves carried to office, or indirectly, through the force of public opinion as it was shaped by vocal minorities, mass hysteria, yellow journalism, and political opportunists and posturers. Legalism, the other nemesis to sound policy, was reflected in the application of domestic concepts of peacekeeping, adjudication, and contractual relations to an international sphere for which they were unsuited. It too found expression directly through the outlook of policymakers, often themselves products of the legal profession, or indirectly through a political system dominated by lawyers and organized around making and interpreting law.

Kennan charged that this moralistic and legalistic outlook, deep-seated and pervasive, had repeatedly obstructed a clear definition and effective pursuit of the national interest. In developing his case he made the McKinley administration his first and most elaborate exhibit. He complained that it had gone into the Spanish-American War for "subjective and emotional reasons," acquiring in its wake colonies for reasons no better. He criticized the "high-minded and idealistic" open-door policy embraced in 1899–1900 by John Hay as a classic case of public posturing. That policy, Kennan argued, rested on a deplorably sentimental attachment to China and displayed a disregard for strategic realities in East Asia that would ultimately bring on an unwanted war with Japan. The two world wars served as additional exhibits in Kennan's exposition to demonstrate the capacity of the public, in a fit of self-right-eousness, to enter on a crusade against evil in the world and then to lapse into disillusionment, its emotional energy spent against intractable power realities. Repeatedly Americans had fallen prey to illusions that war as an instrument of policy could bring total victory or, alternatively, that peace could be had through world disarmament, arbitration treaties, the outlawry of war, the action of international organizations, and other means that side-stepped "the real substance of international affairs."[10]

The United States, which had begun the twentieth century "with the concepts of a small neutral nation," would have to find a new basis for its policy if it were to meet the challenge that Kennan saw the Soviet Union posing even as he wrote. To improve on past performance, policymakers needed to take a more rational and calculated view of international politics. The answer was to be found in "realism," a term that spotted the Kennan corpus and became a buzzword as dear to undergraduates and armchair strategists as to authentic makers of policy. It signified precisely what Kennan's historical analysis revealed the United States needed: a more orderly, clearheaded formulation of policy built on well-defined national goals, dis-playing a firm grasp of international conditions, and leading to the mobili-zation of power sufficient to overcome anticipated obstacles and realize the desired goals. The purpose of American policy had always drawn from a fund of "basic decency." If policy could be effective as well, it might do much to further "the cause of peace and of world progress."[11]

With their profound aversion to the workings of ideology on policy, Ken-nan and other "realists" fancied themselves pragmatists. They decried the dangers of seeing the world in terms of any "ism." Ideologies blinker and blind, obscuring reality and justifying in the name of high causes extreme inhumanity and wanton destruction. The horrors witnessed by Kennan and his contemporaries in their own lifetime—savage purges in the Soviet Union, a war engulfing much of the world, and a holocaust that swallowed up peoples by the millions—seemed the bitter fruits of ideological zeal. They had gone to war to expunge German and Japanese fascism, but even after victory they found ideology still stalking the globe in the form of Soviet and Chinese communism. Kennan's own reaction against ideology had taken shape earlier, during his apprenticeship as a diplomat in Central Europe and the Soviet Union in the late 1920s and the 1930s. He had come away with an impression of Marxism as a distorted view of the world and of its Bolshevik proponents as psychotics capable of "manifold brutalities and atrocities."[12]

Kennan proved notably reluctant to state that the American view of the world also suffered from the distorting effects of ideology. He never explicitly identified moralism and legalism as foreign-policy ideologies unto themselves or as part of some large ideological system. Americans might be mistaken, naive, inconsistent, or deluded, but not ideological. His "isms," he contended, had to be understood as tools by which "highly vocal minorities— politicians, commentators, and publicity-seekers of all sorts"—manipulated the public for their own selfish ends. He thus in effect redirected his critique away from the influence of a clearly identifiable, powerful, pervasive ideology and toward a vaguely defined democratic ethos that put a premium on public posturing by policymakers and others. As he had observed in *American Diplomacy*, the American political system at the turn of the century had been "unsuited, really, to the conduct of foreign affairs of a great power," and nothing since had changed it.[13]

Kennan's solution was to insulate foreign policy from the democratic process and thereby minimize the influence of moralism and legalism. The people should have their say only in an occasional referendum. Day-to-day decisions should be the privileged preserve of experts well versed in international realities and devoted to the national interest but unswayed by the popular emotions, "permissive excesses," and parochial interests that dominated American politics. As intimate and trusted advisers, these experts would at last put within the grasp of the nation's elected leaders "a mature and effective foreign policy, worthy of a great power."[14]

The dismissive treatment of ideology in *American Diplomacy* might be seen as arising from the pleasant pipedream of a former Cold War bureaucrat. Kennan and other realists nursed a deep faith that detached, coolly analytic experts, sitting around committee tables in the Pentagon, the State Department, and the White House, could in their collective wisdom grasp the "realities" of international affairs. Only "bold, ruthless, self-confident minorities, armed with insights higher than" the mass public's, Kennan contended in his *Memoirs*, could offer the guidance that a "lost and blinded child" required.[15]

This seductive and elitist vision that animated *American Diplomacy* rested on some dubious assumptions. It assumed that moralism and legalism were superficial political problems, not expressions of broader and deeper cultural values and needs. It assumed that experts were supermen who carried no intellectual baggage (or at least traveled light), who were largely untainted by ethnocentric assumptions, national biases, or cultural presuppositions, and who on reflection would largely agree with each other on fundamentals. Finally, it assumed that the experts and the policymakers they advised could function within the American political system without succumbing to its essential requirements. They would somehow create and sustain a schizophrenic policy, American in name but not in its basic aspirations. Taken together, these assumptions reveal an irony—that George Kennan, sworn foe of the ideological impulse, had made realism his ideology and, to compound the contradiction, had persuasively urged others to do the same.

Kennan's handling of foreign-policy ideology disqualifies him as a guide to lead current policy critics out of the interpretive morass they now find themselves in. Their problem and ours is to understand ideology, not ostentatiously to condemn and root out one manifestation while tacitly embracing another. One discerning student of ideology has extended this point as though with Kennan in mind. "Discussions of sociopolitical ideas that indict them *ab initio*, in terms of the very words used to name them, as deformed or worse merely beg the questions they pretend to raise."[16]

The obvious work to consider as an alternative to *American Diplomacy* is *The Tragedy of American Diplomacy*, the preeminent historical treatment of foreign-policy ideology in terms of economic interest. Its author, William Appleman Williams, came to maturity in the Midwest in the midst of the Great Depression, attended the U.S. Naval Academy, and served in the Pacific during World War II. In 1947 Williams left the navy to take his doctorate in history at the University of Wisconsin. He began his academic career in 1950, at the very time Kennan was settling in at Princeton. In 1959, after nearly a decade of exploring his discontent with U.S. policy, Williams at last published *Tragedy*, the work on which his reputation was primarily to rest.[17]

Williams' treatment contrasted sharply with Kennan's in its essential emphases. A policy that Kennan had condemned for its innocence, inconsistency, ethnocentrism, and inept execution Williams found to be just the reverse—hardheaded, sophisticated, strategically consistent and coherent, and tactically adept. Where Kennan saw the United States directed by misplaced sentiment and miscast lawyers and politicos, Williams detected the guiding hand of economic interest and an interlocking business and political elite that he credited with insight and skill. Most to the point for our purposes here, where Kennan displayed reticence about describing American policy in explicitly ideological terms, Williams did not; on the contrary, he emphatically insisted on the centrality of ideology. In doing so he embraced what can be classified as an interest-oriented approach. Ideology was functional, a tool used by the grandees of American capitalism to maintain their economic power and with it their sociopolitical control.

For Williams the 1890s was a transitional decade (as indeed it was, in a different sense, for Kennan). Led by a shrewd, farsighted McKinley, the United States ended the old pattern of territorial expansion and took up the new one of informal open-door imperialism. By then the foreign-policy elite, including publicists and strategists sensitive to the requirements of a maturing capitalist economy, had reached a consensus on the latter course. To avert "the threat of economic stagnation and the fear of social upheaval" at home, they set about securing the overseas markets capable of absorbing the burgeoning surplus of farm and factory and supplying the raw materials that American industry depended on.[18] Their favored method was the promotion of free trade and indirect control of crucial markets rather than the creation of costly colonial regimes.

China at the turn of the century provided the testing ground for this new open-door policy. Williams described the policy as "a brilliant strategic stroke," far from the blunder Kennan made it, and he located its origins in "the proposition that America's overwhelming economic power would cast the economy and the politics of the weaker, undeveloped countries in a pro-American mold." The open door, effective in China, was soon applied globally, so that as early as the 1920s "the pattern of American expansion under the principles and procedures of the Open Door Notes came to maturity."[19]

The open-door ideology was thus central to understanding the course an ascendant America followed in world affairs. That ideology set the United States at odds with those revolutionary regimes, first in Mexico and Russia and later in China, that challenged free-trade imperialism in the name of genuine self-determination and "balanced and equitable development."[20] During the economic crisis of the 1930s, that same ideology turned the Roosevelt administration against Japan and Germany, both obstacles to overseas economic expansion. After World War II it again proved a source of conflict as American policymakers, still firm in their belief that democracy and prosperity at home depended on continued economic expansion abroad, attempted to force the Soviet Union to play by American rules and thereby precipitated the Cold War.

Williams' conception of ideology, so central to his interpretation, was shaped in part by a progressive tradition that had once been a vital force in American politics and among historians but was in eclipse by the time Williams embarked on his study of American foreign policy. He shared the progressives' suspicion of monied interests, their doubts about foreign entanglements, and their disposition to see the hands of self-interested elites behind bad policies.[21]

Williams also drew, in a free-wheeling way, on Marxist theory. Marxism served primarily by helping him refine the insights of his progressive forebears without breaking with them. It helped him elaborate the idea of a socially destabilizing crisis of overproduction that had forced U.S. foreign policy to search for markets. It helped explain how a consensus about the needs of the economy and its implications for foreign policy could arise and be "internalized" in the thinking of disparate groups within the elite. (It thus spared Williams the resort to a conspiracy theory popular with earlier progressives.) And it helped to highlight the deleterious impact of the United States on dependent economies.

Every bit as much as Kennan, Williams described American policy in order to prescribe for it. Americans would have to learn "to sustain democracy and prosperity without imperial expansion." Averting continued and costly collisions between the United States and powerful revolutionary forces would require radical changes. In the conclusion of *Tragedy* Williams offered his recommendations: liquidating the Cold War, channeling development aid through the United Nations, and reordering American domestic life. The last he well knew was the crucial step, for without a change in the domestic economy American foreign policy would continue to operate along well-established lines.[22]

Though appealing to many in its boldness, Williams' interpretation provoked a critical counterattack. Some charged that Williams carried a priori conclusions to his work and often ignored or even distorted historical evidence. Others shunned the battle over footnotes and instead concentrated on Williams' tendency to circumscribe the ambit of foreign policy ideas, limiting them to the specific needs of a particular group. His stance made it difficult to account for intellectual confusion, irresolution, misperception, and other commonplace human aberrations.

Williams compounded these problems by introducing an element of conceptual confusion. Though he claimed that the open-door ideology was the product of objective economic forces, little of *Tragedy* is devoted to demonstrating the link between the requirements of the economy and the concerns of policymakers. Indeed, Williams has on occasion seemingly rejected a clear-cut economic determinism. Ideas, he noted in a 1966 essay, may "originate as instruments of specific interests" only in time to "break their narrow bounds and emerge as broad, inclusive conceptions of the world." Thus he has conceded that the idea of the open door might have drifted away from its original economic moorings, if such they were, and even have blended with other ideas such as paternalism, racism, or nationalism that may have only a tenuous link to the economic system.[23]

Williams' *Tragedy* brought to bear on U.S. policy a more sophisticated and self-conscious understanding of ideology than is evident in Kennan's *American Diplomacy*. Even so, *Tragedy* suffers from an interpretive ambiguity that deserves attention for the limitations it reveals about any conception of ideology that is tied tightly to economic self-interest. *Tragedy* insists on the centrality of the connection, but Williams has fair-mindedly conceded that ideas generated by the economic system can become self-perpetuating or at least be sustained by noneconomic forces. Having made this concession, he leaves us wondering how central economic self-interest is—and whether an insistence on its centrality may not blind us to the importance of concerns that are neither rooted in nor sustained by economic forces or calculations. Policymakers may conceivably act on ideas that are in some (or even most) cases noneconomic in origin or nature.

This confusion is the result of Williams' excessively narrow conception of ideology colliding with his sensitivity to historical complexity, and it raises legitimate doubts about his prescription for policy change. A dramatic alteration in the domestic economic system may not induce any dramatic transformation of foreign policy, particularly if those who direct that policy are responsive to ideas from a multiplicity of sources, including noneconomic ones. This line of reasoning leads logically to the conclusion—directly at odds with Williams' own basic belief—that a socialist America might itself also pursue a foreign policy that was no less exploitative and domineering than that of the old capitalist America.

★ ★ ★

Working definitions of ideology that are either dismissive or reductionist will not help us carry forward the analytic task begun by the critics of recent U.S. policy. As a look at Kennan and Williams suggests, a flawed or incomplete notion of ideology is likely to yield, in addition to a false diagnosis of the problems afflicting U.S. foreign policy, a misinterpretation of the roots of the problem and misdirected proposals for solving it.

Still in search of a good handle on ideology, we would do well to consider a third approach, one that attempts to understand ideology in relation to a cultural system. It has been championed by cultural anthropologist Clifford Geertz and by a number of political scientists (such as Gabriel Almond and Sidney Verba) who are intrigued by the concept of political culture. They have emphasized the degree to which ideology is inescapable (even by policy experts) and have argued that it is much more than simply a tool wielded in the self-interest of ambitious politicians or calculating capitalists. According to advocates of this approach, ideologies are integrated and coherent systems of symbols, values, and beliefs. They arise from those "socially established structures of meaning" that Geertz associates with culture.[24] Ideological constructs, which culture not only inspires but also sustains and constrains, serve as a fount for an instructive and reassuring sense of historical place, as an indispensable guide to an infinitely complex and otherwise bewildering present, and as a basis for moral action intended to shape a better future.

At the heart of the cultural approach is, first of all, a refusal to posit a single, simple reason for the origins and persistence of a particular ideology. Such an approach may sound conceptually fuzzy and interpretively messy. But if we accept the notion that societies are indeed complex in structure and function and that they are difficult to capture in sweeping, "scientific" generalizations, then we are justified in looking with skepticism on laws that neatly define the relations between group interests and group beliefs or assert the existence of a "base" that determines the "superstructure." An open-minded inquiry into the roots of ideology should leave room for noneconomic impulses, in particular those stemming from racial or ethnic identity, strong nationalist preoccupations, an evangelical faith, and pronouncedly regional concerns. These impulses figure prominently in the American case, as the account that follows will make clear.

Though the cultural approach runs against any urge to reduce successful ideologies to a single dimension, it can nonetheless easily accommodate an interpretive emphasis on the importance of social class. There is certainly much to be said in favor of using the distribution of economic power within a society as a means to understanding ideologies that rise to prominence or achieve "hegemony" (to use the currently fashionable language of Antonio Gramsci). The sponsoring "ideologues" in the case of U.S. foreign policy were usually white males possessed of at least a modicum of wealth from birth. Privilege not only smoothed their way to positions of political prominence but also left its stamp in some significant ways on their views of the world.

Once generated, ideas acquire—in that loose, oft-used, and suggestive phrase—"a life of their own." The other distinctive feature of the cultural approach is, then, its insistence on looking for the diversity of ways in which ideology is sustained. An ideology may owe its survival to cultural impulses that played no, or only a marginal, role in its rise. It may attract the support of new sponsors that value it for particular reasons of their own or for its contribution to some vaguely felt need for continuity or stability. A ready example of this possible disjunction between the origins and the maintenance of an ideology is the translation of divine predestination, a notion appropriate to the sectarianism of one generation, into the secular terms of national predestination by subsequent generations with different problems of identity and purpose to work out. Moreover, ideologies may become institutionalized and hold sway even after they have ceased to serve any obvious functional role or advance any clearly identifiable class or group interest. For instance, the views that rationalized the father's control of black slaves continued to define the son's and grandson's perceptions of blacks even after emancipation had eroded the base of concrete self-interest. An ideology may, in other words, survive as a form of "folk wisdom," thanks to those carriers and repositories of culture—the family, the school, clubs, churches, and places of work.

Further consideration of ideological survival leads to two additional points directly applicable to the case of American foreign policy addressed in this volume. One is the tendency toward ideological persistence in countries with a stable political culture. Spared the shock of a great social revolution or foreign invasion and occupation, the United States has enjoyed this kind of stability to a remarkable degree compared to most other nations. Not surprisingly, then, the continuity in institutional structures and in social and political values has been accompanied by an ideological continuity in the realm of foreign policy with few if any equals among great powers in modern times.

The corollary, and in large measure the consequence, of this continuity in American foreign-policy ideology is the absence of a self-consciousness about that ideology. Because of a remarkable cultural stability, Americans have felt no urgent need to take their foreign-policy ideology out for major overhaul or replacement but have instead enjoyed the luxury of being able by and large to take it for granted. Precisely because Americans could afford to leave their ideology implicit and informal, they have tended to regard as unusual if not aberrant most other ideologies—such as those espoused by communist, fascist, or strongly nationalist regimes—which are couched in explicit, formal, even formulaic terms. But a foreign-policy ideology that is carefully manufactured, neatly packaged, widely advertised, and readily available off the shelf is not necessarily more genuine or more influential. In fact, the case could be made that ideologies assume formal, explicit, systematic form precisely because there is resistance to them within the culture, whereas an ideology left implicit rests on a consensus and therefore exercises a greater (if more subtle) power.

A search for an American foreign-policy ideology inspired by the cultural approach would have us looking for a relatively coherent, emotionally charged, and conceptually interlocking set of ideas. These core foreign-policy ideas would have to reflect the self-image of those who espoused them and to define a relationship with the world consonant with that self-image. They would in all likelihood derive from and be sustained by a diversity of domestic values or arrangements. They would have to be central enough to the national experience to help us account for key developments, as well as powerful enough to have performed for generations of Americans that essential function of giving order to their vision of the world and defining their place in it. That is to say, these ideas would have supplied, as any ideology does, "a world image convincing enough to support the collective and individual sense of identity."[25]

While pushing us toward a definition of foreign-policy ideology that is both spacious and flexible, the cultural approach has the added virtue of warning us against the dangers of foreshortened historical perspective, even one that goes back to the 1890s, as in Kennan and Williams. Along with most other historians, they see in that decade the inauguration of modern American foreign policy. Though they agree on little else, they both assert that with the Spanish-American War and the attendant acquisition of colonies and dependencies, American policymakers entered the thicket of international politics from which their successors have yet to emerge. Surely, they contend, so dramatic a shift either reflected or set in motion a major reconceptualization of policy assumptions. While plausible, such a supposition may in fundamental terms be unfounded or at least exaggerated. If cultures have a tendency toward persistence, with important systemic changes usually assimilated gradually, then we should look for a corresponding durability and continuity in the realm of ideas. Contrary to Williams, we may find a foreign-policy ideology that predates the rise in the late nineteenth century of a corporate order and that easily responded to its needs without basic transformation. Contrary to Kennan, we may find twentieth-century policy less a battleground between old ideas and new than a monument to a long-established outlook on the world.

The way to discover this ideology, it would seem, is to take the longest view possible on the attitudes and values of the groups that have supplied the foreign-policy elite, a miniscule portion (perhaps about 1 percent) of those who are intimately and actively concerned with the course of American foreign policy. This elite, including not just prominent policymakers but also other participants in major policy discussions and debates, have left behind abundant evidence of their views that goes back to the eighteenth century. Though these views are not codified in formal, systematic terms, it is possible to identify their main components and to trace their interrelationship. To do so, one need only look at this elite's private musings and, more important, the public rhetoric by which they have justified their actions and communicated their opinions to one another and to the nation.

Public rhetoric may seem peculiarly suspect as evidence to be taken at face value. The cynical would contend that carefully staged public appeals are occasions not for frank and nuanced expression but for cant intended to fool the gullible and mask true intentions. One might argue that rhetoric is a form of persuasion, that to treat it instead as confession would be profoundly mistaken.

But such a skeptical view may be too clever by half. Public rhetoric is not simply a screen, tool, or ornament. It is also, perhaps even primarily, a form of communication, rich in symbols and mythology and closely constrained by certain rules. To be effective, public rhetoric must draw on values and concerns widely shared and easily understood by its audience. A rhetoric that ignores or eschews the language of common discourse on the central problems of the day closes itself off as a matter of course from any sizable audience, limiting its own influence. If a rhetoric fails to reflect the speaker's genuine views on fundamental issues, it runs the risk over time of creating false public expectations and lays the basis for politically dangerous misunderstanding. If it indulges in blatant inconsistency, it eventually pays the price of diminished force and credibility. Public rhetoric is tainted evidence for the historian seeking a widely shared ideology only when it violates these rules and falls unpersuasively on the ears of its ostensible audience. Indeed, comparisons of public rhetoric with private statements, a sensitive test that cynics might justifiably insist on, suggest that the policy elite do recognize the cost of violating these rules and do generally observe them. Interpretive naiveté may reside not in taking rhetoric seriously but rather in failing to listen carefully for its recurrent themes and values.

In the United States, foreign-policy rhetoric has been peppered with widely understood codewords. References in speeches, school texts, newspaper editorials, and songs to liberty, providential blessings, destiny, and service to mankind have been fraught with meaning shared by author and audience. Precisely because of their explanatory power and popular appeal, such simple but resonant notions became essential to the formulation and practical conduct of international policy. Policymakers steeped in these notions used them to reduce complicated problems to manageable proportions, to devise a personally appealing response, and to marshal support at home for the choices they had made. The "mere rhetoric" found in the historical record may thus be viewed as a way of coming to terms with pressing problems or unfamiliar situations, and it should be taken with complete seriousness for both the deep-seated attitudes it reveals and the action it may portend.

To argue that rhetoric is revealing evidence is not to argue that it and the ideas it conveys should be considered apart from the needs and interests of the elite who have shaped and articulated that rhetoric. On the contrary, the American foreign-policy ideas embedded in public rhetoric have been strikingly functional. Indeed, it is the central argument of this volume that the fundamental propositions of American foreign policy are rooted in the process of nation building, in domestic social arrangements broadly understood, and in ethnic and class divisions. These propositions are products of those who have predominated in domestic no less than foreign affairs.

A crucial caveat must be offered at this point. An understanding of a nation's ideology provides no certain insights into its behavior. Ideologies are important because they constitute the framework in which policymakers deal with specific issues and in which the attentive public understands those issues. For both groups, ideologies elucidate complex realities and reduce them to understandable and manageable terms. But such an approach needs to be tempered by an awareness of the dangers of interpretive rigidity, given the complexity of both human psychology and the decisionmaking process of governments. It is important, to begin with, to accept the view that the relationship between ideas and action is not rigid. The simple idea or set of ideas on which a policy may initially rest invariably has to leave room for diverse nonideological considerations, such as a need for access to export markets and raw materials, preservation of essential national security, attention to the preferences of the electorate, and even the promptings of personal political ambition. Interpretive prudence also urges us to accept the notion that ideological permutations may occur as a result of changes in the cast of policy personalities. Far from being fixed or static, the ideas that make up a foreign-policy ideology may be reassembled by different leaders or in different ages in different ways. While all policymakers are borrowers (in Henry Kissinger's phrase) of "intellectual capital," the bank of experience on which each draws may significantly differ.

★ ★ ★

These general observations clear the ground for a treatment of the rise of the core ideas in the ideology of U.S. foreign policy. It takes us back to the late eighteenth and the nineteenth centuries, when the American political elite moved toward a consensus on the fundamental issues of international affairs. That consensus was consonant with the elite's cultural values and the broader conception of nationhood they espoused. What was the nation to become, and how was its identity to be reflected in its international behavior?

This process, in which Americans sought to define themselves and their place in the world, should be seen as a form of what one historian has aptly called "imaginative ideological labor," which is common to ascendant nationalist movements in midcourse. Building on the shared outlook and interests inspired by previous socioeconomic developments, nationalists in this stage engaged in clarifying the idea of the nation and giving it concrete expression by creating historical myths, propagating values, and constructing institutions. These efforts were meant to undermine competing loyalties, such as regionalism, and erect "an ideological and institutional structure of immense power, which—within negotiable limits—[would determine] the possible forms of political activity and belief."[26]

The chapters that immediately follow should be read primarily as a history of nationalist ideas relevant to policy but not, at first, always incorporated into it. Ideology exercised a limited influence over the decisions made during the nation's first century, since the government was rendered cautious by its relatively limited resources and the sometimes sharp political disagreements dividing the informed public. While those chapters are not systematic studies of policymaking, policy does deserve a place in them because it helps illuminate the emergent ideological construct in at least two respects. Policy debates served in key instances as forums for resolving the conflict between divergent national visions. Moreover, policymakers in the eighteenth and nineteenth centuries occasionally paid tribute to the hold that elements of the ideology already exercised by acting on its promptings.

By the early twentieth century, three core ideas relevant to foreign affairs had emerged, and they collectively began to wield a strong influence over policy. The capstone idea defined the American future in terms of an active quest for national greatness closely coupled to the promotion of liberty. It was firmly in place by the turn of the century, after having met and mastered a determined opposition on three separate occasions—in the 1790s, the 1840s, and the 1890s. A second element in the ideology defined attitudes toward other peoples in terms of a racial hierarchy. Inspired by the struggle of white Americans to secure and maintain their supremacy under conditions that differed from region to region, this outlook on race was the first of the core ideas to gain prominence. The third element defined the limits of acceptable political and social change overseas in keeping with the settled conviction that revolutions, though they might be a force for good, could as easily develop in a dangerous direction. Attitudes toward revolution, like those toward race, were fairly consistent through the formative first century, but unlike views on race, they were only sporadically evoked in that period. It was not until the 1910s, in response to an outburst of revolutionary activity abroad, that the power and the place of this element in the ideological construct was confirmed.

Now tightly interrelated and mutually reinforcing, these core ideas could provide national leaders with a clear and coherent vision of the world and the American place in it. In other words, by the early twentieth century those ideas had assumed the status of an informal but potent ideology that would point the direction for subsequent foreign policy, as well as set the tone and define the substance of American life to an unprecedented degree. But before we can describe, let alone evaluate, the recent policy consequences of that ideology, we are obliged to consider its origins. To that task the next three chapters are directed, with each devoted to one of the core ideas.

2 Visions of National Greatness

We have it in our power to begin the world all over again.
— Thomas Paine, "Common Sense" (January 1776)

The stunning possibility of Americans reinvigorating a gray, spent world was glimpsed and articulated at a crucial moment in 1776 by Thomas Paine. He was an unlikely figure to hold high this vision of a glorious future. An indifferent student and restless apprentice to his staymaker father, Paine had run away from home at sixteen and led the life of an itinerant ne'er-do-well. He had gone through two wives and failed at six different occupations before finally resolving to immigrate to the colonies. He was then thirty-seven, in dire straits financially, with little to recommend him besides letters from Benjamin Franklin and an incipient pamphleteer's love of the language and a hot issue. He reached Philadelphia in November 1774 just as the British were cracking down politically. When news arrived that the king had pronounced the colonies in rebellion, Paine put his pen to work in behalf of the American cause.

"Common Sense," published in January 1776, argued powerfully for independence as the only course left that would secure the rights to which Englishmen were entitled. Paine's main target was those sunk in "fatal and unmanly slumbers" who still believed reconciliation possible. The weapon he used against them was the concept of two spheres: that England belonged to the European system and that America belonged to its own. Perhaps inspired by his acquaintance with Franklin, who had long suspected that the respective interests of colony and metropolis might easily diverge, Paine now made that point publicly, explicitly, forcefully. London controlled and restricted American trade. London, distant and ill-informed, could not properly govern Americans. And London dragged Americans into her expensive imperial wars.

To material obstacles to reconciliation, Paine added a political element— a commitment to freedom—that further served to distinguish the two spheres.

The New World had become "the asylum for the persecuted lovers of civil and religious liberty," while in England "a corrupt and faithless court" abused liberty, and elsewhere in the Old World liberty was simply denied. Americans were thus marked out as the keepers of the flickering flame of liberty. It was in this latter context that Paine, in the pamphlet's stirring conclusion, introduced Americans to the unprecedented opportunity that independence would present to them. Theirs would be the "power to begin the world over again," he announced. "The birthday of a new world is at hand, and a race of men, perhaps as numerous as all Europe contains, are to receive their portion of freedom from the events of a few months. The reflection is awful, and in this point of view, how trifling, how ridiculous, do the little paltry cavilings of a few weak or interested men appear, when weighted against the business of a world."

The impact of "Common Sense" was instant and enormous, claiming a readership unmatched in the colonial experience. The pamphlet's direct and forceful style enabled Paine to reach across the lines of class, occupation, and ethnic origin to speak to a mass audience. In making his compelling call to take the next small step from resistance to independence, a step that would render "this continent the glory of the earth," Paine drew widely for inspiration. From a body of thought handed down from the Renaissance, he culled the notion that virtue was essential to the survival of a republic but that virtue inevitably declined. Harried in one place, it would seek refuge elsewhere. Paine made America that refuge. Paine also drew on Puritan millennial notions of a global spiritual rebirth and the special role to be played in that rebirth by a chosen people living under providential blessing. Americans would be that people. He incorporated as well John Locke's notion of political and economic progress as the product of individual conduct guided by calculations of utility and self-interest, not by the dictates of tradition and external authority. By serving themselves Americans would serve the world. Finally, "Common Sense" reflected the Enlightenment preoccupation with a new world order devoted to the betterment of mankind, not to power politics and the aggrandizement of princes. Americans would set relations between nations on a new basis.

Paine, looking back on "Common Sense" thirty years later, observed that he had written it to help men "to be free."[1] That entailed, most obviously, an end to British tyranny and hereditary monarchy—a clear goal that was widely understood and accepted and soon achieved. However, the young nation had considerably more difficulty deciding what steps were necessary to realize Paine's vision of independent Americans "beginning the world over again." In the new scheme of things, was the government to command a large or small sphere of responsibilities? Which economic, ethnic, and regional interests was it to serve? Who could be trusted to oversee its affairs? Finding answers to these explosive, and potentially divisive, questions was in turn inextricably tied up with the equally knotty problem of defining the relationship that a nation of free men should establish with the wider world, which was still dominated by monarchies and despotisms. What kind of foreign policy was appropriate to men of such quality? What was to be their mission in the world?

These questions would not be soon or easily resolved. The resolution was particularly troublesome because Americans were divided over a sensitive issue—whether domestic liberty could flourish alongside an ambitious and strongly assertive foreign policy. Two major conflicting tendencies quickly emerged on this issue. It would take a century and three major debates to determine which conception of national greatness was to dominate American thinking about foreign affairs.

★ ★ ★

For Americans a practical choice between the two alternative foreign-policy courses was delayed for a time. They first had a war against Britain to fight and win. By 1783 they had, with French aid, succeeded in this task. Even so, the pygmy nation of three million enjoyed an independence more nominal than real, and its weak confederate government was beset by intractable problems on all sides. Without the power to tax, it could not field an army or build a navy. An unpaid national debt mounted yearly. Commerce went unregulated and unprotected against abuse on the high seas and in major foreign markets. The British continued to garrison parts of the territory conceded in the peace, and native Americans, encouraged by London and Madrid, threatened settlers all along the frontier. Moreover, Spanish control of New Orleans impeded the export of American produce down the Mississippi and fanned a secessionist spirit among discontented American frontiersmen. Only in 1789, with the ratification of a federal constitution, did the central government gain the powers to meet these problems. Americans had finally agreed on a workable substitute for the British political system they had rejected. Now other fundamental choices lay ahead, for—as they soon discovered—in defining their foreign policy they would also be defining their character as a nation.

George Washington, who was to preside over the new state's crucial first eight years, at once summoned to his service Alexander Hamilton and Thomas Jefferson. From their respective posts, one as secretary of the treasury and the other as secretary of state, they were to advise Washington on the inherited agenda of foreign-policy issues and on the additional problems posed by the outbreak of war in Europe in 1793. In the process they were to press on him and the nation the two antagonistic visions of America's role in the world. An awareness that each decision might set enduring precedents made their contest increasingly emotional and bitter. It was to split the Washington administration, give impetus to political factionalism, and inspire a national debate that stands among the most passionate and abusive, even hysterical, in American history.

The Jefferson who entered the Washington administration in 1790 carried with him a preoccupation with liberty that suffused his notion of a good society, of national mission, and of an appropriate foreign policy. In Europe, where diplomacy had carried him between 1784 and 1789, he had found "the general fate of humanity . . . most deplorable . . . suffering under physical and moral oppression." But in America men might find the felicity and abundance that was their right. With ample land each individual was assured not just a livelihood but personal independence and its twin, liberty. Jefferson repeatedly stressed that farmers were "the most virtuous and independent citizens." Cities, industry, centralized political power, and gross inequalities of wealth and privilege were all the enemies of his ideal—a social order dominated by yeoman farmers.[2]

In foreign affairs a policy of aloofness was calculated to be the best way of preserving the liberties Americans had achieved and of allowing them to develop still further as a free people. Geographic distance from a rapacious and turmoil-prone Europe already promised peace. That promise could be made secure if Americans could bring themselves "to abandon the ocean altogether . . . [and] to leave to others to bring in what we shall want, and to carry what we can spare." But Jefferson recognized that Americans—farmers not least among them—could not in fact abandon foreign trade. Since agrarian prosperity and the purchase of essential manufactured goods depended on access to foreign markets, Jefferson stood ready to negotiate commercial treaties and to protect trade against abuse. For that, however, the country needed no more than a few diplomats and a small navy. "To aim at such a navy as the greater nations of Europe possess, would be a foolish and wicked waste of the energies of our countrymen."[3]

On becoming secretary of state, Jefferson sought, with the support of James Madison in Congress, to promote conditions conducive to the flowering of American liberty. In broad terms, that meant securing the adjoining lands and foreign markets important to the prosperity of an agrarian economy and to the vigor of the republican values which that economy nurtured. He regarded an England still unreconciled to the loss of her American colonies as the main threat to these goals. Subordination was at all costs to be avoided, harmful as it was to American expansion and commerce as well as pride. Though the British navy commanded the high sea, Jefferson was prepared to insist that the ocean was "the common property of all, open to the industry of all." The United States would have to rely on commercial retaliation to wring trade concessions from Britain. "It is not to the moderation and justice of others we are to trust for fair and equal access to market with our productions, or for our due share in the transportation of them; but to our own means of independence, and the firm will to use them." It would also help to cultivate France as a strategic equipoise, as well disposed toward the United States as she was antagonistic to Britain. By embracing republicanism in 1789 France became an alliance partner, which was not only convenient but also politically natural. Looking inland, Jefferson wanted guarantees from Spain for exports from New Orleans that would consolidate the nation's hold on the Mississippi valley. Eventually new land to the west was needed to extend the "empire" for liberty. In this way the new secretary of state hoped to make secure and prosperous the agrarian republic on which his dreams centered.[4]

Alexander Hamilton was by contrast entranced by a vision of national greatness in which liberty figured less prominently. Born in the West Indies (the "bastard brat of a Scotch pedlar," as John Adams uncharitably described him), Hamilton went to New York to study, joined the revolution, and served during the war as Washington's aide.[5] His subsequent political career revealed Hamilton as a man of flawed brilliance. He was blessed with an abundance of energy and intelligence and a tough political sense, but he was also governed by a driving ambition that sometimes left good sense behind in the dust. He helped push through the new constitution (despite his private concerns that it did not give the federal government enough power), and his subsequent political impact as first secretary of the treasury and a leading figure in the Federalist party was enormous. Government policy from 1789 to 1795 was inseparable from Hamilton's vision and administrative achievements.

The conception of national greatness that Hamilton was to act on in the 1790s had taken shape the decade before. The revolutionary struggle had taught him the costs of war, while his views on human nature—that "men are ambitious, vindictive, and rapacious"—carried him to the pessimistic conclusion that conflict was the law of life. States no less than men were bound to collide over those ancient objects of ambition: wealth and glory. Even republics could not escape this grim condition, as the experience of Sparta, Athens, Rome, and Carthage all proved. Americans would have to recognize, Hamilton cautioned, that they too lived in a world "yet remote from the happy empire of perfect wisdom and perfect virtue."[6]

These hard truths in turn dictated that Americans recognize the dominant role of power, self-interest, and passion in international affairs. The still-vulnerable country should move warily until it acquired the strength essential to assert its interests and influence. The first step was the creation of "a vigorous national government" under the direction of an elite (described by Hamilton as "a few choice spirits, who may act from more worthy motives" than the common rabble). They would ensure a stable political order and take the lead in developing the economy. That step was to be at once followed by the construction of a strong navy to protect commerce from jealous European powers. Given time to develop and mature, Americans could become strong, stave off demands that they serve as "the instruments of European greatness," and eventually establish their own greatness. As a force in its own right, the United States would be "ascendant in the system of American affairs . . . and able to dictate the terms of the connection between the old and the new world!" Hamilton's was a grandiose vision seemingly at odds with Jefferson's determination to make foreign policy serve the essential requirements of American liberty.[7]

The policies that Hamilton fought for after 1789 proved consistent with these views. A sound financial system and peace with Britain were essential, and he guarded them tenaciously. Without a steady source of revenue the government would fall back to its former feeble state, unable to keep order at home or protect its international interests. Since 90 percent of the revenue came from import duties on trade with Britain, any interruption of that trade would disable the government. Yet Madison and other hotheads in Congress angry over continued British abuse of American commerce called for retaliation in kind, seemingly without giving mind to the harm that would result. They also failed to take account of the awful possibility that provocations offered by both sides might touch off a war for which the new nation was not yet prepared. In that event the mighty British fleet would sweep American commerce from the sea, bombard the chief Atlantic ports, and mount invasions from Canada and along the coast. Thus might the prospects for national greatness be dashed.

Too weak to make the British play by American rules, the United States would have to accept British rules and—were it possible—operate under the cover of a British alliance. To signal acquiescence and to neutralize the intemperate opposition at home, Hamilton arranged a diplomatic mission to London, headed by John Jay. To ensure its success, Hamilton personally prepared its instructions and clandestinely informed the British chargé d'affaires of Jay's purposes and his own desire for accommodation.

Murmurs of discontent with the Hamiltonian program came to an abusive crescendo in 1795 following the arrival of Jay's treaty. That program, leaders of the emergent Republican party had been charging with some heat since mid-1792, was putting liberty at risk by concentrating power in the hands of the executive and promoting an aristocracy of wealth. Already, even before Jay's arrival, they had come to fear both an Anglicization of American politics that would subvert republican virtue and an indulgence in luxury and social pomp more appropriate to a royal court than an agrarian republic. Some were troubled by dark dreams of a sellout to Britain and the restoration of monarchical control. The new, one-sided treaty demonstrated most obviously Hamilton's acceptance of costly British control of American trade in order to safeguard his mercantile allies and his fiscal system. But it also confirmed his subservience to London and the corrupting style of court politics there. This economic subordination and political emulation, Republicans feared, would prove the undoing of American liberty. Earlier Madison had warned against "the influence that may be conveyed into the public councils by a nation directing the course of our trade by her capital, and holding so great a share in our pecuniary institutions, and the effect that may finally ensure on our taste, our manners, and our form of government itself."[8]

Both Madison and Jefferson charged that the new treaty was an act of appeasement that served as an invitation to continued British abuse. The treaty also confirmed a dangerous structural dependency (equally alarming to a later generation of leaders in newly independent states). It was in Jefferson's view "nothing more than a treaty of alliance between England and the Anglomen of this country against . . . the people of the United States." As the public attack intensified, Jay was denounced as an archtraitor groveling before the British court. (Paine described him as having served as "minister *penitentiary*.") At mass meetings illuminated by torchlight his effigy was hanged. And his treaty was widely ridiculed. One bit of doggerel described it as "truly a farce, fit only to wipe the national ——— ."[9]

Hamilton, characterized with grudging respect by Jefferson as "really a colossus to the anti-republican party," rushed to the defense of his diplomatic handiwork. Some of Hamilton's arguments occupied familiar high ground. The nation, "the embryo of a great empire," needed at least a decade of peace to grow stronger. A test of power with Britain in the current state of national weakness "would probably throw us back into a state of debility and impoverishment from which it would require years to emerge." But

Hamilton was no less assiduous in pointing out the base motives—''vanity and vindictiveness''—that actuated his opponents. He accused some politicians, still unreconciled to the new government, of wishing to use the treaty to bring it down. Others, ''fawning or turbulent demagogues,'' he suspected of playing on public passion to advance their own ''irregular ambition.'' Still others, ''deeply infected with those horrid principles of Jacobinism,'' he saw as dancing to the French tune and seeking to draw the United States into war against Britain.[10]

Thanks to Washington, Hamilton got the last word in the debate. Washington had been deeply stung by the obloquy directed at him following his open endorsement of the Jay treaty, but he remained silent until September 1796, when his imminent departure from office provided an opportunity for a reply in the guise of a ''farewell address.''[11] The address, despite its peppering of platitudes (''honesty is the best policy''), has long been regarded as a seminal document notable above all else for its earnest if somewhat fuzzy injunction against ''permanent Alliances.'' Though Washington offered his views disarmingly as the ''counsels of an old and affectionate friend'' of his countrymen, he in fact used the occasion to fire a broadside against administration critics, those ''foes of order, and good government,'' who seemed infatuated with France. Hamilton lent considerable assistance in preparing the blast—so much, indeed, that he had almost as good a claim to authorship of this address as he had of the Jay treaty.

The address advanced that paradox dear to authoritarians in power: liberty might be undermined by its very exercise. Nowhere was this more true than in regard to foreign policy. Vigorous and possibly divisive debate was dangerous, for by challenging political authority and stirring up factional strife, it sowed the seeds of disorder and thereby put liberty in peril. Behind the outbreak of dissent was the insidious influence of political parties, described in the address as ''potent engines, by which cunning, ambitious and unprincipled men will be enabled to subvert the Power of the People, and to usurp for themselves the reins of Government.'' They divided the nation and introduced ''foreign influence and corruption'' into the councils of the government itself. Freed from party passions and foreign (read ''French'') meddling, the United States would, Washington promised, emerge ''at no distant period'' in the role Hamilton prized—''a great Nation'' secure within its own sphere and able to deal on its own terms with Europe.

Hamilton stood triumphant. He had so dominated the cabinet that Jefferson had retired in frustration at the end of 1793. He had rescued his treaty from attack and seen it through the Senate in July 1795. He had committed Washington's prestige to a thinly veiled attack on his enemies. And though his foreign birth barred his way to the presidency after Washington's retirement, he continued to exercise inordinate influence over John Adams' cabinet even after giving up public office. When French attacks on American shipping, followed by insults to American emissaries (the famous XYZ affair) introduced the prospect of war, Hamilton seized the opportunity to pursue the military command and glory he had long dreamed of. Under Washington's nominal direction he began putting together an army to meet the French. With that force behind him, he reasoned, he might also overawe the Francophile Republicans and even contemplate the conquest of the adjoining Spanish territories of Florida and Louisiana as well as the detachment of South America from Spain.

John Adams, stiff and fiercely independent, bridled at the pretensions and interference of a man he privately denounced as "the most ruthless, impatient, artful, indefatigable and unprincipled intriguer in the United States, if not in the world."[12] He at last turned on Hamilton, checking his projects and driving his friends from the cabinet. (The result was a rift in the ranks of the Federalists that made Jefferson's election to the presidency possible.) Aaron Burr completed Hamilton's downfall, fatally wounding him in a duel in 1804.

Ironically, Hamilton dead proved more influential than Jefferson alive and at last in power. Jefferson's fundamental views on the relationship between liberty and foreign policy had passed unchanged through the scorching controversy of the 1790s. He still wanted no involvement in European affairs greater than commerce required. "Though I cordially wish well to the progress of liberty in all nations, and would forever give it the weight of our countenance, yet they are not to be touched without contamination from their other bad principles." His inaugural address in March 1801 proved an eloquent and politically healing affirmation of his faith in republican government and in the special providence of Americans as "a happy and prosperous people" working out their destiny apart from the "exterminating havoc" of Europe.[13]

But a system of government stamped in the Hamiltonian mold remained in place to a surprising degree, while Jefferson launched on a course in foreign relations guided perhaps more by expediency and the promotion of his own agrarian vision of national greatness than by his fear of a strong executive as a danger to liberty. The result was to move Jefferson closer to Hamilton in the style if not the substance of his policy. He responded vigorously to France's acquisition of the Louisiana territory. The loss of New Orleans put at risk the overseas trade essential to Western farmers, whereas the purchase of Louisiana and the enormous expanse of territory that went with it would sustain the prized agrarian way of life for generations. To block France and secure this land, Jefferson threatened an alliance with Britain and passed beyond the limits of what he considered his constitutional powers (much as Hamilton might have done) to gain possession of that territory and to rule its inhabitants, perhaps as many as a hundred thousand, without their consent or participation.[14] Not content with doubling the size of the nation at one stroke, he sought to shake Florida from the feeble grasp of Spain, and later still, after leaving the White House, he looked forward to the eventual acquisition of Canada and Cuba.

A strong federal government seemed less alarming when it was no longer in the hands of the "Anglomen" party. Similarly, national greatness became an attractive objective when it looked forward to a continental republic rather than a maritime state dependent on the British navy and economy. Jefferson himself betrayed impatience as he gave up hope that natural population growth would lead to absorption of new territory "piece by piece" (as he had phrased it in the 1780s). He looked instead to the federal government as the responsible agent for wringing or seizing adjoining territory from other powers and amalgamating it with his republican system.[15]

When the resumption of war in Europe in 1803 resulted in renewed violation of American commerce, Jefferson again inadvertently paid his respects to the ghost of Hamilton. Jefferson dealt circumspectly with Britain and left office admitting the failure of commercial retaliation, a weapon he and other Republicans had earlier urged on Hamilton. Merchants flouted it; Federalist New England talked of secession; and all the while the fiercely struggling European powers continued to prey on American commerce. War and the further augmenting of state power would prove the only recourse left to Republicans entangled more deeply in the international economy than they cared to admit, their burgeoning agricultural production more dependent on foreign consumers than ever before.

Jefferson had come to terms with a world that did indeed seem to be governed, just as Hamilton had said, by self-interest and strength. And in doing so, he had made a compromise fatal to his own earlier pristine vision of the good society and a minimal foreign policy. These developments raise in turn a set of still haunting questions. Was the early Jeffersonian vision of a nation devoted above all else to liberty and equality impossibly utopian in a strife-torn world? Had that vision been overwhelmed by his compatriots' taste for prosperity and power and their inability to contain their energy within narrow bounds? Or was there something in the outlook of even Jefferson the libertarian that made the vision of national power impossibly seductive?

★ ★ ★

Jefferson's successors, the last of the Virginia dynasty in the White House, carried forward the vision of liberty tied to an expansive foreign policy. James Madison and James Monroe, with the considerable assistance of John Quincy Adams, pushed the national advantage against a Spain in imperial decline. They made good on Jefferson's interest in Florida, delineated on advantageous terms the southern boundaries of the Louisiana Purchase all the way to the Pacific, and in the doctrine associated with Monroe's name openly advanced a portentous claim to political oversight over the hemisphere.

Three Tennesseeans—Andrew Jackson, Sam Houston, and James K. Polk—carried forward the latter-day Jeffersonian vision as the Virginians left off. Jackson consolidated the nation's hold on the southeast interior. As warrior and frontier diplomat in the teens, he chastened Britain no less than Spain and subdued the Indians. Later, as president, he eliminated native Americans as a significant presence east of the Mississippi and looked on benignly as Houston led Texas out from under Mexican control. The electoral triumph of Polk, a dark-horse Jacksonian Democrat, on an expansionist platform in 1844 prodded a previously deadlocked Congress into voting Texas' annexation early the next year, on the eve of Polk's inauguration. Thereafter, true to his campaign pledge, the dour and driven Polk laid claim to the entire Oregon territory and pressed to the brink of war with Britain. No sooner was Polk certain of a peaceful settlement than he turned on Mexico in May 1846. The war, which began over the Texas boundary, ended with one-half of Mexico—her California and New Mexico territories—and a hundred thousand of her citizens falling permanently into American hands.

This process of contiguous territorial expansion, begun with the Louisiana Purchase in 1803 and rounded out with the Gadsden Purchase in 1853, was an impressive achievement. This tripling of the nation's size depended, most obviously, on growing American military power that rendered insecure the grip of Russia, Britain, France, Spain, and Mexico on their respective North American territories. It also took money, some $48 million, just to secure legal title. Population growth was another important ingredient. An ever more numerous body of Americans, reaching thirty-two million by 1860, filtered steadily westward. This "irresistible army of Anglo-Saxon emigration" (as one expansionist of the time characterized it) created irredentist enclaves, undermined foreign control, and provoked confrontations that Washington repeatedly turned to American territorial advantage.[16]

Easily overlooked, yet just as essential to expansion, was an additional element—a guiding vision. The fate of liberty and the mission of the United States had become intertwined, just as Paine had insisted they should be. "Providence has showered on this favored land blessings without number, and has chosen you as the guardians of freedom, to preserve it for the benefit of the human race," President Jackson declared in his farewell address.[17] On the surface he seemed merely to reiterate the familiar commitment to liberty understood in passive terms. But increasingly American leaders were coming to accept a close relationship between liberty and the active promotion of national greatness defined more and more in terms of territorial expansion.

The Jefferson of the early 1800s had played a crucial role in promoting this tendency by surmounting the apparent contradiction between his own early ideas on liberty and Hamilton's on greatness. To be sure, the latter-day Jeffersonians still rejected Hamilton's narrow preoccupation with power, and they disagreed with him over the precise nature of the greatness Americans should seek. But they quietly made their peace with him on the need for an assertive foreign policy. Vigor in acquiring new agricultural lands was essential to sustain a republican political economy in which individual opportunity, autonomy, and virtue might flourish. Without the addition of new lands, a territorially confined republic with a growing population would degenerate. Cities would grow up, commerce and manufacturing would displace agriculture as the primary occupation, with the result that the population would succumb to the temptations of luxury, immorality, venality, and corruption. Confinement and inactivity were thus the national nemesis; expansion was its salvation and a matter of moral urgency for all true republicans.

Without power at the center, the national ambitions of the latter-day Jeffersonians might be frustrated and their republican ideal doomed. This conclusion drove them to accept the concomitant possibility that new acquisitions might require, just as the Louisiana Purchase had, a strong executive exercising the traditional tools of statecraft: the power to coerce, the right to deceive, the freedom to bluff and maneuver through crises—in general, the latitude for policymakers to act promptly and as they saw fit. They thus firmly turned their back on the early Jeffersonian fear of creating concentrations of power that might not only undermine a liberal order at home but also in time destroy altogether the American example to the world.

This important shift in the conception of American mission was reflected in a public rhetoric that ever more frequently pictured the United States as a dynamic republic, its people special bearers of freedom and always on the move. John L. O'Sullivan, well known as a proponent of this optimistic and energetic new creed that he himself dubbed "manifest destiny," proclaimed:

"We are the nation of human progress, and who will, what can, set limits to our onward march?" These remarks and others like them constituted a significant elaboration of the theme first advanced by Paine—that Americans held in their grasp the chance "to begin the world all over again." The Texas, Oregon, and Mexican War debates in Congress and in the press during the mid and late 1840s produced emphatic statements on the boundless possibilities of this "mighty nation, fast approaching, and destined soon to surpass the greatness of any European power," to exceed the size of any empire, and to overtake even the Chinese in population.[18]

Charges by critics that expansion was inimical to liberty drew passionate if familiar responses. Liberty required constant progress and "almost unlimited power of expansion," insisted one Senator in the February 1848 debate over the objectives behind the Mexican War. A colleague seconded his view. "By action alone—by ceaseless constant action" Americans could preserve liberty. "Let us expand to our true and proper dimensions, and our liberty will be eternal; for, in the process, it will increase in strength, and the flame grow brighter, whilst it lights a more extensive field." To attempt, on the other hand, to "set bounds to the indomitable energy of our noble race . . . would be treason to the cause of human liberty." A passive America would stagnate and ultimately fall prey to the fate of Europe, where a concentrated population had given rise to great social ills.[19]

Advocates of a dynamic republic shored up their case with a variety of other mutually supporting ideas. Perhaps most serviceable was the notion, already well established, that the United States stood in a pivotal position in human history. The center of civilization moved ever westward. It had sprung up in Asia, moved across the Mediterranean, and lodged most recently in Britain. With the British Empire in decline, the United States stood at the cutting edge of this process. Americans had already begun their own westward march across a continent. In time they would extend their vitalizing influence to Asia, where civilization had begun at the dawn of man.

The concept of the dynamic republic was further supported by a new physics developed well before the 1840s. John Quincy Adams was particularly keen on spelling out its most important law: the United States, "a great, powerful, enterprising, and rapidly growing nation," exercised an ever-stronger gravitational pull on adjoining lands. In 1823 he applied the law to Cuba. Tied to Spain by an "unnatural connection," the island "can gravitate only towards the North American Union, which by the same law of nature cannot cast her off from its bosom." Adams and other devotees of the new physics sometimes likened adjoining territory to ripening fruit, which political gravity would deposit in the outstretched hands of awaiting

Americans. For example, Madison, referring to Canada in 1805, noted: "When the pear is ripe it will fall of itself." But when fruit ripened too slowly to allow gravity to do its work, impatient Americans would speak of Washington "shaking the tree" or "plucking the fruit" before some others grabbed it.[20]

Finally, the dynamic republic, its exponents of the 1840s contended, was not subject to the same laws of history that had brought the downfall of Athens and Rome. Fashioned from different stuff, the United States had "a peculiar aptitude for expansion, a principle which no other Government ever did possess," and in its favored destiny was safe from the tyrants, traitors, and senseless warfare that had brought down free peoples in other ages.[21] Any taint of force or fraud that diminished the reputation of the United States as it acquired new territory was more than offset by the high purpose—the triumph of republican ideals and institutions—to which that territory would be dedicated.

The breathtaking series of territorial advances scored during the first half of the nineteenth century, though justified in terms of the dynamic republic, nonetheless raised unsettling questions. How far and how fast could Americans press their claims and advance their ambitions before betraying the cause of liberty? Mutterings, largely limited to New England, were heard over the dispossession of the American Indian, especially under Jacksonian Democrats. Proposals to annex Texas and the prospects of thereby adding a new slave state stirred up still-broader opposition. Polk's handling of the Oregon question prompted charges of imprudence, even folly: his claims in the dispute were excessive; his truculence toward the premier imperial power of the day was needlessly provocative; and the costs of a war would exceed the value of the territory at issue.

It was, however, Polk's policy during the Mexican War that gradually turned this simmering discontent into an explosion of dissent. Polk went to war to push the Texas boundary down to the Rio Grande, indicated that he would seek as spoils of the conflict the cession of the vast Mexican territories of New Mexico and California, and listened with apparent sympathy to the advocates, some within his own cabinet, of taking all Mexico.

At first the outspoken critics of the president's bold and provocative agenda were few in number. Democrats were particularly reluctant to go against a wartime president of their own party. Whigs, on the other hand, were given pause by the memory of the rapid decline the Federalist party had suffered after its unpatriotic resistance to the War of 1812. So critics among them were careful to mix their denunciations of Polk with support for appropriations for an army already in the field and praise for the bravery and sacrifice of troops led by two Whig generals. Moreover, the factional rivalries that beset both parties made the political implications of dissent difficult to calculate and inclined such Democratic luminaries as Thomas Hart Benton, Martin Van Buren, and John C. Calhoun, as well as Whig notables Daniel Webster and John J. Crittenden, to cautious maneuver. Finally, both Whigs and Democrats knew the harm a clear stand against the acquisition of new territories would do their respective parties. Already the Texas and Oregon debates had markedly raised the sectional tensions over the future of slavery and the balance of power between the regions, creating deep divisions within the two parties that had a truly national base. For party loyalists silence or compromise was preferable to an acrimonious and self-destructive debate.

A small group of so-called conscience Whigs implacably opposed to slavery and horrified by the prospect of its extension into new territories initially led the opposition. Joshua R. Giddings from Ohio and such spokesmen of the party's Massachusetts stronghold as Charles Sumner and Charles Francis Adams saw behind the war the hand of a Southern slavocracy. Polk seemed to them bent on pouring out life and treasure in support of a plot to spread a malignant and inhumane institution to new territories, thereby promoting the pernicious political influence of the South. These conscience Whigs provided the only two votes in the Senate and all fourteen votes in the House against Polk's call for war.

As the war continued amid mounting costs and Polk's war aims ballooned, Whigs and to a lesser extent Democrats who had at first acquiesced or sat silently on the sidelines joined the chorus of dissent. The arguments of the critics ranged widely. Polk's war was aggressive and unjust, defended by lies, and presented to Congress unconstitutionally as a fait accompli, and it created opportunities for European intervention dangerous to American security. As the issue of annexation came to the fore, critics warned that Polk was intent on bringing into the union an inferior people unsuited to citizenship. They tackled head-on the agrarian arguments used by supporters of the war. Americans hardly needed more land, contended Thomas Corwin, a leading Whig from Ohio, in a controversial Senate speech in February 1847 calling for an immediate end to the war. ''With twenty million people you have about one thousand million acres of land, . . . allowing every man to squat where he pleases. . . . '' A ''pretense of want of room'' was ''the plea of every robber chief from Nimrod to the present hour.''[22]

The broadest and most penetrating criticism was, however, that Polk's war endangered liberty. Democrats with views close to those of the early Jefferson and Whigs prepared to appropriate his rhetoric now expressed their dismay over the danger that a war of conquest posed to liberty and republican virtue. By trying to subject to American rule the predominantly foreign population of New Mexico and California and possibly even the entire nation of Mexico, Polk threatened to cast the United States irrevocably—and to its eventual sorrow—in an imperial role. Whig editor Horace Greeley urged his countrymen to read "the histories of the ruin of Greek and Roman liberty consequent on such extensions of empire by the sword." He observed that "only idiots or demons" could seek the glory of conquest so harmful to their nation. From the other side of the political fence, John C. Calhoun noted: "There is not an example on record of any free State ever having attempted the conquest of any territory approaching the extent of Mexico without disastrous consequences." Mexico was thus "forbidden fruit." If consumed, he cautioned, it would prove fatal to American political institutions. Jefferson's old lieutenant, Albert Gallatin, spoke as a voice from the past, warning that Polk's war debauched political virtue and betrayed the heavy responsibility Americans carried as "the 'model republic' " specially blessed by providence.[23]

Critics were acutely concerned that imperial commitments would inevitably, sooner or later, enhance executive authority at home. Already in Polk's handling of the conflict were all the warning signs of a dangerous aggrandizement and abuse of political power threatening to republican principles and practice. The president had provoked war, manipulated Congress, established a secret fund, and held under his close personal control a large military establishment—all in the best imperial (or Hamiltonian) tradition. This concentration of executive power, together with staggering taxes, a large standing army, and the intractable problems associated with an imperial policy, would eventually divide the country, undermine free institutions, and introduce an era of despotism and anarchy. Calhoun counseled "masterly inactivity" as the best hope for a republic. "If we remain quiet . . . and let our destinies work out their own results, we shall do more for liberty, not only for ourselves, but for the example of mankind, than can be done by a thousand victories. . . ." A Tennessee Whig agreed. "We are the great *exemplar*." Americans would advance "true republicanism" by setting an example of virtue and peace.[24]

Polk held firm and defied his critics, though at a price to his party and himself. The slavery question, superheated by the prospect of the war bringing in new territories, began to destroy Democratic unity. Meanwhile, the Whigs, though also polarized by that same question, nonetheless succeeded in making political inroads at the expense of Democrats. (The Whigs gained control of the House in December 1847 and would win the presidency the next year.) Polk stubbornly continued to insist on his peace terms, and the equally stubborn Mexicans, even with their armies scattered and their capital occupied, refused to bow. At last, early in 1848, Polk brought the war to an end with help from Nicholas Trist, a State Department functionary sent to Mexico by the president to negotiate a peace treaty. Having added to the reservoir of land for a growing population, Polk provided a final assessment of his achievement late in the year. New land held at bay those tendencies toward "centralization and consolidation" so deadly to republics, at the same time contributing to "the preservation of the union itself.''[25] Polk then honored his 1844 pledge to be a one-term president and retired. He died several months later, worn out by the exertions of office.

The critics perhaps deserve credit for driving Polk to accept a peace treaty not altogether to his liking. But they had not prevailed in the struggle to answer the fundamental question raised by Polk's policy. Was it possible to combine the cultivation of liberty at home with striving for greatness in international affairs? Polk proved that there were pitfalls, not that it could not be done.

Polk's policy had, however, given the country a bad case of territorial indigestion. The issue of slavery, at first only a small cloud on the horizon of national politics, had by the 1850s developed into a brooding thunderhead. Just as the critics had warned, the problem of the place of slavery in newly acquired territory proved dangerously divisive. Already in 1848 antislavery Whigs and Democrats had bolted their respective parties to form the Free Soil party. The process of party realignment was under way. The national Whig party would give way to a Northern-based Republican party, while the Democrats would become a predominantly Southern party.

Despite these troubling trends, the notion of the dynamic republic had lost none of its intrinsic appeal by the 1850s. Indeed, it gained in attractiveness to some politicians intent on combating the rise of sectional antagonism. They found in calls for a foreign policy of greatness and liberty couched in sufficiently broad terms a means of promoting a countervailing nationalism. For example, William Seward, a future Republican leader and prominent secretary of state, chose in 1854 to celebrate the country's achievements and its anticipated future glories, knowing full well that such a stirring vision might help stem the desertions that were carrying his Whig party toward total collapse. The United States, already "a great continental power," would achieve, he predicted, greater eminence still as American commerce and republican ideals transformed Hawaii, China, Japan, South America, Europe, and even Africa. Here was something to appeal to everyone. Against the prophets of doom Seward expressed the same confidence voiced by other proponents of national greatness that the United States was not subject to the forces that had brought down other empires, from the Macedonian to the British.[26]

But as the parties came to differing sectional attitudes toward slavery, foreign policy increasingly assumed a sectional twist. The result was a paralyzing conflict over the specific projects into which the dynamic republic should channel its energy. Many in the South with an eye on Mexico, Nicaragua, and Cuba still dreamed of new slave states that would preserve its strong voice in Washington and its weight in national politics. The North and West tended to regard Southern projects with repugnance; Canada, Hawaii, and commercial expansion engaged their attention. Many Northern Democrats kept a foot in both of the expansionist camps by favoring an assertive policy in any direction.

At last in 1861 the storm broke and convulsed the American people in four years of conflict during which scenes of terrible carnage were repeated month after month. The Civil War gave way to the era of Reconstruction, but even so the paralysis precipitated by sectional crisis persisted. The South was in chaos. Three-and-a-half million former slaves demanded attention. The nation suffered war-induced inflation, while the government labored under a debt of unprecedented size, equivalent to one-eighth of the national wealth. Residual energy and resources, opponents of new foreign adventures insisted, were better applied to domestic developments. "We have already more territory than we can people in fifty years, and more people, by eight or ten million, white and black, than we dare admit at present to a share in our Government," mused a newspaper in 1866 preoccupied with unfinished business at home.[27] Beyond this preoccupation with domestic needs there emerged in the post–Civil War decades an additional check on foreign policy adventures: political partisanship. Expansionist projects developed under the aegis of a Republican-controlled White House or State Department were guaranteed instant, critical Democratic scrutiny.

★ ★ ★

After four decades of national immobility the old vision of greatness and liberty regained its hold on policy in the 1880s and 1890s. The end of Reconstruction together with sectional reconciliation finally removed a prime source of national controversy and division. At the same time, the extension of European imperial rivalries into the Pacific, East Asia, and the Americas began to evoke in the United States both alarm and calls for imitation. New technology applied to weaponry, ships, and communications suddenly made the world seem smaller and more threatening. The vogue enjoyed by the competitive ethic of social Darwinism strengthened this perception that the world was rapidly pressing in. Americans were also discovering that they needed new spiritual and commercial frontiers abroad to replace an exhausted continental frontier and a saturated home market. Recurrent economic crises—first in the 1870s, again in the 1880s, and finally most severely in the 1890s—made foreign markets seem, at least to some, indispensable to the nation's future prosperity.

The dramatic transformation of American life in the post–Civil War decades, some historians have speculated, may also have prepared the way psychologically for this return to an active policy. Industrialization, urbanization, and the arrival of millions of immigrants created internal pressures (or at least elite anxieties) that were ultimately vented in overseas adventures. These trends, as reflected in the troubling fragmentation of the nation into antagonistic blocs of capital and labor and diverse ethnic and regional cultures, may have made the unifying effect of an assertively nationalist foreign policy particularly attractive. Whatever the causes, Washington began to build up the navy in the late 1880s and to move toward a more active role in both Latin America and the Pacific.

The siren call of national greatness was again being loudly and clearly heard. In a widely read book of 1885, the evangelist Josiah Strong gave voice to the expansionist strain common among mission-minded Protestants. He promised his countrymen that God was ''preparing mankind to receive our impress.'' As successors to the British and beneficiaries of the westward movement of civilization, this generation of Americans would turn commerce, missionary work, and colonization toward shaping ''the destinies of mankind.'' Alfred Thayer Mahan, who was embarked on writing the classic text on naval strategy, saw Americans irrevocably caught in a wary, strife-torn world. ''Everywhere nation is arrayed against nation; our own no less than others.'' The United States would have to have a large navy, overseas bases, and a Central American canal if it were to protect its commercial and strategic interests. Henry Cabot Lodge, prominent Massachusetts senator and influential Republican, sought to awaken Americans to their place ''as one of the great nations of the world.'' With ''a record of conquest, colonization, and territorial expansion unequalled by any people in the nineteenth century,'' they should not hesitate now to join other powers in the current race for ''the waste places of the earth.'' National honor, power, and profits as well as racial fitness and pride were the watchwords of these commentators.[28]

A policy grounded on these notions was to plunge Americans into their third debate over the fundamental purposes of their foreign policy. The controversies of the 1890s, brought to a climax by the Spanish-American

War, marked the last stage in the rise to hegemony of the notion of the dynamic republic. In some crucial respects they amounted to little more than a reprise of the clash of the 1840s.

Once more a president precipitated a major debate by seizing the opportunities created by a one-sided war. William McKinley, an Ohio politician of few words and a keen political sense, was an effective proponent of the dynamic republic. After accepting war with Spain in 1898 to free Cuba, he quickly put through Congress the long-delayed annexation of Hawaii and ordered American forces to occupy Cuba, Puerto Rico, Guam, and the Philippines. He followed in 1899 with fresh initiatives: the passage of a treaty annexing the latter three islands and the conclusion of an agreement with Germany on the partition of Samoa. That same year he oversaw the dispatch of the open-door notes in response to a feared partition of China and in 1900 sent troops to help put down the Boxers.

These decisions reveal not a master plan but rather a consistent devotion to those ends that publicists had already linked to national greatness—commercial prosperity, territorial expansion, and military security. The president himself defended his policy in September 1898 with a reference to "obligations which we cannot disregard." The next month, during a swing through the Midwest, he called on Americans to be faithful to "the trust which civilization puts upon us." Echoing the liturgy of foreign-policy activists earlier in the decade, McKinley claimed for the United States a right and duty to establish colonies, help "oppressed peoples," and generally project its power and influence into the world. Americans would benefit, and so would all humanity. To a Boston audience in February 1899 he described control of the Philippines, Cuba, and Puerto Rico as a "great trust" that the nation carried "under the providence of God and in the name of human progress and civilization." He reassured doubters with the claim that "our priceless principles undergo no change under a tropical sun. They go with the flag."[29]

Supporters of the president played on the same range of themes. Americans were "a people imperial by virtue of their power, by right of their institutions, by authority of their Heaven-directed purposes." Such were the views of the young Indiana Republican Albert J. Beveridge, whose perfervid and popular speech given in September 1898 helped prepare the Midwest for McKinley's visit. The United States was "henceforth to lead in the regeneration of the world." He and others made much of the trade and strategic advantages derived from overseas possessions. The Philippines in particular were lauded as a base for promoting the "vast" China trade and protecting growing interests throughout the Pacific. In a world made small by electricity and steam, those islands were not remote but were rendered virtually contiguous to the continental United States by an easily crossed ocean.[30]

An administration intent on gathering the spoils of war did not go unchallenged. Once more critics with a pristine and self-limiting vision of the American future took a stand. They included dissident Republicans, such as Senator George F. Hoar of Massachusetts and former President Benjamin Harrison, most of them of an older generation and active earlier in the antislavery crusade. Democrats were even more visibly in opposition. In the Senate Southern Democrats provided seventeen of the twenty-seven votes against the annexation of the Philippines, just as they had previously led the fight in Congress against taking Hawaii. Democratic notables, including former President Grover Cleveland, former Secretary of State Richard Olney, and the party presidential candidate in 1896, William Jennings Bryan, attacked McKinley's foreign policy. Intellectuals and educators from both parties joined the ranks of the critics, prominent among them David Starr Jordan of Stanford University, William James of Harvard, William Graham Sumner of Yale, the novelists Mark Twain and William Dean Howells, and the humorist Finley Peter Dunne. Political and social reformers, notably Carl Schurz and Jane Addams, rallied to the cause as well. Even the industrialist Andrew Carnegie lent his name and money to the opposition.

This diverse group began to coalesce under the banner of the Anti-Imperialist League in November 1898 as McKinley's full war aims became clear. Their arguments against annexation received national attention during the Senate treaty debate. The outbreak of Filipino resistance to American rule in early 1899 and reports of torture and atrocities committed in the course of "pacification" served further to dramatize the issue to the benefit of the critics.

These critics were quick to rebut the practical argument of expansionists that the changed circumstances in the world and in the American economy required a new outward thrust. Why exchange an impregnable continental position for distant possessions that were vulnerable to sudden attack and would require a costly naval and military buildup to defend? The Philippines were seven thousand miles from California and only six hundred miles from China. Caught up in the vortex of imperial competition, those islands would prove a strategic burden rather than an asset. They would, moreover, drain the United States economically, a point made most emphatically by Carnegie. They would be costly to administer while providing little if any fillip to the pursuit of the China trade.

The burden of the dissent, however, remained (as in previous debates) the incompatibility of liberty with a foreign policy that aimed for greatness. In

June 1898, Cleveland warned that the country seemed poised to "abandon old landmarks and . . . follow the lights of monarchical hazards." Later, in September, Schurz cited the old historical law that a republic "can endure so long as it remains true to the principles upon which it was founded, but it will morally decay if it abandons them." Sumner, in attacking the annexation of the Philippines, invoked the early idyllic Jeffersonian vision, which—though never fully realized at home—remained "a glorious dream." A commitment to limited government, individual freedom, and approximate economic equality had made the United States stand "for something unique and grand in the history of mankind." Echoing the arguments of earlier critics, Sumner contended that "adventurous policies of conquest or ambition" would transform this special "democratic republic" into "another empire just after the fashion of all the old ones." Like other republics that had indulged "in the greed and lust of empire," the United States would begin by attempting to impose its rule on others. It would next have to arm against predatory colonial rivals. The net effect of foreign adventures would soon be seen at home in the form of a burgeoning state apparatus that would dispense patronage and control a large military establishment. Factions would contend for this concentrated power, and in the process inexorably corrupt republican virtue and ultimately overthrow liberty.[31]

Once more critics failed to discredit the expansionist creed. Unlike their forerunners in the 1840s, the critics of the 1890s were not even to have the satisfaction of inflicting some political damage on the offending party in power. Expansionists now had the considerable advantage of being able to point out that their critics' stand in behalf of a pristine Jeffersonian vision of liberty had become thoroughly compromised—by Jefferson himself and by his disciples earlier in the nineteenth century. Roosevelt and Lodge claimed that McKinley merely walked the path Jefferson had marked out. "The parallel between what Jefferson did with Louisiana and what is now being done in the Philippines is exact." Beveridge developed the argument for precedents with greatest effect. The 1890s was not a watershed, he pointed out, but part of a process of expansion launched by Jefferson, "the first Imperialist of the Republic." With each decade Americans had pitched "the tents of liberty farther westward, farther southward" and at each step had turned aside resistance from "the infidels to the gospel of liberty." Liberty was a principle no more universally applicable now than it had been then. The "savage" and "alien" populations in previously acquired territories had been incapable of self-government and so been made "wards" of Washington. If the United States could take Florida from the Seminoles, the northern plains from the Sioux, or California from the Mexicans, if it could treat the

Indians as dependents and govern territories as colonies, then it could also take the Philippines and save Filipinos from "the savage, bloody rule of pillage and extortion." [32]

The combined appeal of liberty and greatness now easily triumphed over a narrow, cautious, self-limiting conception of national mission. The president had steadily raised his demands until they included acquisition of the entire Philippines, and he pushed the treaty embodying these terms through a resistant Senate in February 1899. The vote of fifty-seven to twenty-seven had been close enough (barely over the necessary two-thirds) to tempt the critics into thinking the 1900 presidential election could be made into a great referendum on imperialism. But such hopes soon crumbled. An effort to find a third-party candidate strongly committed to the anti-imperialist cause quickly collapsed. Some of the opposition turned, reluctantly, to the Democratic party and its standard-bearer Bryan. (His free-silver stand was controversial, and his strategy during the treaty debate, which had helped McKinley secure annexation, had revealed poor judgment.) Others sat the election out or held their noses and voted Republican. With his enemies divided, McKinley prevailed this time by a wider margin than in his previous contest with Bryan in 1896. The issue of imperialism was in any case not even joined during the campaign. The staunchest critics, isolated and ignored, fought on for only a few years longer against public apathy before fading away.

★ ★ ★

By the turn of the century the keystone of U.S. foreign-policy ideology had fallen securely in place. Americans had succumbed to the temptations of an assertively nationalist foreign policy. Hamilton had first dangled it before them, Jefferson himself had fallen to its charms, Polk and McKinley had warmly embraced it. Step by step foreign-policy activists had come to occupy the patriotic high ground, defeating doubters and defying critics ever more decisively along the way. Activist leaders embraced a broad definition of national security that would carry the nation toward greatness in the world. In this endeavor they ultimately brought Americans to terms with colonies and naval bases, spheres of influence and protectorates, a powerful blue-water navy, and an expeditionary army.

A multiplicity of arguments justified the search for international greatness. Foreign powers hostile to the United States had to be met and thrown back. Crusading abroad would elevate the national character, strengthen national unity and pride, and smooth the workings of the economy. American energy and vision were too great to confine within fixed domestic bounds. But of all the arguments developed in behalf of a foreign policy of greatness none was to be as fateful as those that invoked liberty.

A policy devoted to both liberty and greatness, activists contended, was far from being a dangerous and unstable union of incompatibles. Instead, greatness abroad would glorify liberty at home. As success followed success and the boundaries of the American enterprise extended steadily outward, a free people's faith in their special destiny would be confirmed and deepened. Secure in their faith in liberty, Americans would set about remaking others in their own image while the world watched in awe.

At the same time liberty sanctified greatness. A chosen people could lay claim to special rights and obligations that rendered irrelevant the Cassandras who spoke of imperialism and the demise of republics. Let the fainthearted cry that the annals of history were filled with those who had reached for greatness and thereby lost liberty. Had they forgotten that the same laws of history need not govern Americans, a special people with a unique destiny? Thus the ascendant nationalists argued that the American pursuit of lofty ambitions abroad, far from imperiling liberty, would serve to invigorate it at home while creating conditions favorable to its spread in foreign lands. In other words, the United States could transform the world without itself being transformed.

By inextricably entangling liberty with greatness, proponents of activism not only met and matched their critics on the critics' favorite ground but also developed an argument with broad appeal. For a people in flux the rhetoric of liberty and greatness established reassuring ties to the nation's mythic beginnings. A nation born out of a struggle against tyranny still held to the ideals of its founders and kept in sight the old promise "to begin the world all over again." Foreign policy could thus supply a sense of national continuity that the domestic sphere was less and less able to sustain.

The proponents of greatness had outflanked their critics, leaving them to mutter dourly from the sidelines about small government, low taxes, and republican virtue. Jefferson had unknowingly contributed to this outcome by pursuing as president a policy substantially at odds with the principles he had professed earlier. The Democrats in the 1840s carried the process another step forward. With their roots in the Jeffersonian tradition, they had to square their expansionist goals with the older dream of liberty. They set about that task with energy. Their success in turn cleared the way for the Republicans of the 1890s—whose dreams of power, progress, and stability were closer to Hamilton's—to secure firmly the bond between liberty and greatness. Though defeated on three occasions, the critics had at least succeeded in handing down a vocabulary of dissent from the 1790s to the

1890s. Their most powerful argument continued to sound in the twentieth century: a foreign policy oriented toward international greatness would prove antithetical to republican principles and subversive of a republican system.

The striking persistence of two visions of American mission deserves scrutiny, the dominant vision equating the cause of liberty with the active pursuit of national greatness in world affairs and the dissenting one favoring a foreign policy of restraint as essential to perfecting liberty at home. How could a fundamental divergence within the American political elite remain so sturdy? How could the outlooks of each side seemingly escape the enormous transformations that characterized the nation's first century?

The appeal of greatness is perhaps most easily understood. The advocates of greatness wished to harness policy to the burgeoning power generated by a commercializing and later an industrializing economy. This economic power created the potential for fashioning the instruments of policy essential to dreams of international greatness. At the same time economic growth created needs and problems that were no less important to the thinking of the advocates of greatness. Markets needed protecting. Divisions at home needed papering over. The national stability, wealth, and power on which an activist foreign policy depended required in turn a strong state with ample revenue, a conclusion that leading policymakers in the 1790s and 1890s accepted instinctively and maintained steadfastly. In both eras Britain provided the model of political centralization and economic development that Americans with a taste for greatness could copy. The Democrats of the 1840s could not accept a strong central government as a good in itself, but there is no question that they were prepared to act like statists to the extent required by their overlapping goals of agrarian economic development and continental expansion.

The policy critics were at odds with the trends that their activist opponents embraced more or less enthusiastically. With liberty their touchstone, these critics reacted with hostility to policies that made the central government dangerously powerful, economic trends that debased or exploited fellow citizens, and developments that in any way threatened to lead the nation away from its heritage of liberty. Arrayed against the dominant political economy, the critics issued by definition from weak and marginal groups in the national life and could form only unstable, transient coalitions. Southern Democrats, whose agrarian values were imperiled by Hamilton and later by the Republican party of McKinley, twice provided the base for political opposition. New England, especially Massachusetts Whigs/Republicans, constituted the other significant base of opposition, first in the 1840s with abolitionists in the lead and again in the 1890s with the regional intelligentsia reinforcing aging politicians (''Mugwumps'') who had ties to the old anti-slavery crusade. Other groups, such as non-Yankee ethnic communities and members of dissenting churches in the 1790s, rallied to the opposition—but not with the frequency or force of either New Englanders or Southerners. By the 1890s dissenters even within these two major groups were so enfeebled that together the strange bedfellows could not muster the Senate votes or popular support to stop a determined McKinley.

The critics' frequently expressed anxiety over the fragility of liberty and the decline of republican virtue may seem in retrospect like empty, ritual invocations. But the dissenters must be given credit for raising—even as late as the 1890s—broad and real issues, not narrow or illusory ones. They cannot be written off as political opportunists or nitpickers fussing over the precise terms of treaties, first with Britain, then with Mexico, and finally with Spain. They correctly regarded foreign adventures as an important indication of national priorities. They saw in those adventures evidence for a growing gap between professed ideals inherited from the past and everyday domestic realities defined above all by commercialization and industrialization. The emerging nineteenth-century order was associated with an aggressive and asocial individualism, geographic mobility, the hierarchies of large-scale organization, growing disparities in wealth, and concentrations of economic and political power. These were all viewed as disturbing features, inimical to the individual self-reliance, rough political equality, and communal solidarity that the critics associated with a good society. Was the American citizen who vicariously controlled Cuba and the Philippines indeed more free and independent than his counterpart of a hundred years earlier? Was the effort to establish liberty on the world stage not a way of distracting Americans from the buffeting that liberty was receiving in the domestic arena?[33]

The critics were powerless to arrest trends adverse to liberty or alter the economic system that gave rise to them. They nonetheless served their countrymen well by emphasizing the steady drift from professed values. They argued that the pursuit of greatness diverted attention and resources from real problems at home and might under some circumstances even aggravate or compound those problems. Foreign crusades unavoidably diminished national ideals and well-being. Ironically the critics, themselves accused of indulging in ritual invocations of a dead past, help us see the activists' celebration of a symbiotic relationship between liberty and greatness as itself a form of ritual, powerful in its nationalist appeal but devoid of any real meaning if measured in terms of the lives of most of their countrymen.

Though out-voted, out-argued, and out-maneuvered, the critics extracted a revenge of sorts. They left lingering the subversive question of whether the central proposition of U.S. foreign policy to which twentieth-century policymakers would fall heir was really a humbug.

3 The Hierarchy of Race

The Number of purely white People in the World is proportionably very small. All Africa is black or tawny. Asia chiefly tawny. America (exclusive of the new Comers) wholly so. And in Europe, the Spaniards, Italians, French, Russians and Swedes, are generally of what we call a swarthy complexion; as are the Germans also, the Saxons only excepted, who with the English, make the principal Body of White People on the Face of the Earth. I could wish their Numbers were increased.... Perhaps I am partial to the Complexion of my Country, for such Kind of Partiality is natural to Mankind. —Benjamin Franklin (1751)

Benjamin Franklin, that paragon of Enlightenment optimism, versatility, and virtue, was also a racist.[1] He divided humanity according to skin color, assigning to each color characteristic traits. Indians he publicly condemned as "barbarous tribes of savages that delight in war and take pride in murder." His private correspondence depicted them as ignorant, congenitally lazy, vain, and insolent. An occasional blow was essential to keeping them in line; even a hint of weakness was an invitation to trouble. A slave owner whose printing establishment profited from slave sales, Franklin regarded blacks as lazy, thieving, and improvident. He defended the severity of slave codes as appropriate to a people "of a plotting Disposition, dark, sullen, malicious, revengeful, and cruel in the highest Degree." Even the "swarthy" German settlers in Franklin's Pennsylvania, derogated by him as "Palantine Boors," seemed undesirable aliens. They were worrisomely clannish, and some among them were even papists.

Franklin's racism was in substantial measure a response to the spur of interest, both national and personal. He dreamed of a free English-speaking people in the Americas increasing in number, territory, strength, and commercial prosperity. Throughout his political career he followed this dream. It carried him toward the advocacy of colonial unity and ultimately of in-

46

dependence from Britain. It made him the proponent of the acquisition and opening of new lands, a task that he identified as the better part of statesmanship. Rulers that acquire new territory (even by removing "the Natives" if necessary), he wrote in 1751, "may be properly called the Fathers of their nation, as they are the Cause of the Generation of Multitudes by the Encouragement they afford to Marriage."[2] To the public good to be derived from the acquisition of new land for an increasing white population, Franklin could add the potential benefit to his private purse. As early as 1748 he had entered the game of land speculation, buying shares in companies with claims in the Ohio valley and Nova Scotia, and for fifteen years he lobbied in London to advance colonial claims to western lands.

The Indians by the simple fact of possessing much desirable territory could not help running directly athwart Franklin's determination to obtain the land needed for future generations of whites. By obstructing the opening of new land and hence the opportunity of whites to get ahead, marry, and multiply, Indians were guilty of one of the most serious crimes in his book: "killing thousands of our children before they are born." Franklin preferred to avoid a collision of interests, and he hated to see docile and accommodating Indians victimized—often indiscriminately killed—by anxious or grasping frontiersmen. Yet he could not help making the Indian his favorite target for racial stereotyping. He thus reflected and reinforced the prevailing prejudices of his countrymen and at the same time convinced himself of the necessity of vigilance and firmness in dealing with so dangerous a people. Surly and violent Indians, especially those that connived with the French against the interests of British America, should be summarily thrust aside and their land expropriated for others to put to better use.

Blacks and Germans were by contrast a less formidable, internal problem— a blotch on the existing pattern of settlement, to be sure, but not a fundamental threat to it from outside. They were either to be assimilated or to be excluded in favor of better stock. Personal involvement in the schooling of Philadelphia blacks disabused Franklin of any belief in their innate inferiority and by the 1770s made of him an opponent of slavery. But his commitment to maintaining the purity of the white settlement drove him to oppose allowing more blacks into the colonies, "as they every where prevent the Increase of Whites." Similarly his commitment to white supremacy led him to look uneasily on the large number of blacks already settled in the South. He regarded them, like the Indians, as a dissatisfied people that unfriendly outside powers such as France might stir to insurrection. The Germans too were of uncertain loyalty. Those already in the country should, if possible, be culturally transformed by free English schools, while those yet to arrive should be kept back in favor of better stock—the English, Welsh, and Protestant Irish.

Franklin's consciousness of color, fully shared by his contemporaries, figured prominently in the thinking of subsequent generations. Their conception of race, somewhat more elaborate and structured than Franklin's, was essentially hierarchical. They drew distinctions among the various peoples of the world on the basis of physical features, above all skin color and to a lesser extent head type (as the illustrations to follow suggest), and guided by those distinctions they ranked the various types of peoples in the world. Those with the lightest skin were positioned on the highest rung of the hierarchy, and those with the darkest skin were relegated to the lowest. In between fell the "yellow" Mongolians and Malays, the "red" American Indian, and the racially mixed Latino. Each color implied a level of physical, mental, and moral development, with white Americans setting themselves up as the unquestioned standard of measurement. "Superior peoples" thus spoke English or some language akin to it, responsibly exercised democratic rights, embraced the uplifting influence of Protestant Christianity, and thanks to their industry enjoyed material abundance. Those toward the bottom were woefully deficient in each of these areas.

This folk wisdom on race was reinforced from early in the nineteenth century by "scientific" investigation. Taken as a group, ethnographers, geographers, and historians offered complex and often contradictory conclusions on the nature of race. Were racial characteristics fixed or subject to change? Did races have multiple and distinct origins or a single common source? How did race relate to culture, civilization, and national character? If the findings of the learned had been an important source of American thinking on race, then their conflicting conclusions might well have cast doubt on the validity of race as a concept. But in fact the learned were important to popular thinking chiefly insofar as they focused popular attention on race by their persistent and often tortured effort to give it an empirical basis. In other words, their interest gave popular legitimacy to race as a fundamental and objective category separating peoples of supposedly unequal gifts.

Blacks above all others served as the anvil on which Americans forged this notion of racial hierarchy and the attendant color-conscious view of the world. Colonists carried with them Elizabethan prejudices that associated the color black and by extension the dark-skinned peoples of Africa with baseness and evil. White stood as the moral and aesthetic opposite, the symbol of virtue, beauty, and purity. An English poem of 1620 played on this contrast by describing the African as "a black deformed Elfe" while picturing the white Englishman as "like unto God himselfe."[3]

By the early eighteenth century Americans were applying explicitly racial

Mongolian.
Ethiopian.

Caucasian.

American.
Malay.

Figure 1. *The Races of Men*

These composite pictures, both presented to school children as The Races of Men, *would have left no doubt about white superiority. In fig. 1 (drawn from a text of 1877) the white race is personified by a noble woman, calm and composed, shown full face, in contrast to the swarthy males with eyes averted.*

TYPICAL MAN.

1   APOLLO BELVEDERE.   2

MONGOLIC.   3   WHITE.   4   AFRICAN.   5

AMERICAN.   6   MALAY.   7   AUSTRALIAN.   8

Figure 2. *The Races of Men*

In fig. 2 (published in 1873) the white, described in the accompanying text as the "normal" race, is represented by classical models and by a more ordinary but nonetheless handsome figure again shown full face. The other races seem wild or dispirited as they gaze vaguely into the distance (except for the "Mongolic" type, who wears a slightly crazed expression).[4]

formulations to blacks. In the South this intellectual legacy combined with economic self-interest to produce the most extreme negrophobia. There exploitation of blacks had become a way of life, and their submission essential to a sense of security among often outnumbered white communities. The black was first abased in the Southern slave codes, and later, in the nineteenth century, his inherent inferiority was vigorously affirmed in response to abolitionist agitation and post–Civil War Reconstruction policy. The folklore of the region stigmatized enslaved blacks as incipient insurrectionists and brooding rapists. Close supervision and control and the threat of severe punishment, including castration for sexual as well as other offenses, served to keep them in check.

These racial views informed the Southern perspective on external affairs already in antebellum days. A horror of miscegenation at home translated naturally enough into censure of foreign peoples who tolerated racial mixing and suffered from its regressive social effects. Southerners, doubting the docility of their own blacks, took fright when Caribbean slaves slaughtered their masters or British abolitionists (and later social revolutionaries in Europe) promoted the radical doctrine of human equality. The emancipation of blacks after the Civil War brought about some shift in race relations, especially toward social segregation, but not in Southern white views of black bestiality and the fears and fantasies that those views stimulated in response to developments abroad no less than at home.

Though whites often disagreed on aspects of the ''Negro question,'' sometimes emotionally so, they nonetheless agreed almost universally on the fundamental issue of white supremacy and black inferiority. By the beginning of the twentieth century the issue of the place of blacks in American society rested on the same foundation that it had three centuries earlier—the protean association of inferiority with darkness of skin color. This strikingly persistent consensus on race was evident in scholarly work, but even more to the point it suffused the popular literature of the time. School texts, for example, consistently put across from decade to decade the same essential message: blacks occupied the bottom rung in the hierarchy of race dominated by whites. Blacks were ''destitute of intelligence.'' A geography of 1789 delicately explained, ''They are a brutish people, having little more of humanity but the form.'' At best these texts presented blacks as victims of slavery, incapable of climbing higher on their own, possibly educable as dependents of paternalistic whites, but also perhaps irremediably backward. A 1900 account probably reflected mainstream white attitudes when it glumly concluded, ''In spite of the efforts to educate them . . . many [blacks] still remain densely ignorant.''[5]

This conception of race, defined by the poles of black and white, carried over into American foreign policy. By its grip on the thinking of the men who debated and determined that policy, by its influence over the press, and by its hold on the electorate, race powerfully shaped the way the nation dealt with other peoples. This included not just the Indian even before Franklin's day but also the peoples of Latin America, East Asia, and Europe as Americans developed their own independent foreign policy.

The idea of a racial hierarchy proved particularly attractive because it offered a ready and useful conceptual handle on the world. It was reassuringly hardy and stable in a changing world. It was also accessible and gratifyingly easy to apply. Rather than having to spend long hours trying—perhaps inconclusively—to puzzle out the subtle patterns of other cultures, the elite interested in policy had at hand in the hierarchy of race a key to reducing other peoples and nations to readily comprehensible and familiar terms. It required no more than an understanding of easily grasped polarities and superficial characteristics. Races were different and unequal. Some were more civilized or progressive, others were more barbaric or backward. By locating white Americans of old stock among the most advanced peoples, the racial hierarchy had the incidental attraction of flattering that elite's ego and lending credence to that other major pillar of American foreign policy, the commitment to greatness.

From the perspective of the chosen few who made and followed policy, the idea of a racial hierarchy had the additional virtue of being congruent with popular attitudes. Americans high and low absorbed an awareness of race in their schooling, in their homes, and in their work place. As a central point of cultural reference on which all were agreed, race could be applied to foreign problems without fear that the concept itself would arouse domestic controversy.

★ ★ ★

The national preoccupation with race was further reinforced and refined by contact with those peoples who fell in the path of the American pursuit of greatness across a continent and overseas. The first of these were the Indians, a cover-all term applied to peoples belonging to several thousand different native-American cultures. For three hundred years, both as colonials and as members of an independent nation, Americans warred against or formed alliances with the Indians, made treaties with them and broke those treaties, until the dominance of transplanted Europeans was established beyond the slightest challenge.

In the process, the Indians suffered enormous loss of life. That part of the Americas north of the Rio Grande boasted a pre-Columbian Indian population that scholars today estimate at ten million. Epidemic disease introduced from Europe carried away millions. Warfare and forced relocation, which brought starvation and exposure, made further substantial inroads. Between the early nineteenth century and 1930 the number of Indians living in the continental United States shrank from perhaps 600,000 to roughly half that figure. White Americans had not inherited the fabled empty continent. Rather, by their presence and policies, they had emptied it.

Successive generations had shared Franklin's view of the Indian as an impediment to acquiring new land cheaply. Just as Southern whites spawned virulent strains of negrophobia, frontier whites were the source of the most intense and violent Indian hating. And though their resort to fraudulent or violent methods collided with humanitarian principles and legal agreements (including formal treaties), the federal government and, it seems fair to say, most Americans endorsed or acquiesced in the practice of Indian extermination and removal. The governor of Georgia, a state synonymous among Cherokees for land grabbing, explained in 1830 that "treaties were expedients by which ignorant, intractable, and savage people were induced without bloodshed to yield up what civilized peoples had a right to possess. . . . "[6] Thomas Jefferson was less blunt but no less devoted to an aggressive policy that would open vast new tracts of land to his beloved yeoman farmer. Later generations along the moving western frontier maintained the proposition laid down by these early Americans—savages would have to go, treaties or no treaties.

The claims of self-interest could not, however, entirely override the dictates of justice, and so there resulted a contradiction in Indian policy that became apparent in colonial times and carried over into the early national period. Missionaries and prominent American statesmen, Thomas Jefferson included, had hoped to dissolve the contradiction by promoting the cultural assimilation of the Indian. Education, conversion to Christianity, and the abandonment of hunting for farming on private land were the key steps toward realizing this goal. Assimilation had the substantial virtue of saving the national honor and preserving the existence of an otherwise doomed primitive people while also ensuring that large tracts of wasteland would be put to better use. Indians would turn part of the wilderness into farmlands for themselves, making the rest available for purchase by whites.

These high hopes were repeatedly shattered by the impatience, sharp dealing, and violence that characterized the actual workings of Indian policy and the day-to-day approach of whites to Indians generally. The government devoted scant resources to promoting assimilation and failed to enforce treaties guaranteeing Indians even their diminished holdings. Those Indians who did make substantial progress towards assimilation, such as the Cherokees, found whites insatiable in their appetite for land and unstoppable in their drive to acquire it. When local conflicts over land developed between whites and Indians, state authorities predictably favored whites. Indian resistance, leading occasionally to alliances with sympathetic European powers, set off in turn brutal frontier warfare that invariably brought Indian defeat and white retribution. The victors then pushed the vanquished aside. Colonial New Englanders and Virginians had set the pattern.They regarded the Indians as dangerous barbarians, to be segregated for better supervision or altogether removed beyond range of contact. A mailed fist and a readiness to use forceful if not brutal methods were essential to keeping them in check.

Andrew Jackson, a Tennesseean and inveterate land speculator who had imbibed that heady frontier brew of land hunger and Indian hating, brought these methods to perfection, and in so doing he became the agent for the destruction of the Creeks, Seminoles, and other Indians of the Southeast. Through a series of military campaigns and imposed treaties in the 1810s, he shattered Indian power and forced open to speculation and settlement Indian land accounting for three-fourths of the territory of Florida and Alabama, one-third of Tennessee, one-fifth of Georgia and Mississippi, and smaller fractions of Kentucky and North Carolina. Later, in the 1830s, Jackson the president set in motion the policy—described by him as "not only liberal, but generous"—of removing the remaining sixty thousand Indians.[7] By the 1850s the Indian question east of the Mississippi had been "solved" to white satisfaction.

The process of subjugation was repeated west of the Mississippi in the latter half of the nineteenth century. Thanks to new technology, especially armaments, railroads, and telegraphs, the next round in the destruction of the American Indian proceeded just as inexorably and even more swiftly. Tribes long resident in the West and some ninety thousand Indians driven there from the East signed treaties with the federal government guaranteeing their land "as long as the waters run and the grass shall grow." These treaties were then universally and systematically violated. Once again local encroachments created tensions, which federal troops invariably settled to the disadvantage of Indians. Some tribes offered no resistance. Such was the case with the California Indians, who numbered one hundred thousand in 1848. In eleven years they were reduced by barbarous treatment to thirty thousand; by 1900 only fifteen thousand were left. Other tribes prudently retreated, seeking in renegotiated treaties to preserve some part of their ever-dwindling patrimony. Some, such as the Sioux, fought back, but even their small and temporary victories were purchased at the price of severe reprisals.

The federal government finally forced most of these battered peoples onto reservations, which were merely confined patches of marginal land where they were to live under governmental protection and supervision. While the Indians sought to salvage the last shreds of their cultural autonomy, their white overseers labored to eradicate the old "savage," nomadic patterns and to settle their charges into a new civilized, Christian way of life.

The army that guarded the peace of the West and policed the Indians was a worthy successor to Jackson's militia. It dealt with Indians according to the principles of group responsibility, expected treachery and bad faith from them as a matter of course, and anticipated their ultimate extermination. General William T. Sherman, who first commanded that Western army (and later supervised its campaigns from Washington), wrote in 1868, "The more we can kill this year, the less will have to be killed the next war, for the more I see of these Indians the more convinced I am that all have to be killed or be maintained as a species of pauper. Their attempts at civilization are simply ridiculous."[8] Northeastern humanitarians protested in vain against outrages no worse than those their ancestors had perpetrated against other Indians in an earlier age.

By the 1870s an American policy of continental expansion initiated in that earlier age had run full course so far as the Indian was concerned. In 1871 Congress stopped making new treaties, and old treaties, the Supreme Court had ruled the year before, were no longer binding. Even autonomy was denied the Indian as the federal government extended its control over reservation life. The Dawes Act of 1887 completed the process of distributing tribal lands and undermining tribal power. Aside from sporadic outbreaks, the Indian now ceased to be a foreign problem and could be neglected as a domestic one. The ties between the Indian and foreign policy, however, were not so much broken as transformed. The rationale used to justify the defeat and dispossession of one people would in the future serve to sanction claims to American superiority and dominion over other peoples.

With the brutal abasement of the Indian in real life went a tendency to ennoble him in myth. In the course of the nineteenth century whites showed a generous impulse, the prerogative of victors, to downplay old antagonisms and assign the Indian a flatteringly high place in the hierarchy of race. Viewed in the romantic afterglow of his defeat, he emerged near the top, just below whites and far above the lowly blacks. The Indian stood there as a melancholy, even tragic figure. He had been the victim of an abstraction, American progress. His sacrifice had been necessary, noted one school text as early as 1813, "for the increase of mankind, and for the promotion of the world's glory and happiness."[9] A child of the wilderness—simple, brave, enduring,

Figure 3.

These illustrations provide two commonplace perspectives on the Indian. Figure 3, from a child's geography text of 1848, depicts the Indian as cruel victimizer.

Figure 4. American Progress

Figure 4, a painting by John Gast of 1872 entitled American Progress shows the Indian as victim, retreating along with the other creatures of the wild before the forces of civilization. In each, noble white women occupy a central position—as pitiful defender of the next generation and as the majestic embodiment of the irresistible forces of progress.[10]

and dignified—he had proven constitutionally deficient in those qualities of industry and self-discipline essential to getting on in a world being rapidly transformed by the forces of civilization. So, like the wilderness, the noble savage in this racial myth would simply have to fade away, thereby confirming that general law of nature: where two races meet, the inferior yields inevitably to the superior.

★ ★ ★

Latinos, the Spanish-speaking peoples of the Americas, occupied a position midway up the hierarchy of race. Their position there was fixed by the hold on the American imagination of the "black legend" with its condemnatory view of Spanish character. That legend had been part of the intellectual baggage that the English colonists had brought to the New World, and it was subsequently amplified by American merchants and diplomats who made direct contact with the newly independent Latin American states early in the nineteenth century. The resulting critique of Latin culture was perpetuated by school texts, kept fresh in cartoons, retailed in political rhetoric, and even incorporated into the views of policymakers, so that by the early twentieth century it had come to exercise a pervasive influence on the American approach to Latin America.

Narrowly construed, the black legend highlighted the cruelty with which Spanish conquerors had dealt with native-American populations. Driven by a taste for "carnage and plunder" (in the words of a 1794 text), these adventurers had overcome the Indians by a combination of brutality and deception and then exploited them unmercifully.[11]

More broadly understood, the legend stood for all those undesirable characteristics that were Spain's unfortunate legacy to much of the New World. An 1898 account written to justify the war against Spain drew on what had become a widely accepted notion of that legacy. "Spain has been tried and convicted in the forum of history. Her religion has been bigotry, whose sacraments have been solemnized by the faggot and the rack. Her statesmanship has been infamy: her diplomacy, hypocrisy: her wars have been massacres: her supremacy has been a blight and a curse, condemning continents to sterility, and their inhabitants to death." Henry Cabot Lodge, an outspoken proponent of that war, characterized the foe as "mediaeval, cruel, dying" and "three hundred years behind all the rest of the world." Returning from a tour of Cuba, Redfield Proctor delivered a major Senate speech in March 1898 flatly accusing Spain of "the worst misgovernment of which I ever had knowledge."[12]

From this legacy derived those qualities that Americans most often associated with Latinos—servility, misrule, lethargy, and bigotry. Latin governments were but parodies of the republican principles that they claimed to embody. John Randolph, a Virginia congressman, had looked south in 1816 and morosely observed that South Americans struggling for liberty would end up under "a detestable despotism. You cannot make liberty out of Spanish matter." Secretary of State John Quincy Adams agreed. Latin Americans, he observed in 1821, "have not the first elements of good or free government. Arbitrary power, military and ecclesiastical, was stamped upon their education, upon their habits, and upon all their institutions." The somnolent populations of that region, debilitated by their heritage and enervated by a tropical climate, neglected their rich natural resources, while the Catholic faith lulled them into intellectual passivity. "A priest-ridden people," Jefferson had predicted in 1813, were beyond "maintaining a free civil government."[13]

Color-conscious Americans came to incorporate yet another element into their view of Latinos, a horror over the wholesale miscegenation that had further blackened that people both literally and figuratively. With appalling freedom, white Spaniards had mixed with enslaved blacks and native Indians to produce degenerate mongrel offspring. This sexual license among the races set an example particularly disturbing to Americans dedicated to defending the color line at home. The woeful consequences of crossing that line were everywhere apparent in Latin America. All Latin countries fell under censure for lax racial standards and indifference to the social consequences of polluting the blood of whites. But the darker the complexion of the people in question, the sharper was the attack. In this respect Haiti, populated by descendants of African slaves, was repeatedly singled out as an example of what happened when dark-skinned people were left to run wild and to murder their masters and then each other.

The black legend provided Americans with the basis for a wide array of negative stereotypes. These were usually assigned—so far as the gender can be determined—to the Latin male. He was depicted, depending on the circumstances and the prejudice of the observer, as superstitious, obstinate, lazy, cowardly, vain, pretentious, dishonest, unclean, impractical, and corrupt. However, alongside this dominant conception of Latin incapacity and the image of the swarthy if not black Latin male that accompanied it, there developed a more positive picture of the Latino as an imminently redeemable, even desirable white. In this alternative embodiment, the Latin usually took the form of a fair-skinned and comely senorita living in a mongrelized society yet somehow escaping its degrading effects. This distinction so favorable to Latin women was drawn by early firsthand American observers, invariably males traveling alone, and it stuck in the minds of those at home, to be summoned up when the times called for saving Latins either from themselves or from some outside threat. A macho Uncle Sam would rush in and sweep the Latin lady off her feet, save her from her half-breed husband or from some sinister intruder from outside the hemisphere, and introduce her to the kind of civilized life she deserved.

Americans could thus choose their images of Latin Americans to fit the circumstances. During the period of continental expansion, the negative image of the male fated to give way before his betters was the most serviceable. Denigration of the Mexican, for example, developed apace with American interest in his land. The first wave of Americans to visit Mexico in the 1820s reported that they found a dark-complected, cowardly, and cruel people addicted to gambling and plagued by loose morals. A visitor to Mexico City early in the decade concluded that most of its people ''want nothing but tails to be more brute than the apes.'' Early Anglo settlers in Texas were quick to accept this harsh estimate. The folklore about ''niggers'' and ''redskins'' that many of them had brought from their homes along the Southern frontier predisposed them to a low regard for another dark-skinned people, the Mexicans, who stood in their way. As the contest for control of Texas and the Southwest proceeded, fellow Southerners and other Americans picked up and developed this theme of Mexican inferiority as a justification for American claims. Such a ''colored mongrel race'' had no claim to Texas, the influential senator from Mississippi, Robert J. Walker, insisted in 1836. A decade later, in the debate over Texas annexation, Pennsylvania's Senator James Buchanan, soon to become Polk's secretary of state, called for pushing aside ''the imbecile and indolent Mexican race.''[14]

Once war began, James K. Polk and his expansionist supporters justified their aggressive course by denouncing the enemy in the conventional and contemptuous terms as ''ignorant, prejudiced, and perfectly faithless.'' In this same spirit a New York paper declared, ''The Mexicans are *aboriginal Indians*, and they must share the destiny of their race.'' So widely accepted had this negative stereotype become that even those who resisted the call of conquest and regeneration characterized the Mexican as a ''half-savage'' who would be difficult if not impossible to improve or assimilate. Whig critics of Polk's policy freely derided the Mexicans as a race that was ''mongrel,'' ''a sad compound,'' ''slothful, indolent, ignorant,'' or simply ''miserable.''[15]

When by contrast Americans saw themselves acting benevolently, they liked to picture the Latino as a white maiden passively awaiting salvation or seduction. During the Mexican War proponents of sweeping annexation indulged this fantasy. One patriotic poet imagined a union between "The Spanish maid, with eye of fire," and the Yankee, "Whose purer blood and valiant arms, / Are fit to clasp her budding charms." Cuba, which had awakened the interest of territorially acquisitive Americans as early as Jefferson's day, even more strikingly evoked this tendency to feminize the Latin. For example, in the 1850s, when calls for acquiring the island were frequently sounded, one enthusiast rhapsodized about Cuba as Uncle Sam's beloved "Queen of the Antilles . . . breathing her spicy, tropic breath, and pouting her rosy, sugared lips." Later in the century, Spanish atrocities committed in an effort to suppress a Cuban independence movement reawakened the vision of a feminine Cuba not so much ready for the taking as ravaged and desperate for rescue from her Spanish master, who fairly bristled with traits associated with the black legend.[16]

The American drive for hemispheric preeminence at the turn of the century brought to the fore yet a third image: The Latino as a black child. Americans had intervened in Cuba to oust the Spaniards, appropriated Puerto Rico as their own, and encouraged a Panamanian secessionist movement against Colombia in order to obtain canal rights. The unexpected resentment and sullen defiance which these supposedly benevolent actions evoked proved puzzling and irritating. To compound the problem, Americans soon found themselves up against the psychologically troubling implications of continuing to portray the Latinos as mates. The picture of Uncle Sam in close proximity to a female Latin America carried strong sexual overtones and suggested the disturbing possibility of racial mixing. Americans uncomfortable over this prospect yet unwilling to surrender claims to dominion found a way out by making the Latino into a black child. This new image was a hybrid, drawing on the chief characteristics of the two previously dominant stereotypes, the racially degenerate male and the dependent woman.

Again Cuba can serve as an example. The Cubans were initially pictured as hapless victims of Spanish brutality and colonial oppression. Cartoons that appeared during the Cuban insurrection played on the theme of womanhood outraged, while the reconcentration policy pressed by the Spanish commander ("Butcher" Wyler) and the sinking of the *Maine* were depicted as entirely consistent with the cruel and treacherous Spanish character. But criticism of Spain did not in the end translate into respect for the insurgents. That the Cubans were not to be taken as even approximate equals was clear in the response of Anglo policymakers even before the war began. Both the Cleveland and McKinley administrations expressed a preference for the possibility of ordered Spanish rule over the certainty of anarchic Cuban self-government. Once the war came McKinley denied the Cubans recognition as a belligerent and afterward placed them under the control of an American military government. Closer contact now impressed on Americans the fact that many Cubans were swarthy, even black. Their army was a contemptible ragtag band ("made up very considerably of black people, only partially civilized") whose leaders were insufficiently grateful for American succor. They might wish independence but were certain to mismanage it if left on their own.[17]

These discoveries quickly transformed the cartoon Cuban into a petulant child whose place on the racial hierarchy was made clear by his stereotypical black features and his minstrel drawl. This picture of Cuban infantilism helped Americans to ignore the protests of this obviously immature and turbulent people against outside intervention and control, and it provided justification for a policy of keeping them in an appropriately dependent relationship to the United States. Thus the Cuban as mistress gave way to the Cuban as Southern black, "very poor and densely ignorant," as a text of 1900 quick to adopt the new imagery observed, but "capable of advancement under proper guidance."[18]

Americans thus entered the twentieth century with three images of Latin Americans at their disposal. One, the Latin as half-breed brute, could be invoked to justify a contemptuous aloofness or a predatory aggressiveness. The second, of the feminized Latin, allowed the United States to assume the role of ardent suitor or gallant savior. The third of an infantile and often negroid Latin, provided the justification for Uncle Sam's tutelage and stern discipline. In each case Americans stood in relation to Latinos as superiors dealing with inferiors.

These images, which had already helped rationalize the drive to expel Spain from North America and then to push the Mexican border south, also supported the ripening claim of the United States to the role of natural leader and policeman of an American system of states. That claim was embodied in the Monroe Doctrine, which began its career in 1823 as a bold but only partially enforceable pronouncement against the extension of European influence in the Western Hemisphere. By the 1890s it had evolved into a major principle of American policy, which not even Britain could safely ignore. With Europe fenced out, American policymakers with inherited pretensions to superiority over Latinos, and with ever-increasing power to make good on those pretensions, moved steadily toward making the hemisphere a U.S. preserve. Cubans, Puerto Ricans, and Colombians had already learned the practical implications of dominance by a people gripped by the black legend. Other Latin Americans, similarly stigmatized, would soon be subjected to the same hard education.

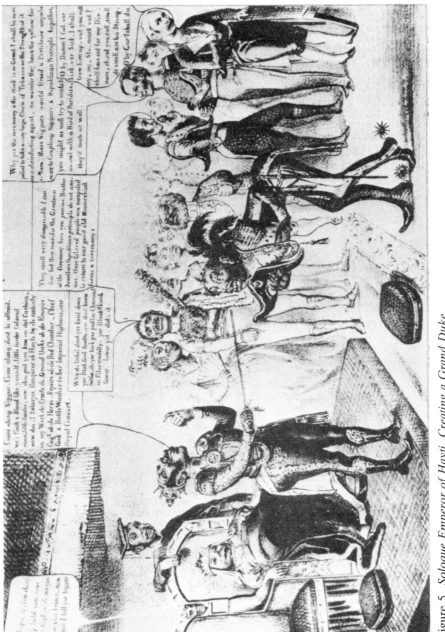

Figure 5. *Soloque Emperor of Hayti, Creating a Grand Duke*

This collection of cartoons captures the Latino in his various guises—as backward black, wrongdoing child, cruel brute, and supplicant woman. In the anonymous parody of Haitian politics (fig. 5), published in the 1850s, a disdainful American resident is made to remark on the incompatibility of "Niggars" and republican principles.

Figure 6.

Chile is depicted as a youthful offender in an 1891 cartoon (fig. 6) in which Uncle Sam is about ready to administer a spanking as punishment for an attack on American sailors on shore leave.

Figure 7. *The Spanish Brute Adds Mutilation to Murder*

The picture of the Spaniard as brute (fig. 7) was done in 1898 following the sinking of the Maine *in Havana harbor. It makes its point by playing on the earliest version of the black legend, emphasizing Spanish inhumanity.*

Figure 8. *The Cuban Melodrama*

In the other melodramatic piece (fig. 8), dating from 1898, Uncle Sam has interposed himself between the imploring Cuban maiden and the dark Spanish villain.

Figure 9. *Miss Cuba Receives an Invitation*
MISS COLUMBIA (to her fair neighbor): *"Won't you join the stars and be my forty-sixth?"*

Following Spain's defeat, Cuba was pictured by American annexationists as a "fair neighbor" (fig. 9) and by others as a prodigal and dangerous delinquent, whose skin

Figure 10. *UNCLE SAM TO PORTO RICO: "And to think that bad boy came near being your brother!"*

color and clothing as well as demeanor contrasted sharply with immaculate and well-behaved young Puerto Rico (fig. 10). [19]

★ ★ ★

The peoples of East Asia, sometimes designated "the Mongolian race" but more popularly referred to as "Orientals," were to win a permanent place in the American imagination by the latter half of the nineteenth century. In that period they came to stand, like the Latinos, somewhere midway on the racial ladder. Their place, however, is difficult to pinpoint since their image tended, again like the Latinos', to be unstable.

In broadest terms, Orientals were seen as inscrutable and somnolent. An observer developing that image in a favorable direction might hold them up as a people of promise, on the verge of shaking off a stagnant cultural tradition and improving their position in the hierarchy of race. Viewed in this light, they would appear admirably trustworthy, clean, and industrious. On the other hand, the image could evolve in a way that made Orientals into a disturbing, even dangerous, bundle of contradictions— subhuman yet cunning, unfeeling yet boiling inwardly with rage, cowardly and decadent yet capable of great conquests. In this latter guise they embodied the worst vices, were indifferent to the appeal of free institutions, and poisoned whatever environment they entered.

Thus Americans created for Orientals, just as they had for Latinos and Indians, two distinctly different images: a positive one, appropriate to happy times when paternalism and benevolence were in season, and a negative one, suited to those tense periods when abuse or aggrandizement became the order of the day.

The Chinese were the first East Asians to appear on the American horizon. Initially the Chinese had been seen secondhand, through the writings of European observers who filtered imperial China though the soft haze of their Enlightenment preconceptions. From a distance China appeared an ancient civilization whose cultured people and achievements in the fine arts and benevolently despotic government gave much to admire. But alongside this positive view prevalent among the American elite, there developed another strain of thought that was critically condescending toward a people who did not embrace free trade, who suspiciously held foreigners under control, and who followed pagan rites and such immoral practices as infanticide and polygamy. A 1784 geography embracing this latter view described the Chinese as "the most dishonest, low, thieving people in the world."[20]

In the early nineteenth century the image of a China distant, refined, and exotic began to give ground to that of a China repulsive, reactionary, and heathen as American visitors, above all the prolific and opinionated missionaries, broadcast their impressions back home. The country was a "moral wilderness,'' its people ignorant, depraved, and dirty, reported the pioneer evangelists.[21] Soon, in the 1850s and after, the arrival of Chinese immigrants to work in the labor-hungry economy of the American West swung the balance decisively against the Chinese. As had happened with other foreign peoples, the closer the contact and the larger the numbers of outlanders involved, the more elaborate and negative the American appraisal. By 1880, with over a hundred thousand Chinese in the United States, an intense nativist movement had grown up in the West, the main area of Chinese settlement. It demanded the exclusion of Chinese from the country and resorted to both mob violence and steady political pressure at all levels of government to achieve that goal.

Propagandists of the nativist cause reached many Americans formerly ignorant of or indifferent to the Chinese. The image they supplied was of an inherently inferior and intolerable foreign element "swarming" out of "a contiguous semicivilized empire" onto American shores. According to this image, the Chinese posed multiple threats. They came as servile "coolie" laborers who would take away the livelihood and destroy the dignity of white workingmen. They lived "huddled together . . . almost like rats" in pestilential ghettos, "Chinatowns" that endangered the health and welfare of the larger white community. Behind the apparently placid public demeanor of these Orientals lurked the sexually demonic. The "Chinamen" not only drove their own women into prostitution but also sought to debauch vulnerable white women—or so it seemed in the sexual fantasy of their foes. At their most alarmest critics of the Chinese saw in these immigrants but the first wave of a great yellow tide that would sweep the entire continent.[22]

The nativist movement won the West, and its indictment of the Chinese was powerful enough to gain wide acceptance elsewhere, including the White House. In 1888 the incumbent, Grover Cleveland, pronounced the Chinese "dangerous to our peace and welfare," while his Republican challenger, Benjamin Harrison, attacked them in much the same terms, as an "alien" race whose assimilation was "neither possible nor desirable."[23] A series of treaties and congressional measures between 1880 and 1904 made exclusion of Chinese the stringently applied law of the land. The negative image of Chinese immigrants produced by this campaign would linger in the American imagination long after it had served its purpose.

But the nativists did not, even in their heyday, have a monopoly on interpreting the Chinese. The American community in China, which had grown in numbers and influence through the nineteenth century, had continued to emphasize the negative qualities of China as it was—weak, vulnerable, and backward. To that extent their evaluation simply reinforced the nativist message. These Americans, however, were more concerned with China as it might become under the patronage of American diplomacy and the invigorating influence of American finance, trade, and mission work. Enthusiastic agents of change, they made a case for China's enormous potential for progress that appealed powerfully to their countrymen, ever on the lookout for an arena to exercise their greatness and conditioned to expect the westward flow of civilization. Asia would be moved; China would be the pivot; Americans would supply the initial shove. Thus at the same time that Americans were being told that Chinese were loathsome creatures to be kept at a distance at all costs, they were also hearing that China was a promising ward whom Americans had a special responsibility to tutor, protect against danger, and even punish for misbehavior.

It naturally followed that American policy, influenced by these divergent views, was curiously divided for a time. An open-door policy attuned to China's future development coexisted uneasily with the exclusion movement. Finally, in the 1910s the tension between the two competing lines of policy was at last resolved. The conclusive triumph of a sweeping policy of exclusion had by then eliminated anti-Chinese nativism as a political issue, thus ironically opening the way for the ascendance of advocates of a special open-door relationship with China. They would have Americans identify with China, sharing in her triumphs and despairing over her failures. By the early twentieth century Americans were again, after the passage of almost a hundred years, beginning to view China in a more positive light.

The Japanese were the other major "Oriental" people to command sustained attention. Like the Chinese, they too rose and fell in the estimation of Americans. Japan began its career in the nineteenth-century American mind a mystery, sealed off by a seclusion policy even more complete than China's. Mistreatment of shipwrecked American sailors early in that century suggested that the Japanese were, if anything, barbarians insensitive to the dictates of common humanity and the law of nations. The Perry expedition seemingly changed all that. Perry's success in 1854 in opening Japan to broader foreign contact, though in fact due largely to the accident of good timing, came to be celebrated in the United States as the indispensable impetus the Japanese had needed to begin a sweeping renovation. By the 1890s, with that process largely completed, Japan had emerged in American thinking as a nation joining the march of civilization. Its achievements, including extensive domestic reforms and the resounding defeat of China in 1894 and Russia a decade later, evoked praise and admiration but also an undercurrent of concern. How far might this rising Asian power go, and with what consequences to American ambitions in the Pacific?

As had happened with the Chinese, the arrival of Japanese immigrants in

Figure 11. *The First Blow at the Chinese Question*

These cartoons depicting the Chinese suggest the divergent tendencies in American thinking on the "Oriental." As an immigrant, he appears as a grotesque figure regardless of whether the cartoon is meant to support exclusion (as in fig. 11, from 1877) or to criticize nativist excesses (as in fig. 12, by Thomas Nast, done in 1869).

Figure 12. *Pacific Chivalry*

Figure 13.

Two cartoons from 1900 (figs. 13 and 14) show Uncle Sam in his two basic roles—
standing forth as the confident protector of a retiring and grateful young Asia and

Figure 14. *Is This Imperialism?*

advancing valiantly in company with President McKinley to punish outrages against
civilization (in this case by China's own nativists, the Boxers).

Figure 15. *Jumping on Your Uncle Samuel*

Figure 15, done in response to China's 1905 commercial boycott protesting U.S. exclusion policy, portrays Orientals as petulant and ungrateful children abusing Uncle Sam. All these cartoons include the essential features of the Chinese stereotype, pigtail and baggy clothes. The adult "Chinaman" is dealt with contemptuously. As a child, he is the object of condescension. Either way his face is shown contorted in panic or fury.[24]

the 1900s sent the pendulum of American opinion swinging sharply back the other way. The cases of the Chinese and Japanese were more than parallel; they were closely linked. Anti-Japanese nativism flourished in the same region, launched by the same alliance of labor and California's Democratic party, using the same methods—ranging from sporadic local violence to lobbying in Congress; it enjoyed the tolerance of the rest of the country; and after two decades it culminated in the complete exclusion of Japanese on racial grounds.

The arguments previously marshaled against one set of Orientals, the Chinese, were easily deployed against another. The interests of free labor should be protected from "Asiatic competition" and white morals defended against a corrupting race. A new generation of nativists warned of the dangers to the "pure maids of California" sitting in school beside "matured Japs, with their base minds, their lascivious thoughts, multiplied by their race and strengthened by their mode of life." Intermarriage would mean "corrupting the very springs of civilization." Calls were again heard for vigilance in the Pacific against attack by a wily people, especially one that had only recently defeated one European power, Russia, and had had the effrontery to claim Britain as an ally.[25]

By the turn of the century a curious relationship had developed between American images of China and Japan. While they would individually rise and fall in American estimation, they would not both move in the same direction at the same time. Rather, a sort of compensatory principle seemed at work. When (as in the late nineteenth century) the Chinese as a nation seemed irremediably antiquated and as a people at close quarters simply repulsive, Japan was made the embodiment of American hopes for a civilized Asia. Conversely, when the Japanese fell into ill repute (as was beginning to happen by the early twentieth century), China was held up for admiration. Here, then, was the novel spectacle of the different branches of a single race simultaneously moving in opposite directions up and down the racial ladder. It seems that by juxtaposing these two oriental peoples Americans had found a means of keeping their hopes and anxieties in equilibrium. While oriental villains served as the lightning rod of American racial fears, more worthy Orientals could be summoned up to keep alive liberal dreams of a prosperous, stable, and democratic East Asia.

★ ★ ★

In the structure of American race thinking, Anglo-Saxonism—the belief that Americans and the British were one people united by uncommon qualities and common interests—occupied a central position. By the first half of the nineteenth century Americans had begun to claim with pride their place in a trans-Atlantic community of English-speaking people. Dimming memories of fratricidal conflict set off by the American revolution created the conditions favorable to the rise of Anglo-Saxonism in an increasingly firm national consciousness. School texts began to celebrate the trans-Atlantic tie. A poetic paean to ''America and Britons'' often reproduced in the 1830s and 1840s proclaimed, ''The voice of blood shall reach, / More audibly than speech, / WE ARE ONE.'' At the same time the proud American racial lineage assumed an honored position as a standard topic in public rhetoric. ''Out of all the inhabitants of the world . . . a select stock, the Saxon, and out of this the British family, the noblest of the stock, was chosen to people our country.''[26]

By the end of the nineteenth century the Anglo-Saxon spell had further strengthened its hold. Race thinking, widely retailed in properly impressive pseudoscientific terms, had given added plausibility to an older ethnocentric notion of Anglo solidarity and superiority. The racial traits of both peoples, as they were now defined, included prominently industry, intelligence, a keen sense of moral purpose, and a talent for government. Together they stood preeminent in world affairs. Already the British had achieved much: their empire embraced one-fifth of the world's surface and one-quarter of its people, and their navy dominated the seas. Americans basked in the reflected glory of these accomplishments but they also knew that they, the child and heir of imperial Britain, were well on their way to eclipsing the parent in wealth and power. The United States was bound to become ''a greater England with a nobler destiny,'' proclaimed Albert J. Beveridge, one of the more nationalistic of the Anglo-Saxonists.[27]

The arrival of large numbers of disturbingly foreign immigrants sharpened the sensitivity to racial differences even within the circle of European whites. The nativism of the antebellum period had revealed early on the determination of ethnic Anglos to preserve their cultural hegemony against alien newcomers, then chiefly Irish and Germans. The concerns felt during that era proved mild, however, compared to the anxiety provoked by an even greater influx of still more foreign peoples, from southern and eastern Europe, at the end of the century. From the racial comparisons then drawn by a defensive but culturally dominant Anglo elite, there emerged a clear and fixed pecking order even for whites.

The elite's preoccupation with the differences among whites carried over into the fabric of thinking on world affairs. Anglo-Saxons clearly dominated the international stage. The Germans came next. They had the same qualities as their racial cousins save one—they had lost their love of liberty. This single serious defect set Germans just beyond the Anglo-Saxon pale and made this still-formidable people into a threatening global competitor, to be closely watched. By the turn of the century they were increasingly pictured as latter-day Huns, prone to the aggressive, even brutal behavior characteristic of a militaristic and autocratic system. The Slavs, half European and half Asiatic, were also formidable racial competitors on the international stage. Highly regimented and of rugged peasant stock, they had displayed great endurance, patience, and strength (if not intelligence and a knack for innovation) as they had slowly but irresistibly extended their control over much of the Eurasian land mass.

Lower down in the hierarchy were the Latin peoples of Europe, defined to include the French as well as Italians and Spaniards. They lacked vigor; they were sentimental, undisciplined, and superstitious; and consequently they were of small account in international affairs. Still farther back among the ranks of the unworthy appeared the Jews, depicted in explicitly racial, antisemitic terms. Predictably, farthest back were the peoples of Africa. In the popular literature of the late nineteenth century the ''dark continent'' began to emerge as the fascinating home of ''savage beasts and beastly savages.''[28] Above all other places Africa invited white dominion.

The popular vogue enjoyed by Darwinism further accentuated the tendency for Americans to think of themselves as a race in comparative and competitive terms and to locate themselves in an Anglo-Saxon community of interests. Given an optimistic twist, Darwinian notions served to reinforce preexisting ideas of Anglo-Saxon superiority. By the standards of industrial progress, military prowess, and international influence and control, Anglo-Saxons had an incontestable claim to the top of the racial heap. From that eminence they would point the way toward an era of unprecedented world peace and prosperity. Lesser races, awed and grateful, could follow the lead of the Anglo-Saxon—or drop to the bottom of the heap to meet their fate, ultimate extinction.

But Darwinism also led some contemporary Anglo-Saxonist observers to more somber conclusions. In international competition among the races victory might not go to the refined and peaceful peoples but rather to the amoral, the cunning, the fecund, and the power hungry. Anglo-Americans might then need to cultivate a sense of solidarity and a capacity for cooperation in order to hold at bay the hard forces of barbarism that might overwhelm them singly.

This world view dominated by a belief in the shared superiority of Americans and Englishmen is nicely illustrated in the outlook of Alfred Thayer Mahan, naval historian and influential strategist. Through the 1880s and 1890s Mahan steadily advocated Anglo-American cooperation, for ''in political traditions as well as by blood we are kin, the rest alien.'' He saw ''the best hope of the world'' in the union of the two branches of the race and the extension of their control over the multitude of peoples still in ''the childhood stage of race development'' and hence unfit for self-government. Of the Europeans Mahan regarded the Germans as the most progressive, though by 1897 Germany's international misbehavior began to plant doubts. Slavs, he was certain, were cruel and barbarous, and the Russians, who combined that ''remorseless energy'' of their race with the ''unscrupulous craft of the Asiatic,'' particularly troubled him. He censured the French as fickle and false and the Latino (save for the entrancing women) as backward. The Chinese he viewed as both pitifully inert and dangerously barbaric, thus justifying on the one hand missionary ministrations and on the other strict exclusion from the outposts of civilization in Hawaii and the West Coast. He classified Filipinos as children and after some hesitations endorsed their annexation. Of the ''Orientals'' only the westernizing Japanese won his respect; they were ''repeating the experience of our Teutonic ancestors.'' Blacks stood at the bottom of Mahan's racial hierarchy. They had been ''darkies'' and ''niggers'' since his youth, and even conversion to abolitionism had not shaken his conviction that they were the most primitive of all the races.[29]

The appeal of Anglo-Saxonism and the related notions about the racial inferiority of other peoples, especially those of color, became dramatically apparent in the 1890s. At home the Southern effort to create a caste system fixing blacks in a place of permanent inferiority intensified; Congress passed new laws against Chinese immigrants and began to debate doing the same to some Europeans; the executive snuffed out the last embers of Indian resistance. Abroad involvement in Cuba and China both betrayed, as suggested above, the workings of deep-seated racial assumptions. In Hawaii and the Philippines, where a policy of intervention gave way to one of outright annexation, the issue of race emerged in more explicit form. Indeed, so prominent and pervasive an influence was race thinking that it figured in the armory of arguments of Americans on both sides of the question. Then, as in the debates of the 1840s and 1850s, race served equally as a reason for a cautious, self-limiting policy and as justification for a bold, assertive one.

In the case of Hawaii, whose future had been argued intermittently in Congress since the 1850s, racial considerations had proven as important as economic, strategic, and constitutional ones. The vigor and superiority of Anglo-Saxons, one side contended, was evident in the way New England merchants, sea captains, and missionaries had gained a foothold on the islands and in the way their offspring, even though a minority, had won commercial and political dominance. The racially deficient natives had simply given way like the Indians. Annexationists saw as the logical next step acceptance by the United States of the white islanders' wish for union and of the remaining native Hawaiians' need for civilization. Critics, repelled by the prospect of incorporating masses of nonwhites, warned against the perils of miscegenation that would produce a feeble, half-breed race on the islands and stressed that the inherent inferiority of native peoples prevented them from rising to the level of full and responsible citizenship. They would remain mere subjects, unassimilable and forever a millstone around the national neck. In the first major contest over Hawaii's annexation in 1893, the critics prevailed— only to find themselves reversed in the summer of 1898 when racial imperialism, brought to fever pitch by war with Spain, easily won out.

The Philippines issue, which arose later the same year, elicited the same conflicting set of views. Again annexationists argued for the mastery of the Anglo-Saxon with his capacity to rule and uplift. Beveridge assured the Senate after a visit to the islands that the Filipinos were "a decadent race," mere children who had been "instructed by the Spaniards in the latter's worst estate." The United States had a clear duty, McKinley argued, to redeem the Filipinos "from savage indolence and habits," and "set them in the pathway of the world's best civilization." That meant as much as a century of tutelage, according to William Howard Taft after his first exposure to those he described as "our little brown brothers." The opponents of annexation countered with their own battery of well-rehearsed racial arguments. The Filipino lived in an enervating tropical climate; even whites could not long submit to it without impairment. Further, the Filipino bore the indelible stamp of three centuries of Spanish misrule. Hawaii had at least had the benefit of a half century of American influence. Finally, the Filipino carried all those unpleasant traits that had made other peoples difficult to deal with. He was ignorant and servile like the black, impractical and infantile like the Latino, savage like the Indian, and impassive like the Oriental.[30]

Had the issue of annexation been resolved on the basis of racial arguments alone, the opposition might well have stymied the McKinley administration. The foothold that victorious American forces had gained on the islands at McKinley's behest, however, introduced a feature that transformed the debate. Annexationists could play more directly on Anglo-Saxon racial pride. To return the archipelago to Spain would be cowardly and inhumane. To leave the Filipinos to their own devices would be irresponsible and dishonorable. Racial superiority carried obligations that could be ignored only at the cost of throwing doubt on that superiority itself. Though the earlier American record in meeting professed obligations to nonwhite peoples

Figure 16. *Troubles Which May Follow an Imperial Policy*

Filipinos and other newly dependent peoples were variously depicted in contemporary cartoons as hell-raising aborigines, pupils under Uncle Sam's stern tutelage, or black children under his solicitous care. The first two cartoons depict the Filipino in his

Figure 17. *A Powerful Argument against Imperialism*

savage guise. Figure 16, anti-imperialist in sentiment, shows the speaker of the House under siege from the insistent representative from the Philippines, while fig. 17 mocks the anti-imperialist William Jennings Bryan for the company he keeps.

Figure 18. *Uncle Sam's New Class in the Art of Self-Government*

The schoolhouse scene (fig. 18) with Emilio Aguinaldo, the Filipino resistance leader, standing in the corner and two former Cuban guerillas quarreling, draws on the second image.

Figure 19. Emilio Aguinaldo

Compare this caricature of Aguinaldo as a disheveled, sulking delinquent with a contemporary photo (fig 19) showing him composed, erect, and smartly dressed out. Hawaii and Puerto Rico, which offered no resistance, and Máximo Gómez, the Cuban general who cooperated with American authorities, are here flatteringly portrayed as both more mature and white, though even they must docilely accept instruction.

Figure 20. *The Cares of a Growing Family*

The third image, of the dependent as black child, is exploited in the cartoons (figs. 20–22) showing President McKinley, Cuban military governor Leonard Wood, and Uncle Sam respectively perplexed by, industriously devoted to, and good-naturedly condescending toward their charges.

Figure 21. *If General Wood Is Unpopular with Cuba, We Can Guess the Reason.*

Figure 22. *Cuba's Freedom Is Not Far Off*

Figure 23. *The White Man's Burden*

These images were sometimes mixed, as in the last cartoon (fig. 23) showing an aborigine borne forcibly by an American soldier toward the schoolhouse.[31]

pointed to some troubling conclusions on this score, memory now proved conveniently short and selective. Once more annexationists carried the day.

★ ★ ★

The racial views embraced by Benjamin Franklin and carried forward by generations of his countrymen had not been an American invention, nor was race thinking an American monopoly. The American experience with race, and the closely related and formative experience with slavery, deserve to be seen as an extension of a variegated pattern of beliefs and practices extending back millenia and across cultures around the globe. There are, however, no easy generalizations to make about the American case or comparisons to draw between it and other cases. Only the obvious point remains—Americans were hardly unique. Gripped by ethnocentric impulses of seemingly universal force, Americans used race to build protective walls against the threatening strangeness of other people and to legitimize the boundaries and terms of intergroup contact. Moved no less by exploitative impulses, Americans followed other ''master classes'' in employing racial attributes to justify subordination of ''inferior peoples,'' whether as black slaves, Indian wards, or Filipino subjects. Finally, Americans betrayed their common humanity by using the resulting collection of racial notions as an arena for the exercise of libidinous and other fantasies normally held in close confinement.

Americans inherited a rich legacy of racial thought from their immediate European ancestors. Westerners coming into contact with peoples of the ''Third World'' in the fifteenth century had already betrayed signs of racism. Well before Englishmen took that first step on the North American continent, they had absorbed Elizabethan myths about blacks and easily extrapolated them to other nonwhite peoples. These inherited views were greatly sharpened as Anglos began to contend with other expatriate Europeans, native Americans, and even Asians for a place on the new continent. For ambitious yet initially isolated British colonists, a picture of the world's peoples in which lightness of skin was tied to innate worth proved understandably attractive. Had there existed no ready-made Elizabethan notions about race, these colonists would surely have had to invent them. They used the racial hierarchy to underwrite their claim to lands they wanted and, once possession was secure, to justify the imposition of Anglo cultural values and institutions as well as the expulsion or political and economic subordination of lesser peoples. Race also provided a balm for the pangs of conscience over the inevitable instances of false dealing and the broader patterns of exploitation and dehumanization that attended this process of achieving white (and above all, Anglo) hegemony.

The attitudes toward race that developed in domestic affairs from black-white relations, and in the interstice between foreign and domestic affairs where the Indian and the immigrant were to be found, were in one sense a mosaic made up of pieces from different regions of the country. Each region had fought the war for racial supremacy in its own way and in accord with the economic prize in question, the nature of the opposing people, and the power disparities between them. Seizing Indian land in New England in the 1680s differed from holding a black population under control in the antebellum South, just as evicting Mexico from the Southwest and subordinating the resident Latino population differed from the struggle to control the immigrant tide washing the urban East at the turn of the century.

But the overall pattern of the mosaic was clear enough. Americans of light skin, and especially of English descent, shared a loyalty to race as an essential category for understanding other peoples and as a fundamental basis for judging them. They had, in other words, fixed race at the center of their world view. Public policy in general and foreign policy in particular had from the start of the national experience reflected the central role that race thinking played. As Americans came into closer contact with an ever-widening circle of foreign peoples in the last decade of the nineteenth century, racial assumptions continued to guide their response. Those crying for a strenuous foreign policy invoked the need to enhance the racial vitality of the Anglo-Saxon stock and to honor the tutelary obligations superior races owed lesser ones, while those skeptical about foreign crusades and colonies either labored to repel charges that they were traitors to their kind or recoiled in horror from races they considered irredeemably backward. Accepted by the turn of the century as an important ingredient in a demonstrably successful foreign policy no less than in the established domestic order, race would pass to subsequent generations as a well-nigh irresistible legacy.

4 The Perils of Revolution

Strait is the gate and narrow is the way that leads to liberty, and few nations, if any, have found it. —John Adams (1821)

Whether the state of society in Europe can bear a republican government, I doubted . . . and [still] I do now.
—Thomas Jefferson (1823)

The American nation was the child of a revolutionary age, and no two Americans were closer students of the tumults of that age than John Adams and Thomas Jefferson. Revolutionaries themselves, they had witnessed the first tremors of the French Revolution from their diplomatic posts in London and Paris in the 1780s. Once back home, they had followed the turmoil deepening in France and then spreading throughout Europe. Still later, in their successive terms as president, they helped the United States to weather the gales, domestic and international, blown up by the French Revolution. Finally, in retirement the two septuagenarians patched up their old friendship and launched on a remarkable correspondence about revolutions past and present. "You and I ought not to die, before We have explained ourselves to each other," wrote Adams in mid-1813, initiating the exchange. Jefferson took up the challenge, though characteristically disavowing any desire for controversy, "for we are both too old to change opinions which are the result of a long life of inquiry and reflection."[1]

From one perspective, the views on revolution that Adams and Jefferson had entertained over a lifetime make them a study in contrasts. Adams, almost obsessive on the subject of revolution, approached political upheaval with extreme caution and eyed assaults on the social order with abhorrence. So numerous and stringent were the strictures and safeguards he imposed on revolution that he in effect came near to placing an acceptable one beyond the reach of mere mortals. His Calvinist heritage and his legal training, with the respect it imparted for a conservative adherence to precedent, order, and procedural niceties, combined to push him toward this position. Personality carried him farther still. Adams, the wearer of "the scratchiest hair shirt over the thinnest skin in American history," was by nature suspicious of the common man, wary of his peers, and on guard against even himself.[2] Introspective, brittle, and abrasive, he regarded with foreboding the upheaval, passions, and uncertainties associated with revolution, even one conducted at a distance. A lifetime in politics, where his fellows seldom met the measure of his high standards, strengthened his pessimism about man's nature and his anxiety over political tumult.

Adams provided the fullest exposition of his thinking on revolution in a series of essays published in 1790 and 1791.[3] For a revolution to succeed, Adams explained, its leaders had to recognize three crucial points: the inherent flaws in all men, the ineradicable differences among men, and the need for a form of government that took practical account of these first two conditions. Revolutionaries should not aspire to some notion of ideal perfection.

> Cold will still freeze, and fire will never cease to burn; disease and vice will continue to disorder, and death to terrify mankind. Emulation next to self-preservation will forever be the great spring of human actions, and the balance of a well-ordered government will alone be able to prevent that emulation from degenerating into dangerous ambition, irregular rivalries, destructive factions, wasting seditions, and bloody, civil wars.

All men sought to achieve distinction in the eyes of their fellows, making each person in effect a slave to society, which would by its opinion of him determine his worth. Because men differed widely in the extent and nature of their talents, their relative place in society would inevitably differ as well. Working from these basic considerations, it was the task of what Adams habitually referred to as "the science of government" to restrain misconduct and channel passion in ways beneficial to society.

This was to be done through "an equilibrium of power" within the government. To begin with, the legislature should be constructed in such a way that the general populace would serve as an equipoise to those members of society distinguished by their wealth or aristocratic background. Within their respective chambers rich and poor could seek distinction and the advancement of their divergent interests. At the same time both groups within the legislature needed to have at hand a separate executive that might serve as an "impartial mediator" and "defense against each other's vices and follies." Thus might the interests and passions of the two main classes within society be given an outlet and yet at the same time be restrained, so that neither class would gain the ascendancy and behave "arbitrarily or tyrannically."

The ultimate task of revolution was to pave the way for such a government and the liberty it would guarantee. Rummaging through history and his own accumulated experience, Adams pronounced few revolutions even temporarily successful. Proponents of political change had time and again misunderstood the limits of man and the "science of government." Among the European states, only the English had produced a sound constitution, "the most stupendous fabric of human invention."[4] Americans had done well to adopt a similar, balanced constitution, but even that might not safeguard their political virtue.

According to Adams, revolutions often ran into trouble long before they reached this stage of constitution making. While revolutions should be launched, in the first place, only "against usurpations and lawless violence," they more often challenged "lawful authority" instead. While they required "virtue and good sense" on the part of both the people and their leaders, they most often gave rise to moral license and a popular cry for economic leveling. Thus, under the leadership of hotheads who "commonly take more pains to inflame their own passion and those of society" than to understand the principles of a sound constitution, revolutions degenerated into foredoomed efforts to reorder society and root out those natural inequalities among men such as talent, wealth, and fame. As the political virtues of restraint, moderation, and prudence went out of season, iconoclasm and attacks on traditional religion and morality undermined the bulwarks of the social order. So many and so serious were the risks that attended a revolution, Adams somberly concluded, that resistance to despotism was justified only where "the fair order of liberty and a free constitution" could be rapidly realized and prolonged anarchy avoided. He warned that those who acted against his judgment would soon find that "a thousand tyrants are worse than one."[5]

It is tempting to pit against Adams the views of Thomas Jefferson. One was the nemesis of revolution, the other its enthusiastic champion. Fascinated and hopeful, Jefferson watched the latest turns in the revolutions of his time. His faith in the inexorable march of liberty and in the ability of men to "be governed by reason" made him a stranger to the dark gloom into which such upheavals seemed to plunge Adams. Revolution was the means whereby men shattered the artificial constraints that stunted their development. However, people could not hope to make the "transition from despotism to liberty in a feather-bed."[6] Once challenged, an entrenched aristocracy was sure to fight to preserve its interests. The common man had no choice but to make whatever sacrifice was necessary to overcome that resistance and bring an end to oppression.

Revolution, then, was not something to decry or fear for its violence; instead, it was an inevitable feature of a benign natural order. Jefferson liked to compare revolution to a thunderstorm that would have to break from time to time to clear the air of the accumulating cloud of political evils. It was, in another of his metaphors, manure essential to the healthy growth of the tree of liberty. Particular revolutions might fail, just as thunderstorms sometimes inflicted damage, but each attempt at liberty put within easier grasp that greatest of all prizes. "At every vibration between the points of liberty and despotism, something will be gained for the former. As men become better informed, their rulers must respect them the more." Taking the long view, Jefferson regarded the American Revolution as evidence of progress achieved and a token of the political inheritance other peoples were destined to receive.[7]

Jefferson and Adams clearly approached revolution in two different frames of mind. But too much can be made of the gulf between them. By the time these two were able to contemplate revolution in the leisure of retirement, their views had moved strikingly toward a convergence. To be sure, traces of the old disagreements remained. Adams, unable to control his ancient urge for self-justification, pointed out that he had seen the dangers in the French Revolution from the start, while Jefferson, "fast asleep in philosophical Tranquility," had entertained only "crude and visionary notions."[8] Jefferson, for his part, continued placidly to intone his faith in liberty and the ultimately beneficial effects of revolution.

Reflection, however, now forced both to moderate their earlier positions. Adams' anxieties about revolution were diminished by his growing conviction that the American political experiment had turned out far better than he had expected and now stood firmly as an inspiration to the world and as a model of "the means and measures" of constitution making. Jefferson, on the other hand, had been chastened by the spectacle of the American spark of liberty leaping the Atlantic only to be extinguished in a sea of blood. His optimism that the flame of freedom might one day consume "the feeble engines of despotism" remained, but he now realized how much longer it would take "light and liberty" to advance and how much more it would cost. "Rivers of blood must yet flow, and years of desolation pass," perhaps as long as five or more generations in Europe and Latin America.[9]

Time, moreover, had brought the two elderly philosophers closer together in their view of man's revolutionary potential. Putting aside his stark picture of fallen man, Adams began to look for those variations in the makeup of different peoples that might serve as a more discriminating gauge of their capacity to gain and hold liberty. Jefferson, meanwhile, came to acknowledge that the unseen bonds tied by king and priest had impaired the rational faculties of some peoples and hence their ability to carry a revolution through to a satisfactory conclusion. Only belatedly did Jefferson and Adams sufficiently recognize that neither reason nor passion existed in the abstract but rather that both operated in widely different national contexts.

From Adams' and Jefferson's latter-day reflections on revolution can be distilled a series of points that constitute their seasoned opinion—and, more important, that defined the basis of their countrymen's thinking on the subject for a long time to come. These views drew heavily on memories of the American Revolution. Cleansed of even the few taints of social violence and radicalism that besmirched it, the independence movement in which the youthful Adams and Jefferson had had a hand emerged in their mature thinking, just as it did in nationalist mythology, as a model of revolutionary moderation and wisdom. Against this model all struggles for freedom were to be judged, whether directed against foreign masters or homegrown tyrants.

According to the rules Jefferson and Adams had laid down, those contemplating revolution had to be careful, in the beginning, to act only against authority rendered illegitimate by persistent violation of individual or property rights or by defiance or subversion of the will of the majority. Once begun, the ultimate fate of a revolution depended on close adherence to a moderate course. In broadest terms the quality of a people—their fortitude, integrity, literacy, devotion to justice, and intelligence—determined whether they would pass safely through what Jefferson called the "hazards of a transition from one form of government to another."[10] Europeans enjoyed the best odds; those outside the mainstream of European civilization, such as Latin Americans or Slavs, were a long shot. But much also depended within any country on the ability and willingness of the better classes to play a leading role. Otherwise, the initiative would pass to urban mobs with a frightful capacity to unleash a reign of terror that only some new despotism could end.

Adams and Jefferson also agreed that anyone attempting to bring the revolutionary enterprise to a successful close would have to pay appropriate attention to constitutional arrangements. "A well tempered constitution" (to use Jefferson's phrase of 1788) was essential to balance contending political interests and to check concentration of power in one body or office, thereby guarding the abuses those wielding such power might commit against the very persons or property that government existed above all to protect. Yet putting together such a formal constitutional mechanism was also, as Adams reminded Jefferson, "an art or mystery very difficult to learn and still harder to practice."[11] Dutiful foreign students would look to the American constitution as a model, and the success of their attempt to construct a system hospitable to liberty would be measured against that model.

Finally, both Adams and Jefferson had come to agree that the spirit of revolution was infectious and that it could, for better or worse, spread far beyond its place of origin. Though Americans had secured their own revolution, they were still not immune nor should they be indifferent to revolutionary outbreaks beyond their borders. Ordered liberty achieved by others would confirm for Americans their leading role in a secure world of free peoples. Revolutions gone astray, on the other hand, would leave Americans feeling repudiated, isolated, and anxious. All fresh revolutionary outbreaks, even distant ones, bore careful watching.

★ ★ ★

The first wave of revolutions spanning the late eighteenth and early nineteenth century evoked a deeply ambivalent American attitude, mirrored in the musings of Adams and Jefferson. Just as Americans were bringing their own seminal struggle for liberty to a successful constitutional conclusion, France began its own revolution. Were not the very people whose support had helped Americans win their freedom from Britain about to embrace the American example? As the French went instead their own deviant way, Americans surrendered their initial optimism and began to nurse in its place an anxiety over the perils of revolution. Latin America's struggle for freedom from Spanish control, following the crest of revolutionary activity in France, served merely to confirm the darker view.

For Americans the French experience was pivotal—and traumatic. Though Americans would go through the same cycle of hope and disappointment with other revolutions, France constituted the first test of their revolutionary faith, and hence observers felt the importance of the outcome with an intensity never again equaled. From the start Americans regarded every step in that drama going on across the Atlantic as an omen of the ultimate fate of liberty for people everywhere. Between the fall of the Bastille in July 1789 and the outbreak of war in Europe in 1793 all the omens were good. With little bloodshed a popular assembly had organized, restricted the king's power, and then gone on to create a republic and repel restorationist forces. In the major American cities democratic societies celebrated these achievements and called on Americans to emulate the French by pressing the cause of liberty still further at home.

Jefferson shared these popular enthusiasms. From the start he had praised the French Revolution as a legitimate effort to right centuries of injustice. French success, which to Jefferson seemed assured, would be but the beginning of the liberation of all Europe, and it would strengthen the cause of liberty in the United States. "I have so much confidence in the good sense of man, and his qualifications for self-government, that I am never afraid of the issue where reason is left free to exert her force," he wrote from France in August 1789. He incautiously added, "I will agree to be stoned as a false prophet if all does not end well in this country. Nor will it end with this country. Here is but the first chapter of the history of European liberty." Rather than see the French Revolution fail, he wrote in 1793, "I would have seen half the earth desolate."[12]

But there is also evidence that even in this initial stage of the crisis Jefferson worried that revolutionary goals might race ahead of the political capacities of the French people. The peasantry in particular, he noted, was plagued by ignorance and habituated to political passivity. Moreover, liberty was new to the entire French people, and thus, he repeatedly warned his French correspondents, prudence would dictate only modest measures of political change at first. An American-style bicameral legislature with its built-in restraints was most in keeping with the needs of the moment. Jefferson would have frozen the progress of the Revolution as early as March 1789, well before the taking of the Bastille, so that the French could gain more experience with self-government and prepare themselves for a full measure of liberty at some later date. Though he responded to the ensuing tumult into the mid-1790s with expressions of approbation, a barely concealed anxiety always lurked below the surface of his commentary.

As the Revolution took a more radical and violent turn after 1793, increasing numbers of Americans set it beyond the bounds of legitimacy. The execution of the king, the victory of the Jacobins over their moderate opponents, and the climactic Reign of Terror provoked these American critics into an open assault. Federalists took the lead, forcing their Republican opponents to reply and making that distant struggle in France into the stalking-horse of the two emerging political factions in the United States.

Federalist leaders seized on this foreign revolution gone awry as a means of neutralizing the influence of their "Jacobin" foe, the Republicans. Alexander Hamilton decried the "horrid and disgusting scenes" enacted under Marat and Robespierre—assassination, internal insurrection, and the "dissolution of all the social and moral ties." In France, he proclaimed, "the cause of true liberty has received a deep wound." Washington, who at first regarded the French Revolution as an offshoot of America's own and as a force reshaping the fate of Europe, came to share Hamilton's pessimism, if not his sense of alarm. He had feared from the start that the French were not "sufficiently cool and moderate" to find their way between the twin dangers of "despotic oppression" and "licentiousness." The "tumultuous populace" of Paris and "wicked and designing men, whose element is confusion" had taken control and wrecked the revolution. Yet a third Federalist, Gouverneur Morris, whose dispatches from Paris proved influential with his political associates at home, pronounced the French like "cattle before a thunderstorm." In their unrestrained pursuit of liberty they had set under siege both religion and morality, the two chief safeguards of political temperance and private property. Morris concluded that only some despot could restore order to a society thus threatened by "a giddy populace."[13]

None in the Federalist camp had been quicker than John Adams to speak out against the bad French example and its inflammatory effect on his countrymen, whose insurrectionary tendencies had to him been long and all too plain. Early in the Revolution he had denounced the French for mocking religion and chasing after the phantom of equality of persons and property. Their choice of government by single assembly foolishly ignored his science of government and predictably yielded an unmitigated string of political and social disasters: anarchy, license, despotism, war, pestilence, and famine. Without balanced government, Adams had predicted in 1790, the French would have "no equal laws, no personal liberty, no property, no lives." The events of the next few years left his gloomy judgment unchanged. "Dragon's teeth have been sown in France and come up monsters."[14]

The Federalist case against the French Revolution and its American sympathizers gained broad acceptance by the late 1790s. Exploiting to the full an aggressive French policy on the high seas and the insulting treatment of American diplomats in the notorious XYZ affair, Federalists stirred up a fever of anti-French sentiment in mid-1798. In the midst of the ensuing war scare, they put through legislation curtailing the civil rights of suspected "Jacobins" on American soil and suppressing subversive ideas. The democratic societies and other defenders of France, assailed for their "seditious" activities, fell silent.

The once sanguine Jefferson now bemoaned the excesses of the French government and the opportunity it had created for Federalist attack on Republicans, the true friends of American liberty. The rise of Napoleon in 1799 relieved Jefferson of any further obligation to defend France's revolution, now clearly at its end. Later he would recall that revolution and its aftermath as "a mournful period in the history of man," filled with "horrors," "madness," "crimes," "human misery," and "fatal errors." It was "the unprincipled and bloody tyranny of Robespierre, and the equally unprincipled and maniac tyranny of Bonaparte'' that had finally crushed liberty. ''Who could have thought the French nation incapable of it?'' he asked in 1802 before the resumption of his correspondence with Adams supplied one answer.[15]

If France had conclusively established the dangers of social revolution, revolts in the Americas against France, Spain, and Portugal suggested the limits of anticolonial struggles. Peoples long oppressed by foreign rule were bound to want liberty, but the conditions that had held them down might also leave them incapable of either winning or maintaining it. Jefferson perhaps even more than Adams emphasized the apparent contradiction between colonial aspirations and colonial capabilities.

As early as 1787 Jefferson had become convinced that Latin America contained ''combustible materials'' about to burst into a flame of liberty. When Santo Domingo ignited in 1791, Jefferson recoiled in horror. There a ''people of color,'' an underclass of black slaves and freedmen, had taken the doctrines of the French Revolution seriously and in the revolt that followed massacred their French masters. White refugees reaching American shores in 1793 aroused in Jefferson not only sympathy for their plight but a dark concern that the revolutionary contagion that had already passed from France to the Caribbean would in due course reach the southern United States, there to inspire still more ''bloody scenes.''[16]

Once more Americans acted to hold revolution at bay. Authorities in the South restricted the import of West Indian blacks and enacted severe slave codes to keep native insurrectionists under control. Any public discussion of the horrors stalking Santo Domingo was taboo in the South lest such news reach the ears of the region's own black population. The shock of watching atrocities repeated year after year, however, knew no regional bounds. The final product of this violent revolution, a republic established in 1804 by former slaves, could only be ''black despotism and usurpation,'' announced a Pennsylvania congressman, and should be treated as a pariah by civilized nations. President after president for half a century agreed, withholding diplomatic recognition from the republic of Haiti.[17]

Revolution in the Spanish colonies in the 1810s fared only somewhat better in American opinion. Here, Jefferson noted with satisfaction in 1811 on first word of this new unrest, was ''another example of man rising in his might and bursting the chains of his oppressor.'' Spanish Americans, unlike the French, had the good sense to seek only moderate political change and, unlike the Haitians, to avoid racial carnage. But American observers such as Jefferson and Adams nonetheless came to suspect that Latinos were not yet ready for liberty. Catholic superstition, a heritage of Spanish despotism, and a racially mixed population—the key elements in the black legend—seemed to them serious impediments to the progress of liberty. Jefferson put it bluntly, and in terms strikingly similar to those Adams used: Spanish Americans were "immersed in the darkest ignorance, and brutalized by bigotry and superstition" and hence were "as incapable of self-government as children." Jefferson could hope for no more than "military despotisms" to replace the existing Spanish tyranny. It would take several generations of education, American assistance and example, and perhaps even a Spanish protectorate before they would be fit for "ordered liberty."[18]

Through the 1820s and 1830s the dominant national attitude, a composite of New England–based Federalist conservatism and Southern racial sensitivities, came increasingly to coincide with Jefferson's deep skepticism that such a thing as Latin liberty could exist. Between 1821 and 1824 the former Spanish colonies and Brazil secured their independence and gained diplomatic recognition from the United States. The Monroe administration, however, bestowed its blessing only after considerable debate in which a hard-headed interest in promoting trade and displacing European influence prevailed. The new states had little to recommend them as fellow republics or models of liberty, a point Secretary of State John Quincy Adams made insistently within the administration as he played for time to settle negotiations with Spain and to determine the viability of the insurgent regimes. His convictions about Latino shortcomings were given public voice by Boston's *North American Review*. "What sympathy or concern can Americans have for people of a different stock, law, institution, religion?" that prestigious journal asked in 1821. "Their violence, laziness, are but the natural consequence of the degeneracy of a mixed race, ruined by tyranny, and afflicted by the evil influence of tropical climatic conditions." Even Henry Clay, Adams' opponent in the recognition debate, conceded evidence of Latino ignorance and superstition, the result of living under Spain's "odious tyranny." Despite his faith that progress would follow the end of tyranny, Clay too occasionally lost his patience, as in 1821 when he denounced independent Mexico as a "place of despotism and slaves, of the Inquisition and superstition."[19]

Most American observers could not maintain Clay's patience and optimism. The gloomy prospects they entertained were confirmed by the behavior of the new states. They flirted with monarchy (and in Brazil and for a time in Mexico actually embraced it), retained their ties to the Old World and the papacy, embraced abolitionism, and sank under the weight of military despotism and public ignorance and vanity. To be sure, Latin America was better off than before its revolutions, but there could be no doubt that the defects of its peoples left them little better suited than Europeans to carry their experiment in liberty to a successful conclusion.

The early 1820s marked the end of the first revolutionary era. Liberty had proven stillborn in Latin America. The French dalliance with freedom had brought forth a monster that only the strong hand of a Bonaparte could slay. Bonaparte's final defeat, in turn, made possible the restoration of the hated old order under the sponsorship of the Congress of Vienna. The North American offspring alone survived. Americans could only hope that their success as a free people would be enough to inspire a new generation of patriots in other lands, who would in time expand the now narrowly constricted sphere of liberty. But France's bloody and prolonged agony, deeply etched in the American political consciousness, stood as a reminder of just how beset with perils the revolutionary road to liberty would be.

★ ★ ★

The second wave of revolution witnessed by Americans would build and break in the middle decades of the nineteenth century. Its climax came with the revolutions of 1848 in Europe; its tragic denouement was acted out in Paris in 1871. The American response proved a repetition of the pattern evident in the previous era of revolutions. American nationalists extolled their own revolution without embarrassment as ''the greatest political event in history'' and hence the natural agent ''in the political regeneration of the world.'' By continuing to offer an example of how revolution might lead to free government, the United States was ''inviting the oppressed nations of the earth to do as we have done, and to be as free and happy as we are.'' The words were uttered by Senator Lewis Cass in 1852, but the same sentiment echoed a thousand times in the halls of Congress and in public meetings, where the rituals endorsing the global struggle for freedom and affirming the American role as model were repeated time and again. To foreigners who actually embraced the cause of revolution, Americans still applied the stringent standards handed down from Adams' and Jefferson's day. And, despite some differences over just how rigidly to apply them, Americans at mid-century, like an earlier generation, repeatedly pronounced the results disappointing, if not outrageous.[20]

Greece and Poland provided the prologue to this period of renewed revolutionary activity in Europe. The Greek struggle, begun against Ottoman overlords in 1821, had unusual appeal for Americans. It pitted a Christian people against infidels, making the contest, in the words of Edward Everett (one of the foremost champions of Greek freedom), "a war of crescent against cross." The Greeks, moreover, had a sentimental claim as the descendants of the ancients, that "splendid constellation of sages and heroes," which made Jefferson, Adams, and others trained in the classics feel a "missionary enthusiasm" for the Greek cause. Popular excitement, at its peak in the fall and winter of 1823–24 and again in 1827, was reflected in the press, public meetings, and the activities of fundraising committees in New York, Philadelphia, Boston, Albany, and Cincinnati. This philhellenism, however, was to end in partial disappointment. In 1830 Russia, Britain, and France acted together to secure the independence for which Greeks had fought and Americans had cheered. But rather than establishing order and liberal institutions, Greeks seemed unable to end the factionalism that had earlier plagued them, until at last the imposition by the three intervening powers of a Bavarian prince as head of state brought tranquillity and a monarchy. To Americans it seemed that the Greek condition was only marginally improved by the exchange of one foreign despotism for another.[21]

The Poles, another brave people under the despot's heel, provided a reprise to the Greek drama, though with an even less happy outcome. Poland had been partitioned in 1795. The Russian-controlled portion went into open revolt in November 1830. Ten months later it was all over. Overwhelming military power prevailed and tightened the grip of oppression on the country. In that brief interval when freedom for a downtrodden people thought to be acting on the American example seemed possible, Americans again rallied in the major cities, collected funds, and contemplated the significance of their own revolutionary heritage. "Remember that not a freeman falls, in the most remote quarter of the world," James Fenimore Cooper enjoined in September 1831 as the Polish revolution entered its death throes, "that you do not lose a brother who is enlisted in your own noble enterprise."[22]

The revolutions that engulfed all Europe in 1848 and 1849 raised American hopes to their highest. A community of youthful republics was about to sweep away the tottering old monarchies of Europe, or so it seemed. The French once again toppled their king. Italians, Hungarians, and Czechs turned against the Hapsburgs; Romans drove the pope from his lair; Germans attacked the authoritarian regimes prevailing in their separate states; and even Britain was briefly shaken by revolutionary plots. This revolutionary surge heightened the robust and self-confident mood in which Americans found themselves as a result of their recent territorial gains effected at the expense of Mexico and after some hard bargaining with Britain. The spectacle of all Europe suddenly shaking off the bonds of despotism provided Americans with an invigorating—and for those worried by the divisive slavery question a diverting—reminder of their national mission as the agent of liberty and the model of revolutionary progress.

Of all the 1848 revolutions, the struggles in France and Hungary most captivated Americans. The Hungarian republic, declared in April 1849, was dead by the following August, the victim of Austrian forces aided by the Russians. The Hungarian cause, however, remained alive in the United States through the efforts of the exiled leader Louis Kossuth. His arrival in New York in December 1851 produced an unprecedented pitch of excitement all the more notable because he represented a cause in extremis. By mid-1852, though, enthusiasm was gone, the republican rituals completed, and Kossuth on his way to permanent exile in England with little substantial to show for his grand American tour. Still, the American dreams for Hungary, as for Greece and Poland earlier, were pleasant while they lasted.

France by contrast inspired political nightmares for the second time. Americans still recalled the excesses that had followed the Revolution of 1789 and that had given way in turn to Bonaparte's empire and then to a restored monarchy. After this unrelieved series of disasters, the French had taken a hopeful, moderate turn in 1830 when they had expelled the Bourbons and put in their place a constitutional monarchy with Louis Philippe on the throne. Americans took comfort in the reassuringly prominent role played by the sensible Lafayette, the good order observed by the French, and their sound judgment in settling for the limited gains of a constitutional monarchy. Against a backdrop of public celebration, President Andrew Jackson offered his congratulations to France for the "heroic moderation which has disarmed revolution of its terrors."[23]

The events of 1848—the fall of Louis Philippe's regime and the establishment of a republic—had Americans again watching with barely concealed anxiety lest the French again fall into anarchy or raise up some man on horseback. Both fears were promptly realized. The "June Days," a popular uprising that briefly convulsed Paris, provoked a violent reaction and set the star of Louis Napoleon in the ascendance. By 1852 he had reestablished the empire. American faith in French political capacities was at low ebb. The *Boston Courier*, sounding like an echo of John Adams, observed with exasperation in December 1852, "The French . . . have spent an infinity of blood and treasure, they have blackened the pages of their national history with an infinity of folly and crime, but they have learnt nothing."[24] Others of a more Jeffersonian persuasion conceded yet another setback but insisted with somewhat diminished conviction that the cause of liberty would in time resume its inevitable advance.

The events in the streets of Paris in 1871 made such tempered optimism even harder to sustain and strengthened the conclusion that the French were constitutionally prone to fits of political fever. Defeat at the hands of Prussia had destroyed the last vestiges of Napoleonic prestige. With peace negotiations in train and the homefront in political confusion, an insurrection broke out in Paris in March of that year. A communal government with its own military force was quickly established and a set of radical policies implemented. These included attacks on the Catholic church, abrogation of rents, and confiscation of property. Before its violent suppression in late May, the Paris Commune had supplied American observers with a large catalogue of horrors to ponder and denounce. Once more Paris, that "dissolute and wicked city," had spawned the mob with its "irrepressible passion for insurrection and street barricades." Memories of "the worst scenes of the Revolution of '89" and the 1848 "revolution of pillage" by "a mob of malcontents" were widely recalled in an American press uniformly hostile to the Commune and singularly relieved by its suppression. Would that the republic established in the wake of this revolutionary paroxysm would finally take heed of the lessons of political moderation Americans had so long tried to teach.[25]

It would be incorrect to attribute the vehemence of the American reaction solely to dismay over French political ineptitude and inability to learn from experience. Events in Paris touched sensitive political nerves at home. They revealed, the editors of the *New York Times* frankly conceded in the immediate aftermath of the Commune, "the deep explosive forces which underlie all modern society."[26] American cities were filling with their own "mob of malcontents," many of them recent European immigrants who had brought with them the same brands of anarchism and socialism that had inspired the communards. These immigrants had swelled the ranks of labor, which not surprisingly had begun to challenge property rights and foment class conflict. Here were the seeds of revolution on American soil, exclaimed alarmed conservatives and nativists. To make sure those seeds did not germinate, they would seek immigration restrictions, beat back labor demands, and post a close watch on heterodox ideas.

The end of this second era had left Americans more convinced than ever of the perilous potential of revolution, but they did not hold their conviction with equal intensity. The differences among Americans on this question can be measured in terms of personal philosophy and temperament, as the cases of Jefferson and Adams make clear. Those differences had something of a political dimension as well. Federalist hostility to revolution was carried forward in the suspicion of radical politics nursed by the conservative wing of the Whig party, while the early Republican enthusiasm was later reincarnated in the late 1840s and early 1850s among Free Soilers, who saw in European revolutions a reflection of their own struggle against the extension of slavery. Americans also divided along ethnic and class lines, with the recent immigrant communities, above all the Germans and the Irish, hopeful for the liberation of their homelands and less easily swayed by the "sanctity of property" argument. Those of Anglo descent, on the other hand, were quicker to grasp the dangerous implications of an underclass of foreigners rooting for revolution abroad.

The lines separating Americans can also be traced in regional terms. The bastions of political order and social conservatism were to be found in New England and in the South. For example, both regions had greeted the French upheaval of 1848 with coolness, and the South later displayed a notable lack of hospitality toward the touring Kossuth. Southerners, with their hierarchical social order and special kind of property to defend, had been alienated by the cry of European revolutionaries for equality. The French decrees in 1848 abolishing slavery in their colonies were precisely the consequences they feared radical doctrine would produce. The Midwest was by contrast more favorably disposed toward revolution. Its population was disproportionately immigrant and its spokesmen in Congress such as Lewis Cass, Stephen Douglas, and Sidney Breese formed the core of the "young America" group, which took the 1848 revolutions in Europe and the simultaneous extension of the domain of the North American republic as signals that liberty was about to sweep the globe. The Kossuth visit, to take one example, evoked a welcome in the Midwest equaled only by cosmopolitan New York.

These regional variations held beyond the Civil War, with the Midwest strikingly less alarmed by the Paris Commune than were the South and New England. Burgeoning cities, especially in the mid-Atlantic states, constituted a middle ground where a large foreign-born working class at ease with notions of radical political and social change faced a well-entrenched elite, preponderantly Anglo in origin and anxious over the mounting challenge to their local hegemony.

★ ★ ★

The third wave of revolutions witnessed by Americans began to build in the 1890s and reached a shattering climax in the late 1910s. The scene of upheaval had shifted from old Europe to its periphery, where Americans least expected revolutions to occur or liberty to arise. And while Americans again experienced the cycle of hope and dismay, this response was now, for the first time, linked to a tendency on the part of policymakers in Washington to scrutinize revolutions and to try to keep them within safe bounds. The United

States was no longer the fragile and vulnerable nation of the 1790s seeking to set Europe at a distance, nor was it, as it had been in the mid-nineteenth century, so deeply engrossed in affairs close to home that it could do nothing bolder than cheer good revolutions, grant them prompt diplomatic recognition, or if they failed offer asylum to vanquished heroes. As Americans in the late nineteenth century cultivated interests both official and private in Latin America, East Asia, and Europe, revolutionary upheavals necessarily impinged upon those interests and inexorably rendered obsolete the former, largely passive American policy. Where those old twin revolutionary bugaboos—violence and radicalism—seemed a threat, policymakers began to use the full panoply of tools at their disposal. They might manipulate arms sales, financial aid, and diplomatic recognition. They might intrigue with factions sympathetic to the United States and good order. They might coordinate their actions with other major powers. They might even dispatch American troops.

From Cuba and the Philippines came the first tremors announcing a new age of revolution. The Cuban struggle for liberation evoked sympathy, at least until American intervention and occupation of the island in 1898 not only eliminated Spanish control but also transformed Washington's perception of the situation. Policymakers now had to weigh Cuban aspirations for liberty against American strategic and economic interests, not to mention racial doubts about Latino political maturity. Out of these conflicting impulses they forged a compromise: limited independence appropriate to a fledgling state in need of guidance and protection. In the Philippines the revolution against Spanish colonial authority proceeded largely beyond American view until military intervention there too gave the United States the upper hand and set U.S. interests and tutelary obligations at odds with "native" demands for liberty and independence. That revolution altogether discredited itself by turning against liberating American troops, and Washington, already opposed to even nominal independence, decreed that a formal decision on the ultimate fate of the islands would have to await the suppression of "outlawry" and evidence of progress toward political order.

Within a decade of disposing of these two outbreaks, Americans were confronted by still others—first in China and Mexico and later in Russia. In all three countries the old order crashed with such speed and resounding finality that Americans were tempted to entertain those old sweet dreams of freedom's advance. But not for long. As each of these revolutions "went astray," old American prejudices again rose to the surface.

Of these latter three revolutions, China's proved the least unsettling. American observers cheered when in late 1911 and early 1912 the Chinese threw out the Qing dynasty and set up a republic, all with a minimum of fuss. Old China, associated in American thinking with stagnant tradition, vulnerability to foreign exploitation, and pervasive poverty, ignorance, and vice, seemed about to take up the path Americans had trod. With missionaries in the lead, China's supporters predicted an era of economic development, democracy, and cooperation between the youngest republic and the oldest. "Now the [Chinese] people are awake," one mission spokesman announced.[27] He and others anticipated fresh opportunities to promote civilization and Christianity, and they called for prompt recognition of the young republic. Despite public and congressional pressure, the Taft administration refused to move, preferring instead to maintain its policy of cooperation with the major powers active in East Asia.

After two years of stalemate the election of Woodrow Wilson finally put policy in the hands of a man with a keenly felt "desire to help China." Wilson regarded the United States as "the friend and exemplar" of the Chinese people, with an obligation to encourage "the liberty for which they have so long been yearning and preparing themselves." In early 1914 he set the American diplomatic seal of approval on the Chinese Revolution and to underline his sympathy withdrew official support from a banking consortium guilty in his view of an exploitative attitude toward the new China.[28]

But by then the signs were multiplying that China would not even achieve the minimum political stability that observers regarded as essential to the security of American missionary and economic enterprise in China. More and more of the Revolution's former friends began to look to a strongman to hold down the latent forces of anarchy. Yuan Shikai, one of the foremost figures in the last years of the empire and now president of what was nominally a republic, was that strongman. Yuan and his successors managed to keep a tenuous grip on the country while assiduously safeguarding foreign life and property. For Americans, now disillusioned over a revolution that had changed China so little, a modicum of stability was enough to satisfy their diminished expectations.

Mexico's revolution commanded greater interest and quickly proved more troubling than China's. As it deviated farther and farther from the norms of a good revolution, the chorus in favor of intervention grew louder and louder. Proximity contributed to the calls for action, especially as the drift toward war with Germany made stability on the American doorstep a growing strategic concern. The destruction caused by the warring political factions that the Mexican Revolution had unleashed also challenged the United States to play its self-assigned role of policeman of the Americas. To revolutionary chaos was added revolutionary radicalism, expressed in an anticlerical policy and such economic goals as nationalization of subsoil rights, regulation of foreign-owned mines, a minimum wage, and land reform. Together chaos and radicalism endangered the lives of a large American community in Mexico (some fifty thousand in 1910), outraged the Catholic hierarchy in the United States, and threatened American investors such as the Hearst and Guggenheim families, U.S. Steel, Anaconda Copper, and Standard Oil that collectively controlled a substantial part of the total Mexican economy.[29]

The Mexican Revolution began with a rapid series of political changes— the overthrow of the dictator Porfirio Díaz in May 1911, the election of Francisco Madero to the presidency of the republic, and Madero's assassination by Victoriano Huerta in February 1913. Huerta's seizure of power deepened the national turmoil. To these unsettling events the Taft administration responded with relative restraint. Though Taft personally had regretted the ouster of Díaz, a strongman so well suited, he thought, to a poor and ignorant country, he had gone ahead and recognized the new Madero government. At the same time he had ruled out any massive military intervention. He suspected that such a dramatic step would fail of popular support in the United States and would in any case set at risk American lives and investment in Mexico. Hoping at least to exercise a calming influence, Taft experimented instead with a show of force along the border in March 1911. This prudent middle course did nothing either to settle Mexico or to silence critics at home. Some from within his own Republican party wanted more forceful action, while others charged that his saber rattling was not only intemperate but served to advance the interests of wealthy investors.

Wilson, also, was to find the Mexican Revolution a puzzle without a solution. No less than in China, he set the United States up as a friend and model. But while he was, initially at least, optimistic about trends in China, the course of the Mexican Revolution disturbed him from his first days in the White House. He doubted that either the Mexican people, passive and ignorant, or their self-appointed leaders, selfish "brutes" and ambitious "barbarians," were ready to establish a free government entirely unaided. It thus fell to the United States as "the great nation on this continent" to guide Mexicans "back into the paths of quiet and prosperity." Or, as he put it more bluntly, he would see to it that "they shall take help when help is needed." The key to Mexico's quest for liberty was setting a constitution in place and seeing that it was respected. With political order thus assured, Mexicans could proceed to deal with the economic and social problems that Wilson came increasingly to recognize as a source of the Revolution.[30]

Wilson's paternalism quickly turned him toward intervention, even though time and again he vowed to respect Mexico's sovereignty and expressed antipathy for the selfish American economic interests hostile to the Revolution. It was his determination to direct the Revolution along enlightened lines that led him to violate Mexico's sovereignty on a massive scale. His actions in turn set against him precisely those nationalist forces most hated by "selfish" American investors.

As the first step toward restoring order and constitutional procedures, Wilson determined on the ouster of Huerta's "government of butchers." To reach his goal, he tried a number of gambits, climaxing in the landing of troops at Vera Cruz in 1914. Wilson's claim that his "motives were unselfish" and limited to "helping [Mexico] adjust her unruly household" failed to shield him from widespread public criticism in either Mexico or the United States. That only a small group of Republican interventionists led by Senator Henry Cabot Lodge approved of this show of force could give Wilson but little comfort.[31]

Huerta's flight from Mexico in July 1914 did not put an end to Wilson's problems. The victorious constitutionalist forces now split, setting the stage for a three-year civil war. Wilson at first thought Venustiano Carranza, the nominal head of the constitutionalists, a cooperative and educable leader. When Wilson learned otherwise, he turned to Pancho Villa, a warlord in northern Mexico with a volatile personality and a reputation in the United States as a Robin Hood figure. Villa was supposed to displace Carranza, restore order, and set the stage for constitutional development. When in 1916 Villa instead launched an outrageous series of raids across the U.S. border, Wilson sent in troops for a second time.

Wilson's decision was influenced by the rise in interventionist sentiment stimulated by Villa's transgressions and probably reflected a desire to improve Democratic chances at the polls in November. A substantial segment of the press (with the Hearst papers in the lead), spokesmen for the Roman Catholic church, prominent Republicans, and the ever-voluble Theodore Roosevelt charged that Mexico had become hopelessly chaotic and that Wilson's relative restraint had been a contributing cause. Villa's raids produced expressions of outrage that "even a little, despicable, contemptible bandit nation like Mexico" would dare defy the United States.[32] As many as twelve thousand American troops marched as deep as three hundred miles into Mexico in Wilson's campaign against Villa, bringing the two countries to the edge of war. Both Wilson and Carranza exercised restraint, however, and finally in early 1917 Wilson called off his crusade and brought his troops home. The prospect of an all-out conflict had taken the edge off public anger, while the mounting crisis in German-American relations commanded the attention of president and public alike.

The revolutionary upheaval in Russia was to prove no less intractable than Mexico's revolution and ultimately a good deal more upsetting. Russia was an unlikely candidate for "ordered liberty." Americans had long identified the czarist regime as the ultimate in political reaction. In Europe it had repeatedly proven itself the enemy of self-determination and at home stood as the model of autocratic rigidity and repression. The Russian government was, the American minister reported from St. Petersburg in 1852, "impelled by a hostility to free institutions, that admits no compromise and yields to no relaxation." The character of Slavic peoples further stacked the odds against political progress. The masses were "ignorant and superstitious barbarians" and "not fit for political freedom," wrote James Buchanan to Andrew Jackson in 1833, drawing on a stereotype commonplace among his countrymen. Was it really possible that a nation so "utterly opposed to all forms of Liberty" could indeed be redeemed?[33]

In 1905 Americans got their first exposure to Russia's revolutionary potential as well as a troubling foretaste of its radical propensities. On "Bloody Sunday," 22 January, czarist troops massacred demonstrators calling for the liberalization of the imperial regime. This act strengthened the opposition and the agitation against the old order. The commentary offered by American observers of this opening phase of the Revolution made predictable points. Nicholas II was a malevolent autocrat, and his archreactionary regime's resistance to popular demands left revolution as the only remedy to the oppressed Russian people, just as it had been the only recourse for Americans of '76. Led by their "substantial citizens"—businessmen, lawyers, and professors—Russians too would secure civil rights and a constitutional democracy. "The spirit of Patrick Henry is abroad in the land of the Tsar."[34]

By late 1905 the earlier enthusiasm for revolutionary ferment had given way to disillusionment and in some quarters even outright hostility. The press, overwhelmingly supportive in January, had dramatically reversed itself by December after having "discovered" that this revolution pointed toward socialism, not democracy, and that its leaders were not good burghers but rather "red anarchists." Despite concessions by the government, dangerous elements had continued to stir up labor unrest, peasant uprisings, and army mutinies, and had even committed acts of terrorism. Editors and other opinion makers in the United States recoiled from a revolution that had turned into a messy, violent standoff.

Politically prominent and socially conservative Americans had anticipated this reversal of opinion and had perhaps even helped effect it with assistance from czarist propagandists. Theodore Roosevelt, John Hay, Elihu Root, and the ambassador in St. Petersburg, George von L. Meyer, shared a distrust of violent change, which they equated with socialism, and regarded the Slav—lazy, illiterate, and backward—as better suited for limited despotism than democracy. In Roosevelt's case hopes that the Russian people would advance toward "self-government and orderly liberty" battled in September 1905 with fears that "a despotism resting upon a corrupt and to a large extent incapable bureaucracy" would block the way. By mid-November his doubts had gained the upper hand and banished all hopes for a moderate revolution. "In social and economic, as in political reforms, the violent revolutionary extremist is the worst friend of liberty, just as the arrogant and intense reactionary is the worst friend of order." Reflecting on these events the next year, Roosevelt attributed the ultimate failure of this revolution to the influence of too many leaders of "hysterical temperament." The Russian upheaval reminded him of another revolution, which Marat and Robespierre had led astray and thereby "made the name of liberty a word of shuddering horror."[35]

The brutal suppression of the vestiges of revolution late in 1905 and a return to normalcy evoked a collective sigh of relief in the United States. The wild-eyed demonstrators had gotten what they deserved, while the harm they had done stood as a salutary reminder to Americans of the need for vigilance against such domestic enemies of law and order as the Industrial Workers of the World and the Socialist party. The celebrated Russian author Maxim Gorki, whom czarist authorities had for a time imprisoned for his views, discovered how far the pendulum of opinion had swung when he arrived in the United States in April 1906 to raise funds and rouse sympathy for the revolutionary cause. Gorki, however, was no Kossuth representing a revolution of national liberation from a foreign oppressor. His cause was a social revolution. Once Americans made this discovery, they responded predictably. When Gorki publicly expressed solidarity with two imprisoned leaders of the United Mine Workers, he was roundly denounced as an interfering foreign radical. To charges of radicalism were added those of immorality when it became known that Gorki was not legally wed to his traveling companion. While the press attacked him, Gorki's sponsors deserted him and New York hotels even refused to accommodate so dissolute and dangerous a figure.

Russia's 1917 revolution occasioned the same cycle of hope and despondency. The collapse of the czarist regime and its replacement by a provisional government in March 1917 evoked enthusiasm. The Russian masses, suddenly endowed with an instinctual preference for liberty, had reduced "the last great, forbidding, seemingly impregnable stronghold of autocracy" and now looked to the United States as the freest of nations to help them.[36] The excited American reaction was accentuated by the crisis atmosphere of wartime. Russia's new found dedication to freedom was certain to strengthen the crusade of the democratic nations against German autocracy. But American faith in the 1917 revolution soon began to crack as the Russian army showed signs of collapse and the Bolsheviks, maneuvering their way to power, opened a campaign to leave the war. Already known from the 1905 revolution as dangerous radicals, the Bolsheviks now also convicted themselves in the American view as traitors. Lenin and his associates had returned to Russia from exile under German auspices making them appear to be German agents bent on disrupting the Allied war effort. Better that some strongman take absolute control than that Russia in her premature try for liberty be allowed to fall instead into the hands of such extremists in Germany's pay.

The Bolshevik seizure of power in November produced precisely those results most feared by Americans. Anarchy reigned, while Lenin and Trotsky predictably capitulated to Germany in March 1918. Some took comfort in the hope that Bolshevism, described by the mass-circulation *Saturday Evening Post* as "despotism by the dregs," would create a popular backlash. The people would soon rally behind some moderate but vigorous leader capable of staying "the destructive hands of the Bolsheviks" and returning the country to constitutionalism and the side of her former allies. Others less certain that Russia could save herself called for intervention. The Bolsheviks are "our malignant and unscrupulous enemies," announced the *New York Times* in December 1917. In a call for action two months later the *Times* argued, "It is not alone the rescue of Russia that is involved, it is the safety of civilization."[37]

Woodrow Wilson's reaction to this third major revolution to confront his presidency was, like the public reaction, heavily influenced by wartime preoccupations. He had welcomed the March revolution for making Russia "a fit partner" in a democratic crusade. Indeed, he was the first head of state to recognize the provisional government. Publicly he celebrated the "naive majesty" of the Russian people, who fought the common German foe. They had been "always in fact democratic at heart," whereas the autocracy that they had just overthrown had not been "in fact Russian in origin, character, or purpose."[38] To encourage the faltering Russian war effort Wilson provided loans and dispatched the elder statesman Elihu Root on an inspection tour. After the Bolsheviks took Russia out of the war Wilson refused for a time to take counteraction, despite persistent lobbying by his allies for efforts to revive the eastern front. Finally in July 1918 he agreed to supply troops to join other Allied forces operating in Russia. Ten thousand Americans eventually served in the maritime provinces in the east and five thousand at the other end of Russia, in Murmansk. In early 1920, with the war won and peace made, Wilson brought the last of the American forces home, even though the civil war between the Bolsheviks and their foes still raged.

Though superficially Wilson may have seemed to recapitulate his Mexican performance, it was not entirely so. To be sure, in Russia as in Mexico and China, he saw himself as the friend of people whose progressive aspirations he claimed to understand intuitively. In Russia, as earlier, he had found that revolutionary leaders were men too small to play the exalted role the times called for. But Wilson had also learned from Mexico the difficulty of directing the course of a sweeping revolution. Intervention even on a limited scale aroused the resentment of the very people it was meant to help and spawned controversy at home. "My policy regarding Russia is very similar to my Mexican policy. I believe in letting them work out their own salvation, even though they wallow in anarchy for a while."[39]

Though this observation by Wilson made in the fall of 1918 accurately described neither his earlier handling of Mexico nor his policy toward Russia at that time, it did indicate what had become his own preferred line of action, from which only powerful pressures could sway him. The sobering experience with Mexico had fortified him against those pressures, though not enough to render him completely immune to the multiplicity of arguments for intervention that had accumulated by July 1918 when he took the plunge into Russia. These arguments, articulated by his advisers and a preponderance of the press, included keeping supplies of war materiel out of German hands, facilitating the withdrawal of Czech forces from Russia along the Siberian railway, and restraining the Japanese, whose territorial ambitions on the Asian mainland Wilson had discovered some years earlier. But the decisive factor was the relentless pressure applied by his wartime allies. And once Wilson had sent the troops in, he could not abruptly withdraw them without damaging relations with his partners in peacemaking and at the same time leaving the Japanese a free hand. Meanwhile Wilson bemoaned the fate of the Russian people subjected to the sufferings of a prolonged civil war and to a "bloody terror" matched only in the worst days of the czars. He left office saddened that the popular hunger for liberty had ended in massive disorder and destruction as power passed from one set of autocrats, "old and distinguished and skillful," to another, "amateur and cruel."[40]

Wilson's own reaction seems moderate in comparison with the deep sense of alarm felt by some of his influential countrymen. That alarm built toward a climax in late 1918 and 1919. With the war over, the Bolsheviks' betrayal of the war effort faded in importance, and concern with the Revolution's radicalism assumed greater prominence. Commentators found abhorrent a regime of maniacs that denied political, religious, and property rights, advocated free love and atheism, and promoted class war not only at home but also abroad. Robert Lansing, Wilson's secretary of state and one of the staunchest anti-Bolsheviks in the administration, compared conditions under the new regime to "the Asiatic despotism of the early Tsars" and to the terror of the French Revolution. Bolshevism, "the most hideous and monstrous thing the human mind has ever conceived," had imposed on Russia the curses of "demoralization, civil war, and economic collapse." A Senate subcommittee's findings went farther: "The activities of the Bolsheviki constitute a complete repudiation of modern civilization."[41]

Posing as it did a direct challenge to American values, the Bolshevik Revolution could not have come at a worse time. Americans were going through a national crisis of self-confidence as the prosperity and exaggerated superpatriotism of wartime gave way to economic crisis and labor unrest. With a sense of their own vulnerability they watched with alarm as the Bolshevik "disease" spread to Germany and Hungary and the Soviets took the lead in organizing the Third International. This could be only the beginning of a long campaign of subversion that even the United States would not escape. Raymond Robins, who had served with the Red Cross in Russia, cautioned businessmen that bolshevism was a bomb that "can blow our system—your system—into the eternal past with the Bourbons and the Pharohs [sic]." The New York Times, developing the implications of Robins' remark, posed the obvious question in January 1919, "Shall we wait for the Bolsheviks to conquer Europe and then carry their despotism elsewhere?" Already, Wilson had warned in the fall of 1918, "the spirit of Bolshevism is lurking everywhere." A year later he suggested that some of the revolutionary "poison" had indeed seeped "into the veins of this free people."[42]

Once again nativist and conservative elements combined in a campaign to save the country from revolutionary contagion. During the Red Scare of 1919–20 the Wilson administration as well as state and local governments brutally suppressed strikes, arrested radicals, and sought to deport the foreign-born who were implicated in "revolutionary" activity. All the while, the courts stood silent. This national hysteria declined only after January 1920 following raids organized by Attorney General A. Mitchell Palmer that netted four thousand suspected radicals in thirty-three cities and in the process massively violated civil rights. By then it was evident that Europe would withstand the red tide and that the peril to the United States had been greatly exaggerated. The domestic left had in any case been effectively silenced. The republic, it was clear by 1921, was safe, but so too was Lenin's Soviet regime. As a worthy heir to the Jacobins and the Parisian anarchists, this

Bolshevik peril would remain to haunt the imagination of the "better classes."

★ ★ ★

By the early twentieth century Americans had witnessed three waves of revolution and repeatedly gone through the cycles of hope, then disappointment, and finally in some cases open hostility. To some extent this pattern of misplaced enthusiasm can be explained in terms of American unfamiliarity with foreign conditions, compounded by the difficulty of securing accurate information in the confusion surrounding a revolutionary upheaval. Moreover, the causes of revolution—the problems of a peasantry, prolonged and exhausting wars, resentments engendered by foreign rule—were either largely alien or increasingly remote to Americans. The propaganda of refugee groups, whether proponents of a new order or defenders of the old regime, further clouded American perceptions. The cumulative effect of ignorance and misinformation is starkly illustrated in the usually sober *New York Times*' treatment of the Russian Revolution. Over a two-year period it predicted the failure of the Bolshevik cause some ninety-one times and announced the flight, death, retirement, or imprisonment of Lenin and Trotsky on no less than thirteen occasions.[43] The *Times* had been deluded, and so in turn were its readers.

More important, however, than mere misapprehension in explaining this persistent pattern of disillusionment with foreign revolutions were the stringent standards that Americans dating back to Adams and Jefferson had used to judge them. Revolution was a solemn affair, to be conducted with a minimum of disorder, led by respectable citizens, harnessed to moderate political goals, and happily concluded only after a balanced constitution, essential to safeguarding human and property rights, was securely in place. In other words, a successful revolution was inextricably tied in the minds of Americans to methods and goals familiar from their own revolution and their own political culture.

In their efforts to explain what seemed to be the almost invariable tendency of revolutions to self-destruct, Americans looked to the personal failings of foreign leaders and the unfortunate traits of foreign peoples. Despotic tendencies, selfish ambition, and simple ineptitude or weakness of character were in various combinations attributed to the leaders of failed revolutions, while the inability of a people to meet the test of revolution and liberty was explained most often in the familiar terms of the hierarchy of race. By comparison with Anglo-Saxons, blacks were thought to labor under the heaviest racial burden. Orientals and Latinos did little better. The Filipinos were thought so unworthy of freedom that American troops crushed their revolution, and the Chinese botched their attempt at setting up a republic. Mexicans, like the Cubans before them, might aspire to constitutional government, but the traits associated with the black legend made the realization of that goal remote except perhaps under American tutelage. Even European peoples had a poor record. Slavs, as the most sluggard of the Caucasian peoples, understandably came to revolution late and failed miserably at it. The French, so close on the racial hierarchy to the Anglo-Saxons, tried mightily to equal the success of their betters, but even here relatively small differences in national character seemed to account for the rather substantial difference in the maturity of their political behavior.

American observers also took note of the differing kinds of revolutions in evaluating their failures. The fate of one type, those against foreign control, depended chiefly on national will and the power that a people could mobilize against a foreign oppression. When such an effort was crushed by brute force, as in the case of the Poles and Hungarians, failure carried no stigma. It was the second type, the social revolutions that ran out of control either because of betrayal by their leaders or because of the irresponsibility of the masses, that most disturbed Americans. Such revolutions were frightening because they combined pervasive violence, despotic practices, and radical doctrines in a frontal assault on individual liberty and private property. Without security for persons and goods against the demagogue and leveler, freedom as American observers conceived it could not survive.

This second type of revolution, Americans had discovered, followed a fairly regular pattern. As those political and social restraints usually guaranteed by constitutions, religion, family, and morality began to slip, life and property fell into increasing peril. In the resulting revolutionary terror, land and goods were redistributed, and the old dominant classes underwent merciless attack. This phase in the revolutionary cycle was captured in images of random, cruel, senseless violence, of women violated, elders slain, children impaled, distinguished citizens brought down by the base. A society thus convulsed would sooner or later turn in desperation to a strongman, a Bonaparte, to restore order. These revolutions consequently ended by making survival rather than liberty the greater good. France supplied the first dramatic example of this pattern in the 1790s and then as if to impress it on the minds of American observers gave short repeat performances in 1848 and 1871. The Russians proved that the pattern was not unique to the French—indeed, that it might repeat itself anywhere with fearsome results.

While the above observations fairly characterize the view of most Americans with an interest in foreign affairs, these observers divided, just as John

Figure 24. *Cinque-têtes, or the Paris Monster*

These illustrations capture the repugnance that governed the dominant American response to social revolution. Such a revolution appears here as a menace to moral order and personal security. Figure 24, prepared in 1798 after three American commissioners to France had rebuffed a bribe demanded by the Directory, depicts that French governing body as a menacing five-headed monster with dagger and torch at the ready. To the right a Jacobin, a devil, and a black share a revolutionary "civic feast" of frogs (!), while behind them a debauched, haglike goddess of liberty sits beside one of her guillotined victims.

Figure 25. *The Emancipation of Labor and the Honest Working-People*

The Paris Commune of 1871 and the activities of the First International evoked
similarly disturbing images, captured by Thomas Nast's 1874 spectral figure of communism (fig. 25), adorned with the insignia of the "French disease," seeking to undo
the honest virtue of the American workingman.

Figure 26. *The Government of Russia*

Cartoons done in 1919 and 1920 in response to the Bolshevik Revolution (figs. 26–28) continue to equate social revolution with indiscriminate death and destruction. The power of the new Soviet government at home depended on the instruments of violence, while abroad the threat the "Reds" posed to civilization and the American way is embodied by a brutal, stereotypically Slavic type.[44]

Figure 27. *On the Threshold!*

Figure 28. *Put Them Out and Keep Them Out*

Adams and Thomas Jefferson had, over precisely how much revolutionary upheaval was tolerable. Those of the Adams persuasion such as Lansing were quick to conclude that under the direction of all-too-fallible man—and foreigners at that!—the revolutionary impulse was all too likely to degenerate and, unless quickly restrained, to rend the fragile social fabric and destroy liberty. Lansing's analysis of bolshevism thus revealed to him that it appealed "to the unintelligent and brutish elements of mankind to take from the intellectual and successful their rights and possessions and to reduce them to a state of slavery." Jeffersonians such as Wilson with a deep faith in the ultimate triumph of liberty were prepared to tolerate greater excesses because of their conviction that emancipation for all mankind was not only possible but imminent. All men longed for freedom, and in time they would have it. Along the way the people would indeed commit "excesses," but they would eventually learn to "preserve their self-control and the orderly processes of their governments." Consequently, Wilson was no more ready to despair over Russia than Jefferson had been prepared to give up on France.[45]

Because of their belief in all people's inherent capacity for liberty, Jefferson and Wilson were inclined to intervene in order to guide revolutions. Adams and Lansing, by contrast, were likely to intervene to arrest them altogether. By the same token, Jefferson and Wilson with their tolerance for disorder and their commitment to the spread of liberty were slower than Adams and Lansing to embrace a strongman. For the former pair the rise of a strongman was a symptom of revolutionary travail, to be welcomed only if he might set the revolution back on track and then withdraw. For the latter a strongman was a welcome figure who might bring order out of chaos. They saw him as the predictable product of the grim revolutionary cycle, first seen in France and later recapitulated in Russia. First moderation gave way to terror, and then terror gave way (as Lansing put it) to a "Revolt against the New Tyranny and restoration of order by arbitrary military power."[46]

In the 1910s, just as earlier, the differences within the broader American consensus on revolution were more than simply a function of personality or political philosophy. Within both the mass public and the small group of Americans actively engaged in foreign affairs, socioeconomic level (and by extension ethnic background) played a powerful, though not always obvious, part. Revolutions and the radical political notions often associated with them held few terrors for an American underclass, much of it of recent European origin. On the other hand, the Adamsian view appealed most to the wealthy and socially prominent who identified culturally with England. They feared the radical potential of all revolutions and the implicit challenge they posed to the principles of order and, perhaps even more important, to the sanctity of property at home.

In alliance with nativists, this privileged elite had repeatedly manned the watch against the forces of disorder and taken the lead in mobilizing the public against any emergent threat.[47] With their disproportionate influence over the press, public schools, higher education, and the church, they worked to perpetuate a political culture inimical to revolutionary upheaval and especially to the violation of property rights. "In no country in the world," Alexis de Tocqueville acutely observed, "is love of property more active and more anxious than in the United States; nowhere does the majority display less inclination for those principles which threaten to alter, in whatever manner, the laws of property."[48] Whatever inequalities of wealth existed among people were natural, indeed essential to progress, and hence were to be borne with good grace. Political change was possible but had to occur slowly and within the existing system. Those who challenged these articles of faith put themselves beyond the pale of political respectability. This elite not only worked to inoculate their own society against the contagion of revolution but also sought to deal with diseased foreign revolutions at the source. Drawing on their status, wealth, and leisure, they laid claim to the high political offices where policy toward those revolutions and the terms of any public debate were set.

The nagging preoccupation with the perils of revolution, most acute among a propertied elite, rounds out the trilogy of ideas central to American foreign policy. Important in its own right, this concern with explosions of political heterodoxy abroad served to reinforce the Anglo's conviction of his superior racial standing and the nationalist's arguments in behalf of greatness. The special American understanding of appropriate revolutionary behavior and grasp of progressive political ideas together confirmed the superior instincts of the race, strengthened the case for an American right to judge and instruct other peoples, and helped neutralize fears that self-assertion abroad might have deleterious effects at home. Conversely, the revolutionary reverses suffered by others confirmed their racial or cultural inferiority and underlined their need for American tutelage. These views on revolutions in general and the Bolshevik specter in particular were now fixed. They would persist in the thinking of policymakers and shape their response to a fourth revolutionary wave that was to burst upon them at mid-century.

5 Ideology in Twentieth-Century Foreign Policy

History is not what you thought. It is what you can remember. *All other history defeats itself.*

—Walter C. Sellar and Robert J. Yeatman,
1066 and All That

Twentieth-century U.S. foreign policy has been much thought and written about. It has been depicted in terms of the pursuit of overseas markets essential to stability and prosperity at home. It has also been treated as an extended struggle between clear-eyed realists on the one side and fuzzy-minded moralists, opportunistic politicians, and a mercurial public on the other. These approaches, whatever their merits, are by themselves incomplete, for they deal inadequately with one of the most notable features of American policy. And that is the deep and pervasive impact of an ideology with its roots in the eighteenth and nineteenth centuries. The power and persistence that ideology acquired has not been sufficiently appreciated. It is precisely that power and persistence that this chapter emphasizes, with the hope that those who consider the era treated here, the years between 1901 and 1965, will henceforth remember ideology as at least one element essential to any overall appraisal.

Americans entered the twentieth century in possession of a coherent foreign-policy ideology validated by a remarkable string of successes. The first generation of national leaders, gripped by concerns with greatness and liberty, race, and revolution, had guided the country safely through the maelstrom of Anglo-French rivalry and launched the quest for continental dominion that had in short order overwhelmed the claims of the European powers, Mexico, and a host of native peoples. Outward-looking Americans at the turn of the century looked back on these achievements as the natural preliminaries to the no less dramatic achievements of their own day.

In the tumultuous era between the Spanish-American War and the end of

World War I, the inherited ideology that had previously served so well continued to provide the American foreign policy elite with a compass to the world and a spur to still-greater achievements. A look at the two dominant figures of that era, Theodore Roosevelt and Woodrow Wilson, reveals the hold of that ideology while also suggesting the diversity of views that the ideological synthesis could accommodate. Roosevelt (the self-avowed Hamiltonian) and Wilson (with his strong affinities for Jefferson) were to play significantly different variations on familiar themes.

Roosevelt, a New York patrician with boundless curiosity, energy, and self-confidence, offers a particularly dramatic illustration of the degree to which the "rise to world power" was an affirmation of core American policy ideas. Roosevelt believed fervently in America's mission. To doubters among his countrymen he had a characteristically forceful and direct reply: "No man is worth his salt who does not believe that the growth of his own country's influence is for the good of all those benighted people who have had the misfortune not to be born within its fold."[2]

The road to national greatness required unremitting struggle, so Roosevelt contended. A compulsive classifier even as a youth, he took a lifelong interest in the natural order and its competitive features. By the 1880s he was avidly Darwinian in his views on international relations (as he was on domestic affairs). Conflict among nations was natural. The fit would prevail and the weak go down to defeat and extinction. "All the great masterful races have been fighting races," he readily concluded.[3] Set in a competitive, sometimes violent world, the American nation had one supreme duty—to seek out challenges and master them, thereby promoting the hardihood essential to survival. With these Darwinian notions Roosevelt mixed what appears to have been a sublimated Calvinism that made him anxious about moral decline. To counter the constant tug of individual self-interest and corruptibility, he championed public responsibility and personal self-sacrifice. But moral flab could doom nations as surely as it could individuals. For the United States, commerce and industry were necessary but base pursuits that had to be tempered by international sacrifice and selflessness. Only by manfully confronting rivals and accepting the burden of rescuing stagnant, declining peoples could Americans maintain their vigorous character and their claims to greatness. .

Roosevelt's "strenuous" conception of national greatness dovetailed neatly with his preoccupation with race. Roosevelt read voraciously and wrote extensively on the subject; in expressing himself he could as easily employ formal pseudoscientific language as the cruder epithets of popular discourse. He regarded the world as a competitive arena for races no less than nations.

The clash between civilized races and barbarian ones was inevitable; progress came only through the civilized man "subduing his barbarian neighbor." Not surprisingly Roosevelt considered Anglo-Saxons (he later came to prefer the term "English-speaking" people) the most advanced race. In 1881, in his first foray as an author, he described them as "bold and hardy, cool and intelligent." The American branch had been further strengthened by the frontier experience where lesser races had served as its "natural prey." With the frontier gone, Americans would have to confirm their mettle by joining their English cousins in the race for overseas territory and in the "warfare of the cradle" against the more prolific lower orders, chiefly eastern Europeans, Latin Americans, and blacks.[4]

Of the "lower orders" Roosevelt had little good to say. He found the passivity and national indiscipline and weakness of the Chinese ("Chinks") contemptible, while the Filipinos stood as no better than savages, who on their own could know only "the black chaos of savagery and barbarism." Among the Orientals, only the Japanese escaped his censure. Indeed, they earned his growing admiration for their prowess in defeating China in 1894–95 and Russia a decade later. Latinos ("dagoes") were—in the familiar clichés—hot blooded yet cowardly, politically incompetent, and shockingly miscegenated. The Indians struck Roosevelt as "squalid savages," their fate the inevitable one of a backward people engulfed by civilization. Only their manliness and their penchant for warfare saved them from his utter contempt. Roosevelt reserved the lowest rung in his hierarchy for blacks, deficient in intelligence and moral vigor and "but a few generations removed from the wildest savagery." Like an earlier generation, he took Haiti's "half-savage negroid people" as prime evidence of the political incapacity of "darkeys" in general.[5]

Roosevelt's attitude toward revolution, also well within the established ideological mainstream, was largely derived from his views on race and was consistent with the conservativism long associated with his class. (Born into an old and wealthy family, TR had received his education from a private tutor and at Harvard, traveled widely, and married into Boston's most exclusive family.)[6] The revolution of a backward people, whether directed against control by an advanced people or driven by an impatience to rush the pace of social or economic change, was taboo and could only end in disaster. In other words, colonial tutelage of the sort he supported in the Philippines was a higher good than self-determination, and evolutionary change, advanced by mass education and moderate programs of political reform, was most likely to promote progress, as the negative example of the 1905 Russian Revolution made dramatically clear. Radical change was bound to be disruptive and retrograde. Talk of class interest and class conflict repelled a man for whom race marked the fundamental divisions between people and race conflict the fundamental challenge to national survival. This outlook effectively reduced the range of acceptable revolutions to those cases in which superior peoples struggled against domination by their inferiors. Thus for Roosevelt revolutions (the American case of course expected) were, like the single condition that justified them, something of an anomaly.

Roosevelt's views had led that up-and-coming New York politician to support an assertive foreign policy in the 1880s and 1890s. Against Germans with pretensions in Samoa, obstreperous and insulting Chileans, the moral derelicts opposed to Hawaii's annexation, and British meddling in the Americas—against all these provocations—Roosevelt had called for the United States to assume its proper role as policeman and colonial master. It should stand on a par with the European powers, help bring "order out of chaos," and build a navy equal to these new national responsibilities. When the culminating debate over the Philippines came in 1899, he repeated his by then well rehearsed call for "the strenuous life" in world affairs that would confirm as well as sustain the superiority of the American people. "We cannot, if we would, play the part of China, and be content to rot by inches in ignoble ease within our borders. . . . " Such an "unwarlike and isolated" America was "bound, in the end, to go down before other nations which have not lost the manly and adventurous qualities. If we are to be a really great people, we must strive in good faith to play a great part in the world."[7]

Like Roosevelt, Wilson embraced the established ideology, but he gave it his own distinctly Southern twist. Born and raised in the Old South, Wilson derived his social position from his family's close ties to the region's prestigious Presbyterian ministry. His studies carried him by stages from the South to the Middle Atlantic states, where he completed his academic apprenticeship and developed his talents as a teacher and scholar. Princeton, where he rose to the presidency, served as his jumping-off point for state and national politics and for the White House, which he entered in 1913, when in his late fifties.

Like many in his region and very unlike Roosevelt, Wilson was a belated convert to the notion that an assertive foreign policy was the key to national greatness. Not until the Spanish-American War did he give even perfunctory attention to foreign affairs. He appears at first to have shared the doubts of many Southerners about the desirability of annexing the Philippines. By November 1898, however, he seems to have reluctantly concluded that it was better for Spain to be displaced by the United States than by a power such as Germany or Russia. The United States stood for "the light of day, while theirs was the light of darkness."[8]

The Senate's endorsement of McKinley's policy of annexation in 1899 and his reelection the next year smothered any lingering doubts Wilson may have harbored—so at least casual and incidental comments suggest. He took up the now dominant notion that the United States had crossed a watershed, leaving the old isolation behind and embarking on a new, "momentous career" in world affairs. He described this transition as "inevitable" and "natural." Americans, who had lost their frontier, needed new markets, and in any case they lived in a world getting ever smaller. As he gradually warmed to the idea of an expansive American foreign policy, Wilson began to sound occasionally like Roosevelt. The times ahead would be "strenuous" as the United States emerged as "a mighty power" destined to act alongside Britain in the role of patient tutor to "undeveloped peoples, still in the childhood of their political growth." The Anglo-Saxons, he proclaimed in 1904, had undertaken to remake the world in their own image. At the same time he warned that "it would be shame upon them to withdraw their hand."[9]

But Wilson did not share Roosevelt's fixation with great-power rivalry and racial struggle. True to his own heritage, Wilson focused instead on moral service that would gently help the weak and suffering and refine the American spirit. Good works abroad would test "our political character, our political capacity, our political principles, even our political organizations." Wilson directed his instinct for service toward an Asia in ferment. The United States had a duty, he contended, "to play a part, and a leading part at that, in the opening and transformation of the East." For example, the Philippines, which had drawn his attention to the Pacific in the first place, challenged Americans to learn colonial administration, introduce order, guide the "natives" through "a long apprenticeship" in self-government, and thereby demonstrate that "we have only their welfare at heart."[10]

Wilson's Jeffersonian preoccupation with liberty and liberal institutions was also evident in his attitude toward revolution. It made him an interested observer and sometimes even a friend of revolution in a way Roosevelt could not be. As a proud Southerner who had grown up in the shadow of the Civil War and Reconstruction, he could identify viscerally with those denied the right of self-determination. He was certain that all peoples sought to be free. Their quest for liberty was like a flame, burning "with an accumulating ardor." Extinguished for a time in one place, that flame would burst forth elsewhere. He was also certain of the universal relevance of Anglo-American political institutions and values. As a student of government, Wilson had long celebrated liberty as the flower of the Anglo-American tradition, its evolutionary advance the benchmark of progress, and constitution making one of man's great accomplishments. The British parliamentary system was his institutional ideal, and the American Revolution stood for him as an epochal event that made "the rest of the world take heart to be free."[11]

The French experience, on the other hand, served Wilson, as it did Roosevelt, as a reminder of the perils of revolution—the terrible consequences of attempting too much liberty too soon. At the age of twenty-three, with memories of the Paris Commune still fresh, Wilson had sought the reason for France's recurrent bouts of revolution and found it in the nature of a people who were "born and nurtured in quasi-servitude" and thus "knew only how alternately to obey and to overthrow." Fifteen years later (in 1894), under the influence of Edmund Burke's writings, Wilson had condemned the French Revolution as the source of "radically evil and corrupting" ideas. The French had proven conclusively that without order there could be neither liberty nor progress. More mature reflection convinced Wilson, just as it had the elderly Jefferson, that the French Revolution with all its demerits at least deserved credit for consuming the old regime and clearing the way for the eventual rise of new, free institutions throughout Europe.[12]

All people might want freedom, but whether they could gain and preserve it depended on race, a third critical element in Wilson's ideological makeup. Even here regional and Jeffersonian influences were at work. Wilson had carried throughout his academic career and eventually into the White House the feelings of paternalism toward and superiority over blacks that one might expect of someone who had grown up with slavery and later accepted unquestioningly the rule of Jim Crow. Liberty, the chief yardstick of progress, was something still beyond blacks. Convinced of their inferiority in this and other respects, Wilson relegated them to the bottom of the hierarchy (and made them the brunt of the "darkey" stories he was reputedly adept at telling). The Anglo-Saxons, measured against the same standard, belonged at the top. Above all, their seminal contributions to the advance of liberty held his admiration. His strong Anglophilia, another contribution of his native region with its heavily Anglo ethnic composition, is reflected in his academic writings praising British political institutions as superior to those of his own country. His preference for things British extended into the realm of manners, literature, and philosophy.[13]

Toward those peoples occupying the intermediate rungs of the racial ladder, Wilson's attitude varied according to their ability to acquire liberal values and institutions either by submitting patiently to tutelage or by carefully copying foreign models. Indians, total failures in this respect, figured conventionally if incidentally as the tragic victims of a justified white hunger for land. He regarded the Chinese, whom he came to know through the writings of missionaries, as an ancient people trapped in a static way of life that was by definition unhealthy. But he also saw the Chinese as "plastic" and thus susceptible to remolding at the hands of vigorous Westerners. The Japanese, as good students of the West, evoked Wilson's respect. They had shown "singular sagacity, the singular power to see and learn." Latinos seem not to have engaged Wilson's interest (though if they had, the incidence of racial intermarriage among them would undoubtedly have shocked this son of the South even more than it did Roosevelt).[14]

Once ensconced in the White House, Roosevelt and Wilson in turn followed a policy toward each of the three key regions of concern to the United States—Latin America, East Asia, and Europe—that reveals both the persistence of old ideas and the differing ways those ideas could be combined and applied. Equipped with a world-class navy, an expeditionary army suited to patrol new national frontiers, and a professionalizing foreign-affairs bureaucracy, they proceeded to act with unprecedented vigor and boldness in world affairs.

Despite their differences, Roosevelt and Wilson carried Latin American policy in a strikingly similar direction. Their immediate predecessors had done much to define that direction when, prompted by the familiar attitudes about national greatness, racial superiority, and political disorder, they began to seek regional dominance. Secretary of State Richard Olney had in 1895 fired the first big gun in that campaign by warning Britain and all other powers against meddling in the Americas. It was time, Olney later remarked, for the United States "to realize its great place among the powers of the earth" and "to accept the commanding position belonging to it, with all its advantages on the one hand and all its burdens on the other."[15] Intervention in the Cuban conflict and the occupation of Cuba and Puerto Rico constituted the next major steps in the American campaign.

Roosevelt continued to develop claims to a tutelary and supervisory role over Latinos. He would not tolerate their debauching their own societies, impeding the advance of civilization in the New World, and inviting by their displays of moral bankruptcy intervention by outside powers. Roosevelt reduced Cuba to protectorate status, his price for withdrawing American troops. When Colombia's leaders obstructed his plans for a transisthmian canal, he added a second protectorate. Brushing aside those "foolish and homicidal corruptionists in Bogotá" (he also called them "contemptible little creatures" and "inefficient bandits"), TR saw to it that a revolution by their Panamanian subjects succeeded and in the process secured his own claims. In 1904 the former police commissioner of New York took the whole hemisphere as his beat. His corollary to the Monroe Doctrine asserted the right to force intemperate Latinos to "obey the primary laws of civilized society." He was determined to make the region "stable, orderly, and prosperous."[16]

Wilson further tightened the Latin American sphere of influence. He thought of his approach as more altruistic than either Roosevelt's "big-stick" style or William Howard Taft's "dollar diplomacy." He often spoke of performing neighborly service and teaching Latin peoples to elect good men. But his self-righteousness, combined with his anxiety over the political ineptitude of wild-eyed Mexican revolutionaries or unruly Haitian blacks, led him to a policy that was strikingly aggressive. He dispatched troops on some seventeen occasions to exorcise the indigenous demons of instability and ignorance, while wartime fears prompted him to seize Denmark's Virgin Islands so that those Old World devils, the Germans, could not.

In East Asia, that distant hotbed of imperial rivalries, American policymakers had also burst into action in the late 1890s. They had annexed Hawaii, seized the Philippines, and proclaimed an open door for China. This flurry of East Asian initiatives gave way, however, to a period of uncertainty. Roosevelt entered the White House proclaiming the Pacific an American lake and East Asia the nation's new frontier. There Americans would be tested just as they had been on the old continental frontier. "We must either succeed greatly or fail greatly."[17] But Roosevelt soon realized that this grandiose vision was beyond reach, and so he moved steadily toward recognizing the dominant position Japan deserved as an advanced state and regional power. That meant Japan, not the United States, would carry the primary responsibility to police as well as tutor China. By thus in effect minimizing the significance of the open door and turning his back on a paternalistic policy toward a weak and embattled China, Roosevelt avoided open-door claims he could not make good on, while at the same time winning from Japan guarantees for the strategically vulnerable Philippines.

Roosevelt's East Asian realpolitik had its limits. Though as a policymaker Roosevelt accepted the primacy of Japanese interests in China, he could not bring himself publicly to repudiate the hardy notion that the United States should serve as China's protector or that China constituted an important market, at least in the long term. Neither could he turn his back on the Philippines even after he had discovered it was "our heel of Achilles." Abandonment of the islands would damage the American claim to greatness and force on the Filipinos "the impossible task of working out their own salvation." A native government there would merely set off a "vibration between despotism and anarchy." The United States thus had no choice, TR concluded, but to stay on for the twenty to forty years required to civilize the islands and in the meantime maintain a Pacific naval presence formidable enough to hold the Japanese to their hands-off policy.[18]

Wilson, for his part, found the idea of an era of U.S. ascendancy in the Pacific considerably more appealing than a disreputable policy of appeasement toward the Japanese. Wilson felt an obligation to help the Chinese become Christian and democratic and to protect them against Japan. Even the distractions of the European crisis could not divert him from the temptations of a missionary policy. But he could not find a way around the strategic constraints Roosevelt had earlier recognized. The Wilson years thus witnessed repeated assertions of a sentimental interest in China with little practical follow-through.

Europe figured a distant third in the global preoccupations of American leaders at the turn of the century. Within a decade-and-a-half, however, entanglement in the Anglo-German rivalry would catapult Europe to the forefront of American foreign policy. The key to this dramatic development was a historic rapprochement with Britain inspired by the Anglo-Saxonism strongly felt by the American policy elite. The British were kinfolk who shared a devotion to ordered liberty, free trade, and international progress and stability. The conviction that an upstart, pugnacious, despotic Germany was the common enemy gave these sentimental notions strong strategic implications. German machinations, real or imagined, in Samoa, China, the Philippines, and Latin America had come to worry American officials. The British, on the other hand, set about carefully cultivating American goodwill.[19]

Roosevelt began the process of translating these "entangling attitudes" into a lasting Anglo-American diplomatic rapprochement. After reaping the benefits of the British strategic retreat from the Americas in the first years of his presidency, TR reciprocated in 1905 by throwing his weight against Germany in the Morocco crisis. Inserting himself as mediator, Roosevelt cautiously but unmistakably worked to shore up the Anglo-French combination and frustrate the troublemaking Kaiser Wilhelm.

Roosevelt's foray into European politics proved but the prologue to the more dramatic actions of the no less Anglophilic Woodrow Wilson. At the outbreak of war Wilson, encouraged by his chief advisers, Edward House and Robert Lansing, bent his policy of neutrality in Britain's favor and put Berlin in a difficult position by holding it to a higher standard in its conduct of naval warfare than he did London. He conceded that what guided him was "not the technical principles of law, but the essential principles of right dealing and humanity as between nation and nation." London he thought more "right" than Berlin. While amicably acquiescing to British measures of economic warfare that contravened American neutral rights, Wilson responded to German submarine attacks with warnings of "strict accountability" and the thinly veiled threat of war.[20] Wilson's stance fell in nicely with British strategy, angered the Germans (on whom the British naval blockade would inflict a heavy toll of dead), and drove from his cabinet William Jennings Bryan, whose minority views set him against European entanglements.

The German decision in January 1917 to unleash its submarines had not immediately forced Wilson's hand. He still hesitated over the prospect of American participation in the murderous European conflict. Finally in April he decided that America would indeed be "privileged to spend her blood and her might" fighting beside the European democracies against a barbaric Wilhelmine Germany, and he asked Congress for a declaration of war.[21] But for Wilson it was not enough to defeat Germany. He wanted also to defeat those banes of humankind that Germany stood for—imperialism, militarism, and autocracy. A victorious war would be for him only the prelude to global reform. An enlightened peace would redeem the bloody sacrifices of the war and break the grim cycle of suspicion, hatred, and conflict.

In the postwar negotiations of 1918–19 Wilson worked to secure acceptance of his fourteen-point blueprint for a better world. That consummately ideological document carried to new limits the old American commitment to an active international policy in the name of national greatness and liberty for all men. It looked forward to an era of Anglo-Saxon cultural supremacy and Anglo-American diplomatic cooperation. Wilson's projected international order would unshackle trade, bring the arms race to a halt, banish secret diplomacy with its alliances and terrible carnage, pull down empires, and most important of all promote self-determination throughout Europe. Moderate, democratic, constitutional revolutions would prevail in Germany, Russia, and the newly liberated nations of the Austro-Hungarian Empire. A coalition of these and other democratic, peace-loving states organized in a League of Nations would bring an end to the terror, tyranny, and aggression in the world and quiet the "universal unrest" of all peoples for justice.[22]

Wilson's new order was not to be. His allies proved intractable and shortsightedly selfish in the peacemaking. The spread of bolshevism into Germany and Hungary reminded Wilson of the difficulties facing "ordered liberty," while the survival of bolshevism in Russia left all Americans confronting a revolution disturbingly antithetical to their own ideals. Adding to these difficulties, Wilson blasted his chances of winning the necessary support at home. Rather than make the compromises necessary to patch together a bipartisan coalition, he rigidly held to the terms negotiated in Paris. When a skeptical Senate rejected his peace, Wilson launched himself on an appeal to "the people" in the fall of 1919, only to suffer a collapse brought on by the unremitting demands of war and peace. Even in the isolation of his sickbed he continued to concoct plans for saving his dreams, until at last in March 1921 he retired from the White House a broken and defeated man.

★ ★ ★

Wilson had been the victim of not one but two sets of critics. On the one hand, a small band inspired by the republican vision of the early Jefferson had challenged Wilson from outside the ideological consensus. A few had first taken their stand in 1917 when the president had asked for war. (In the Senate a mere six had voted nay, and in the House only fifty.) One of the opposition leaders, George W. Norris, a Nebraska Republican, reflecting a populist view still strongly entrenched in the agrarian and non-Anglo ethnic communities of the Midwest, charged that a pro-British elite was taking the United States "into war upon the command of gold."[23] Bankers with large loans out to the allies, munitions makers who profited from keeping the British fighting, and propagandists employed to dress selfish interests up in altruistic terms had conspired against the common man, who would fight, die, and pay. Randolph Bourne, one of the few intellectuals not swept up in the war fever, warned that all the Wilsonian cant about a holy war for democracy only meant Americans would neglect their own democracy while fussing ineffectually over the affairs of others.

The debate over Wilson's peace plans saw Norris, Robert La Follette, Sr. (Republican of Wisconsin), and other like-minded Senators continue to appeal to the ideals of the early Jefferson. The pursuit of greatness abroad killed reform and narrowed liberty at home. Albert J. Beveridge, once an emphatic advocate of greatness through activism abroad, seconded these views. A commitment to reform, an Anglophobia sharpened by the war, and the discovery of the role of business and financial interests as an obstacle to reform as well as a hidden hand in foreign policy had brought about his dramatic change of heart. He now argued that Americans were better served by concentrating energy at home, where "the well-being of a great people and the development of a mighty continent" provided challenges enough. The American mission, as he had come to redefine it, was "to present to mankind the example of that happiness and well-being which comes from progressive, self-disciplined liberty." Rejecting Wilson's "mongrel internationalism," Beveridge called for the United States to get out of Europe and stay out, the better to play its role as exemplar to the world.[24]

The 1920 election, though hardly the "great and solemn referendum" on the League that Wilson wanted, did demonstrate that the electorate had come to share some of the critics' discontents. Wilson's drift into the Anglo-French camp had been a special rebuff to one in seven of his countrymen, some thirteen million either born in Germany or Ireland or the offspring of parents born there. War itself had imposed sacrifice and regimentation on all Americans, while demobilization brought recession and more hardship, especially for labor and farmers. Popular doubts about the wisdom of Wilsonian activism, already reflected in the League fight, deepened as Europe returned to its old degenerate ways. Already in 1920 widespread discontent was reflected in Republican Warren G. Harding's landslide victory (with 61 percent of the vote). As Europe came apart in the 1930s, more and more of the public came to accept the contentions of the neo-Jeffersonians that Wilson's European crusade had cost too much—$100 billion and over 100,000 lives— and had had no purpose beyond advancing the interests of a financial and industrial elite. A poll early in 1937 revealed that an aversion to a repeat of the last war had not abated. Seventy percent of Americans branded Wilson's entry into the European conflict a mistake.[25]

Energized by this growing popular sympathy, critics persisted in their battle against an assertive foreign policy. Initially their chief spokesman was William E. Borah, a Republican senator from Idaho who headed the Senate Foreign Relations Committee between 1925 and 1933. The United States was, in Borah's view, a moral exemplar whose interests were best served by preserving a detached relationship to the world. Involvement in foreign struggles and arms races would only encourage despotic and militaristic tendencies at home. The main task of American foreign policy was to promote trade and arms control and otherwise let others, even Latin Americans and Russians, go their own way without judging their brand of nationalism or style of revolution. Later, in the mid-1930s, Gerald Nye assumed a prominent leadership role. The activities of this North Dakota Republican as chairman of the Senate committee investigating the banking and munitions industry gave credence and widespread publicity to the suspicion that the "merchants of death" had indeed led an unsuspecting nation into war.

Jolted by warnings that Europe was drifting toward another conflict, Nye and other congressmen in a loose alliance with peace groups, progressives, agrarian radicals, and Midwestern ethnics stepped up the effort to inoculate the public against the arguments of an Anglophile elite and to limit presidential discretion. In their determination to prevent another Woodrow Wilson from involving the country in Old World quarrels, they successfully promoted mandatory neutrality legislation, and some even advocated a public referendum on any presidential call for war. By 1937 that latter measure had the support of seven out of ten Americans and a respectable portion of Congress. For a time at least the country was in no mood to embrace the glories of another world war.

The proponents of an assertive U.S. foreign policy had continued, however, to wield their influence. Foremost among them was a group of influential Republicans, including Elihu Root, William Howard Taft, Philander C. Knox, Henry Cabot Lodge, Charles Evans Hughes, Frank B. Kellogg, and Henry L. Stimson. They represented a type familiar in American policy-making circles over the previous hundred and fifty years. They were all white males, blessed with good families, good breeding, good schooling, and good contacts. They were self-consciously Anglo in their ethnic orientation, and without exception Protestant (usually Anglican or Presbyterian). The emergent twentieth-century variant on this type was usually a Northerner or Easterner and increasingly from Northeastern cities. His formal education in private schools and Ivy League colleges and law schools was supplemented by an informal education in foreign affairs promoted by trips to England and the Continent. He practiced corporate law until gaining public office, usually by appointment. His soundness on foreign-policy questions was ensured by the values inculcated in elite social circles, in exclusive schools, and in establishment clubs and organizations, of which the Council on Foreign Relations (established in 1921) was to be the most important.[26]

This group of prominent Republicans constituted the second set of Wilson's critics in the League fight. But their quarrel with the president was, at least in ideological terms, something of a family feud over how best to discharge the obligations of greatness. Far from espousing isolationism, they agreed in broad terms with Wilson that the United States had achieved an eminence in world affairs and with it a duty to promote a better ordered, more just, freer world system. Where they differed with Wilson was over the specifics of his policy. They could not accept the vague and unconstitutional obligations imposed by Article 10 of the League Covenant, which required all member states to join in resisting any acts of aggression. At the same time, they had no problem with making new international commitments. Indeed, Lodge, Root, and Knox promoted a defensive alliance with France, "our barrier and outpost" against a resurgent Germany.[27]

Lodge, as chairman of the Senate Foreign Relations Committee and elder statesman, spoke for this opposition in 1919. He could not accept a League that would infringe on American sovereignty and congressional authority and might wish to meddle where Americans would not want to go. But he also went out of his way to affirm the national commitment to the pursuit of greatness in terms strikingly close to Wilson's own views. Two recent wars had transformed American foreign policy. The war with Spain "marked the entrance of the United States into world affairs to a degree which had never obtained before. It was both an inevitable and irrevocable step. . . . " By entering into the European conflict Americans demonstrated their understanding of their new "world responsibilities." Now, in the wake of the war, Americans had to decide for themselves in what way they were to be "of the greatest service to the world's peace and to the welfare of mankind."[28]

Having defeated the scheme of involvement Wilson preferred, these Republicans proceeded to press their own. Through the 1920 election they urged Harding to make a clear commitment to Europe and establish some connection with the League and its auxiliary, the World Court. These efforts met with little success. However, with Harding's victory and their party back in power, they were to have a second chance between 1921 and 1933. Hughes, Kellogg, and Stimson, who followed each other as secretary of state in those years, proved formidable forces in administrations where the president lacked either interest or experience in foreign policy. All three continued to argue for some formal tie to the new international organizations and kept close diplomatic contact with their counterparts across the Atlantic. Though they eschewed the grandiose language and goals of Wilson, they confidently turned their attention to a wide range of problems relating to arms control, the reduction of international tensions, economic recovery, and political stability. Reinforced by unprecedented industrial and financial power, American influence in Europe rose to heights unknown before the Great War.

Interwar policymakers—Republicans as well as their Democratic successors—drew from the familiar intellectual baggage for their views not only on national greatness but also on revolution. Social revolution was anathema, as it had always been to men of their class. "No summer thunderstorm clearing the air," concluded Herbert Hoover of the Russian Revolution, it was rather "a tornado leaving in its path the destroyed homes of millions with their dead women and children." Adolf A. Berle, Jr., preoccupied with developments in Latin America in the 1930s, declared with succinct finality, "I don't like revolutions on principle."[29]

The Republicans continued Wilson's policy of denying the legitimacy of the Soviet regime in hopes that isolation might hasten the fall of that unnatural form of government or at least impede the export of its hateful propaganda and plots. Calvin Coolidge's flat announcement that he would not deal with the Soviets until they showed a willingness to "take up the burdens of civilization with the rest of us" reflected the official view that prevailed for sixteen years after the Bolshevik Revolution.[30]

Though Franklin Roosevelt at last in 1933 extended diplomatic recognition to a country he regarded as important as a market for American goods and as a counterbalance to Japan, his decision did not expunge older, keenly felt anxieties within the foreign-policy establishment. Not only had the Soviet Union survived, but bolshevism seemed to spread to "backward" regions, stirring up dangerous revolutionary ferment. Bolshevism lay behind the attack on foreigners in China, a view Kellogg duly accepted from his minister in that country. Forces dedicated to "Soviet subversion" also seemed to stalk the Americas through the twenties and thirties, especially in Cuba and Mexico, stirring up political unrest and anti-Yankee sentiment and threatening the United States with "a communist seizure of power" right in its backyard.[31]

Wherever Bolshevik agitators exploited the ignorance and passivity of less developed peoples, the response favored by Americans was to look for a strong man. Kellogg, worried by leftist activities in Italy and China, welcomed the rise of Mussolini and Chiang Kai-shek to power. To put a stop to supposed communist infiltration in Nicaragua, he dispatched Stimson on a mission that paved the way for the dominance of the Somoza family and four decades of political stability if not popular education and social justice. The pattern continued in the 1930s. In Cuba State Department representatives aborted one left-leaning revolution in 1933 and guided Batista toward the position of power he would hold until the late 1950s. Fears of Comintern subversion in Spain and Greece made U.S. policymakers sympathetic to military strongmen there, Franco in Madrid and Metaxas in Athens.

Older attitudes toward race also persisted little changed into the interwar era. They flourished at home in the nativism of the 1920s, itself an encore to the hyperpatriotism and attacks on hyphenates that had marred the war years. With the foreign-born and their children accounting for an alarmingly high proportion of the population (over a fifth), defenders of the old stock and ancestral virtues stirred into action. Congress passed by overwhelming margins laws to keep out undesirable immigrants—Japanese, Filipinos, and southern and eastern Europeans. In the South, Midwest, Southwest, and Far West as many as five million Americans joined the Ku Klux Klan, drawn by its doctrine of white supremacy and its attacks on Catholics, Jews, and other outsiders. The racial hatreds of the time turned most ferociously against blacks, for whom lynchings were but the most brutal of a variety of reminders of their assigned place in the hierarchy of color.

It should thus come as no surprise that the dominant American view of the world still followed that same hierarchy. Anglo-Saxons continued to stand at the top, with western Europeans close behind and those other peoples of Europe recently subject to exclusion lower down. The traits assigned Latinos and Asians, next in the rankings, were surprisingly unchanged. Motion pictures, from the first an important source of the American image of other peoples, merely elaborated on these traits and deepened them by lending a verisimilitude that overtly political caricatures in cartoons lacked. Latins on the silver screen were unpredictable, excitable, and passionate. True to old distinctions between the genders, the males appeared as repulsive "greasers," the women as sultry temptresses irresistible to Anglo lovers. Screen Asians in the 1920s were by and large brutal figures with a pronounced taste for crime, vice (most often opium smoking), and white women. The next decade produced a differentiation that would persist through the Pacific War. By the late 1930s the Japanese had come to personify the degenerate and savage side of the oriental character, while the Chinese had emerged as a foil, the result of a trend toward more positive treatment that began with the movie version of *The Good Earth* in 1937 and continued in the equally popular Charlie Chan series.[32]

These racial attitudes bore striking fruit in the feelings of condescension and contempt that policymakers occasionally revealed. Franklin D. Roosevelt, advocate of the Good Neighbor policy toward Latin America, unwittingly revealed his feelings of superiority when he offered a backhanded compliment to what he described as "these South American things." He observed, "They think they are just as good as we are," and then broadmindedly conceded that "many of them are." In Cuba in 1933 he demonstrated the strength of his paternalism when he acted on what he conceived to be "our duty" to prevent "starvation or chaos among the Cuban people." China, consistent with popular notions, was viewed from Washington and even by its Asian experts as plastic, passive, and in need of American help. Japan was seen as schizoid—"the Prussia of the East," in Lodge's phrase, as well as the best oriental student the Anglo-Saxons had. One side of this split Japanese personality was thought to reflect an indigenous warrior tradition. Treacherous and armed with modern weapons, militaristic leaders controlled their own "emotional population" and pursued a foreign policy of terror and conquest. The other side of the Japanese character was represented by forward-looking, Western-oriented civilians eager to promote international cooperation.[33]

Japan's occupation of Manchuria in 1931 and the invasion of China proper six years later bothered the defenders of Anglo-Saxonism in the East. Stimson and later Roosevelt and his secretary of state Cordell Hull worried that the militarists were in the ascendance. But American leaders also believed that the civilians still had a chance to regain control and reverse a policy of aggression if encouraged by an admonitory and if necessary hard-line U.S.

Figure 29. *Attending to His Correspondence*

No less than films, cartoons from the teens through the thirties reveal the familiar racial repertoire. Latinos were still depicted as dark-skinned truant children (fig. 29) or alternatively as light-complected, comely senoritas (fig. 30). Uncle Sam knew how to handle one as well as the other.

Figure 30. *My, How You Have Grown!*

Figure 31.

Asians also assumed stock form. By the 1930s the Chinese had, as shown in figs. 31–32, evolved into pitiful, inert figures (pictured here as the person under the militarist's heel and as the ponderous dinosaur), while the Japanese assumed the guise of crazed, cruel fanatics.[34]

Figure 32. *The Sleeping Giant Begins to Feel It*

stance. Stimson, confident that his service in the Philippines had given him an insight into "the Oriental mind," was determined to defend the East Asian international order and a U.S. China policy characterized by a "real nobility." Both were threatened by the "virtually mad dogs" that had taken control in Japan. Staging public displays of disapproval, he also fussed and blustered at Japanese envoys in private. Hull, for his part, had by the late 1930s decided that the Japanese were barbarians at the gate intent on joining Hitler in driving the world back into the Dark Ages. Roosevelt bluntly told Japanese diplomats that their policy violated "the fundamental principles of peace and order." With his associates he was even blunter. The Japanese were indeed "the Prussians of the East"; they were "openly and unashamedly one of the predatory nations fundamentally at odds with American ideals; and they were "drunk with their dream of dominion." For Roosevelt it was clear on which side Japan stood in the sharpening global struggle "between human slavery and human freedom—between pagan brutality and the Christian ideal."[35]

The Roosevelt administration increased the pressure on Tokyo, moved in part by the conviction that these Orientals, proverbially respectful of force, would give way. Economic sanctions, a naval buildup, aid to China, and deployment of the Pacific fleet in a more offensive position, however, produced not the desired retreat or even a slowing of the Japanese advance but the unexpected blow at Pearl Harbor. For Americans this "sneak attack" was an extraordinary outrage (though entirely consistent with assumptions about the wily oriental character). A supposedly inferior people had directly and for the moment successfully challenged a superior people carrying out their self-assigned role as arbiters of civilized behavior.

The American response to the contemporaneous crisis in Europe was also influenced by racial notions. Americans displayed increasing sympathy for their embattled British cousins. By late 1941 more than two-thirds of Americans supported any steps short of war to save Britain.[36] During the same period antisemitism left Americans indifferent to the Holocaust then beginning to unfold. Congress, organized labor, and four-fifths of the public surveyed in 1938 opposed admitting Jewish refugees. Entry into the war did nothing to soften this opposition. Restrictive immigration regulations, interpreted by a prejudiced foreign service, held the flow of European Jewry to a trickle. Legal and administrative obstacles, circumvented by the Roosevelt administration with remarkable ease when the British called for help, suddenly became insurmountable when it came to saving lesser folk.[37]

Against this backdrop of mounting world crisis, the activist conception of national greatness at last recovered its hold on foreign policy. Shaken by the excesses of Wilson's crusade and rescued by postwar Republicans, that sweeping notion was to gain a powerful new champion in the person of Franklin D. Roosevelt. Much in Roosevelt's outlook resembled Wilson's. Democracies were a force for peace in the world because they acted on the peace-loving instincts of the common man. Serious difficulties among nations were to be traced to militaristic and despotic regimes that indulged a minority's taste for aggression and conquest at the expense and in defiance of the enlightened popular will. Democracies had to unite against such threats and not allow aggression to pass unchecked. In the struggle for peace and freedom the United States should stand at the forefront. But FDR was no carbon copy of Wilson. He displayed an unabashed and undisguised love of power and political maneuver. Moreover, he lacked the deadly earnestness and dogged deliberativeness of his predecessor. As a policymaker, FDR could be whimsical, casual, and even maddeningly vague and inconsistent.

Roosevelt had not embarked on his presidency with an assertive foreign policy in mind. On the contrary, he sought at first to hold foreign policy problems in Asia and Europe at bay. The depression impelled him to concentrate on domestic relief and economic recovery. At the same time the remembered miseries of war restrained him.

> I have seen blood running from the wounded. I have seen men coughing out their gassed lungs. I have seen the dead in the mud. I have seen cities destroyed. I have seen two hundred limping, exhausted men come out of line—the survivors of a regiment of one thousand that went forward forty-eight hours before. I have seen children starving. I have seen the agony of mothers and wives. I hate war.

Consistent with this impassioned denunciation of August 1936, Roosevelt proclaimed that same year that Americans, though still the custodians of liberty, would have to limit their activity to their own hemisphere.

> Democracy is still the hope of the world. If we in our generation can continue its successful application in the Americas, it will spread and supersede other methods by which men are governed. . . . [38]

Between 1937 and 1941 Roosevelt began to set caution aside. His older views and deeper predilections came to the surface as he campaigned for aid to Britain against Germany and refused to bow to Japanese pretensions to dominance in East Asia. International lawlessness, he declared, was intolerable, whether directed against the small and vulnerable states of eastern and central Europe, the established democracies of the West, European colonies in Southeast Asia, or an ancient and defenseless China. American involvement in this second major international crisis of the twentieth century might prove costly, as Roosevelt was quick to concede, but it also offered a second chance to accomplish what Wilson had failed to do—effect a thorough reform of a flawed international system. The Atlantic Charter, proclaimed by Roosevelt and Winston Churchill in August 1941, stated Anglo-American objectives in familiar terms: a just peace, the right of self-determination for all nations, free trade, and a new league that would serve as a safeguard against yet another outbreak of aggression.

Roosevelt's journey to the Wilsonian station had not been an easy one. It involved the loss and then the recovery of a faith that was virtually part of his heritage. An independently wealthy scion of an old New York family, he had attended Groton and Harvard, traveled widely, and traded on his extensive connections among the well placed to gain public office. Like his cousin Theodore, whom he greatly admired, FDR was a supremely self-confident politician, with a keen sense of noblesse oblige. He was also a champion of the Monroe Doctrine as well as a disciple of Mahan and an ardent navalist, who for a time occupied the post of assistant secretary of the navy, once held by TR. He had expressed strongly interventionist views while serving Wilson in that capacity during the First World War. Later, as the Democratic vice-presidential nominee in 1920, FDR had taken up Wilson's faltering struggle for the League. His defeat demonstrated to a man with presidential aspirations that overseas adventures were out of favor. That discovery combined with a growing personal realization of the high costs of the European war and of the flaws in the peace took its toll on his activist views.

The mounting tide of German, Italian, and Japanese aggression in the 1930s carried Roosevelt back to foreign-policy orthodoxy. His October 1937 speech calling for a quarantine against an "epidemic of world lawlessness" set him on a road that led to the Atlantic Charter of 1941. His route can be traced in his ever-bolder public denunciations of the barbaric forces bent on world conquest and his ever more explicit calls for resistance in the name of civilization. Roosevelt's policies reflected his rhetoric. By the fall of 1941 the United States had become, in Roosevelt's phrase, the "arsenal of democracy," feeding the British war machine, conducting an undeclared naval war against Germany, and enforcing a potentially crippling oil embargo against Japan.[39]

Having regained his Wilsonian faith, Roosevelt had then to face a second struggle, this one against considerable "isolationist" opposition. His chief antagonist was an organization called America First and its most popular speaker, the famed aviator and reluctant activist Charles A. Lindbergh. Mobilizing in the fall of 1940 against the drift to war, America First drew supporters primarily from the upper Midwest and from non-Anglo ethnics nationwide. Those were also Lindbergh's roots. His Swedish-born father, a Minnesota agrarian radical, had joined Norris and La Follette in opposition to intervention in World War I. Like that earlier generation, the younger Lindbergh opposed Americans marching across the blood-stained fields of Europe and championed the values of a simple, agrarian America at odds with the big city and Eastern cosmopolites, the very types most intensely committed to intervention.

While Lindbergh's hostility to a crusading foreign policy was fundamentally inspired by the dissenting Jeffersonian tradition, it was strongly reinforced by a preoccupation with race and revolution drawn, ironically enough, from the dominant foreign-policy ideology itself. Successive tours of Europe between 1936 and 1938 had left him dismayed by that continent's self-destructive instincts and its failure to recognize the threat posed by "the teeming millions of Asia." That threat took palpable form in Soviet Russia, whose "record of cruelty, bloodshed, and barbarism" stood, Lindbergh argued, "without parallel in modern history." Though saddled with an unworkable communist system, the Russians with their semi-Asiatic culture could overrun a divided Europe and destroy "that most priceless possession, our inheritance of European blood." Lindbergh blamed the British for dividing and distracting Europe. They were unable to come to terms with their own imperial decline or to cooperate with the Germans, who stood as a "buffer to Asia" and a guarantor against Europe's committing "racial suicide."[40]

If the United States had a duty to perform in the face of this crisis, it was to cooperate with the "extremely intelligent and able people" of Germany in preparing against the Bolshevik onslaught and in rectifying the injustices of the postwar settlement. Encouraging Britain in its opposition to Germany was a profoundly mistaken policy. "It is time to turn from our quarrels and to build our White ramparts again. . . . " If, however, Europe proved bent on self-destruction, then the United States had no choice but to stand aloof. While barbarian invasion carried Europe back to the Dark Ages, the United States would have to serve as the repository of Western culture and the defender of the hemisphere. Thanks to the rise of air power, hemispheric defense would now be easier than ever before. The Atlantic would become a moat protecting the vestiges of Western civilization.[41]

Beginning in September 1939 Lindbergh went public with his argument that the United States had to assume the role of asylum and model in a world torn by war and oppressed by despotism. Americans had the primary task of cultivating their own liberty. It would thrive on reform, not involvement in foreign wars, as the American experience in World War I had proven.

Lindbergh asked his generation to address the social, racial, and industrial problems before them in order to bequeath to the next generation "a strong nation, a lack of debt, a solid American character free from the entanglements of the Old World." A country whose people and institutions were strong did not need to fear invasion. Why should the public follow the foolish, divisive policy of the Roosevelt administration and its pro-interventionist allies who were "injecting the wars and hatreds of Europe into our midst?" He warned that those who fanned popular passions—the British desperately scrambling to regain their lost supremacy, American Anglophiles, and a Jewish-dominated media—did so for narrow, self-interested reasons.[42]

Lindbergh charged that Roosevelt promoted intervention through resort to "subterfuge and propaganda," practices far more dangerous to American democracy than any foreign threat. The president's policy, ostensibly intended to save democracy, might actually destroy it. War would not only take the lives of millions of Americans; it would also require regimentation at home subversive of economic and political liberty, and it would pile up debt burdensome to future generations. "We seem to have no understanding of our own limitations," Lindbergh sadly reflected in August 1940. "Will our vanity, our blindness, and our airy idealism throw us, too, into the conflict heedless of the future?"[43]

In responding to Lindbergh and like-minded critics, Roosevelt did indeed enjoy the backing of influential and outspoken Americans who shared his view that the mounting world crisis was a summons to return to a policy of active greatness. The Committee to Defend America by Aiding the Allies, founded in May 1940 with encouragement from Roosevelt himself, had a nationwide membership in which Eastern lawyers and college professors figured prominently. The other major interventionist organization, the Century Group, was a tightly knit, behind-the-scenes operation launched in June 1940. Its core of support also came from an American East Coast elite, long the breeding ground for the dominant policy figures and ideas. The Century Group wanted an immediate declaration of war, but satisfied itself with pushing Roosevelt in the direction of gradually increasing support for Britain.

These interventionist groups advocated a policy that was deeply rooted in an ideological view of the world. To be sure, they stressed the security dimensions of the crisis. The Atlantic, they contended, was no longer a buffer but a highway, so that American security depended on preserving the British fleet and maintaining the balance of power in Europe. Since Germany had destroyed that balance, the United States had no choice but to work with Britain to restore it. But older and certainly no less powerful than this realpolitik line of reasoning were their sentimental ties to Britain, their vision of building a better world where international law was respected and democracy flourished, and their faith that the United States assisted by Britain could do the job. They would realize Wilson's dream of a community of free states living at peace in an enlightened international order.

Firm in their beliefs and determined to bend policy to their will, the interventionists had little tolerance for the opposition. The Roosevelt administration reacted to the rise of America First in 1940 with deep concern. To blunt its influence and discredit its leaders, the interventionists launched a smear campaign that made opposition tantamount to treason. Rabid Anglophobes, Nazi sympathizers, Communists, cowards, and antisemites were creating divisions at home at the very time the nation needed to rally together. Roosevelt's secretary of the interior, Harold L. Ickes, openly labeled Lindbergh the "No. 1 Nazi fellow traveler" in the United States. Roosevelt was "absolutely convinced that Lindbergh is a Nazi." The president wanted his critics investigated, and by December 1940 was publicly branding them as subversives representing "evil forces."[44]

By the fall of 1941 Roosevelt and his sympathizers had thrust aside the opposition. With his policy of aid to Britain and China beyond challenge, he stood on the precipice of war. Whether he wanted to take that final step is still not clear. The hesitations that the public and perhaps even Roosevelt himself felt were at last resolved at Pearl Harbor in December 1941. With that attack went the last obstacle to a renewal of the Wilsonian crusade. He told a shocked nation that "a decade of international immorality" had come to a climax. It was time the United States dedicated itself to rooting out absolutely and forever "the sources of international brutality."[45]

★ ★ ★

World War II led to an unprecedented, decade-long mobilization and deployment of national power. No sooner had American leaders been assured of victory over the Axis than they set to work on stabilizing and reforming the postwar political and economic order, as well as on countering what they soon concluded was a serious Soviet threat to that order. By the end of 1950 the pattern of the Cold War was set as arms costs mushroomed, aid programs and alliances multiplied, American troops fought their first limited war in Korea, and Washington made the initial commitments that would lead to the second, in Indochina.

While the assertive new policy of the 1940s did indeed transform the global posture of the United States, it left the inherited foreign-policy ideology essentially unchanged. For policymakers—still disproportionately from elite, Eastern, urban, Protestant backgrounds—that ideology was a birthright, just as public service remained an obligation of their class. This elite group displayed some of the characteristics of a close family. They congregated mainly in New York, Boston, and Washington. Root and Stimson were among their most revered ancestors, while W. Averell Harriman, Dean Acheson, and the brothers Rockefeller, Dulles, and Bundy claimed pride of place among the new generation. They had struggled together under the banner of Roosevelt the interventionist and world reformer; some had even served in the original Wilsonian crusade. From their strongholds in the major foundations and universities and in the foreign-affairs bureaucracy, this elite group recruited gifted outsiders, such as the Kennedy and Rostow brothers and Dean Rusk, and fought the "isolationist" heresy that still lingered among an ignorant public. They catechized those, such as Harry S. Truman and Lyndon B. Johnson, whom chance and the quirks of the electoral process had raised to positions of political eminence.

For this generation of policymakers the grip of the old ideology was strengthened by two new formulations. One emphasized historical lessons that validated the old ideological vision. Those lessons, which were to guide policymakers in the 1940s and after, flowed from a historical mythology known as the great-cycle theory. Its proponents looked back with nostalgia to the high promise of the First World War, when the United States had moved toward a mature, assertive foreign policy in keeping with national ideals and growing national power. Sadly, with a better ordered world almost within grasp, Americans had betrayed the promise. Wilson's maladroit postwar performance (especially his costly failure to build a political consensus) was partly to blame. So too were obstructive, opportunistic, and narrow-minded public figures. And so too was the American public, which proved itself ill informed, unsteady, and easily swayed by the likes of Lodge, Borah, and later Lindbergh. Thus the country had slid from the heights of wartime responsibility into the slough of a naive, timid, and ultimately costly isolationism.

The great-cycle theory, coming into vogue just as American policy passed through another wartime peak, was intended as a cautionary tale pointing to the dangers of yet another lapse. A retreat to isolationism after World War II would be certain to precipitate yet another global conflict. The ghosts of Hitler lying in wait at Munich and Tojo plotting the attack on Pearl Harbor haunted the memory of cold warriors and were regularly conjured up to emphasize the dangers of unpreparedness and appeasement. Concessions to the ambitions of such aggressors would only inflame them to commit greater outrages. Franklin Roosevelt, himself at first excessively timid in the face of growing world crisis, had at last discovered this truth—and set Americans back on the path Wilson had first blazed. It was now up to FDR's successors to hold the nation on course.

Imbedded in this legend of a great cycle was a proposition handed down directly from Wilson and derived from the ideological formulations that predated him. The possibilities for a peaceful and free international order depended on the internal constitutions of the states making up the world community. On the one hand, democracies such as the United States were inherently peace-loving, even to a fault. The underlying assumption here was (in Harry Truman's words) that "the stronger the voice of a people in the formulation of national policies, the less the danger of aggression." On the other hand, nondemocratic states, whether communist, fascist, or nazi, could be counted on to pursue a course of hostility and aggrandizement abroad, just as they would follow a repressive policy at home. "Despotism, whatever its form, has a remorseless compulsion to aggression," declared Truman's influential secretary of defense, James Forrestal, in 1948. To create a peaceful and secure world it was essential to create a community of states committed to self-determination and liberty. Internal reform was the only sure and lasting solution to the threat repressive states would always pose to their neighbors.[46]

The other fresh formulation undergirding the old ideology was geopolitics. To the first generation of foreign-affairs experts in the burgeoning government bureaucracy and in academic social science as well as to prominent latter-day Wilsonians it gave a tough-minded, pseudoscientific vocabulary to supplement the high-sounding, sentimental, and moral rhetoric associated with the old ideology. Geopolitics, which had already figured prominently in interventionist arguments, began with the premise that new technology had so narrowed the gap between nations that developments half a world away could, as never before, vitally affect national security. Dean Rusk stated the fundamental fact of geopolitical life: "If you don't pay attention to the periphery, the periphery changes. And the first thing you know the periphery is the center." Rusk also drew the practical implication of geopolitics: "What happens in one place cannot help but affect what happens in another." Or, in the words of Lyndon Johnson, "We know now that surrender anywhere threatens defeat everywhere." The geopolitical world was like a chessboard. Each major power would seek to control the greatest expanse of space. The more territory it controlled, the greater its population and natural resources, and the greater in turn would be its power and capacity to acquire yet more territory and further augment its power in a cycle that would leave a rival weakened and isolated. In this world of pure power politics, conquest of the entire globe seemed at last a real possibility.[47]

These geopoliticians saw the recent past in terms that complemented the great-cycle theory. The era of isolation and free security, which they contended the United States had once enjoyed, was long gone. The ever more sophisticated tools of warfare had reduced the Atlantic and Pacific to mere ponds and made the Americas vulnerable to attack. Theodore Roosevelt and Alfred Thayer Mahan, advocates of an offensive navy, became for geopoliticians the American prophets of this new strategic order. Wilson was depicted as a reluctant disciple who belatedly grasped the danger that the Kaiser posed to the Atlantic community and developed the collective security implications of geopolitical doctrine. Franklin Roosevelt too had acted on the insights of the prophets as he sought to secure the Atlantic and Pacific, frustrate the Axis assault on the Eurasian land mass from its flanks, and revive the notion of collective security. The two world wars, however, would, seem but skirmishes compared to the struggle ahead. The Soviet Union, controlling the bulk of Eurasia and already probing its perimeters, constituted a strategic threat of an altogether new magnitude. Only by acting on the basis of ''geopolitical realities'' could the United States avoid encirclement and preserve hopes for a free world.

The old ideology, thus doubly reinforced, shaped Cold War policy and inspired the most important expression of that policy, the doctrine of containment. Ideology defined for the advocates of containment the issue at stake: survival of freedom around the world. That ideology also defined the chief threat to freedom: Soviet communism—which the United States had an incontestable obligation to combat. The ideological strains in containment are evident in the thinking of the leading cold warriors, most strikingly George F. Kennan, father of the doctrine. His sharply critical views of Soviet foreign policy and his deeply felt aversion to the repressive nature of the Soviet regime had been nurtured by his training as an expert in those hotbeds of antibolshevism, Berlin and the Baltic port of Riga, during the late 1920s and early 1930s, and they had come to full blossom in the early Cold War years.

Kennan sprang to prominence in February 1946 when he telegraphed from the Moscow embassy a lengthy analysis of Soviet behavior. It won him a ticket home and a prominent place as Washington's resident Soviet specialist. Like others of his writings, this piece was filled with sweeping and seemingly authoritative generalizations, giving voice and intellectual depth to the anticommunism already gripping Washington. Kennan began by drawing on the distinction, commonplace in American analyses of foreign lands, between benighted or evil rulers and their misled or innocent subjects with a presumed instinct for freedom and a special feeling for the United States. Soviet leaders, ruthless and immoral, did not represent the ''natural outlook of the Russian people," he contended, just as Wilson had earlier. Those leaders had to be understood in terms of a revolutionary ideology with its own "neurotic view of world affairs" that had combined with a Slavic heritage of "oriental secretiveness and conspiracy." Like their czarist predecessors, the men in the Kremlin were acutely sensitive to the economic and political superiority of the West, driven by that "traditional and instinctive Russian sense of insecurity," and equipped to understand only the "logic of force" in inter-state relations. The Soviet Union constituted a global danger that appeals to reason and attempts at compromise would not charm away. A direct military challenge to the West was unlikely. But Moscow could be counted on to wage a quiet and indirect war, making the most of the international Communist network boasting "experience and skill in underground methods [that] are presumably without parallel in history." Wherever that network located "diseased tissue," it would feed like a "malignant parasite."[48]

Kennan's fame spread from the foreign-affairs bureaucracy to the informed public in July 1947 when he published an authorized exposition of containment in, predictably enough, *Foreign Affairs*, the journal of the Council on Foreign Relations. Hidden only briefly by the pseudonym "X," Kennan described the aim of the new foreign-policy dispensation in crisp, stylish geopolitical terms: "the adroit and vigilant application of counter-force at a series of constantly shifting geographical and political points, corresponding to the shifts and manoeuvres of Soviet policy."[49]

This famous essay was also suffused with the moral formulations long familiar to the audience of influentials that Kennan wished to reach. "The Soviet pressure against the free institutions of the western world" posed, in Kennan's view, "a test of the over-all worth of the United States as a nation among nations." For confronting them with this test his countrymen owed "a certain gratitude to . . . Providence." By successfully meeting the "implacable challenge" before them, Americans would prove that they could indeed rise to "the responsibilities of moral and political leadership that history plainly intended them to bear." They would in turn find their reward in "either the break-up or the gradual mellowing of Soviet power." It was clear to Kennan that the Soviet system, like any that denied the universal aspiration for freedom, already "bears within it the seeds of its own decay." "The sprouting of these seeds is well advanced," Kennan contended, echoing the hopeful view anti-Bolsheviks had expressed since 1917. Once the fall came, the Soviet Union would be transformed "overnight from one of the strongest to one of the weakest and most pitiable of national societies."[50]

The ideological cast characteristic of Kennan's thinking had also been an increasingly pronounced feature in Washington since 1945. Roosevelt's death in early April had unleashed anti-Soviet currents previously held in check by the former president's conciliatory spheres-of-influence approach to the Russians. FDR had increasingly operated on two levels during the war—publicly still a Wilsonian but privately recognizing the limits of American power and the regional interests of the Soviets, British, and even to an extent the Chinese. An education in international affairs had taught this able student that the United States could neither make democrats of everyone nor act as policeman everywhere. We cannot know how Roosevelt would have resolved the tension between his public rhetoric and his private calculations. But it is clear that his successor soon embraced a Wilsonian policy free of the reservations FDR had come to entertain.

A pair of early meetings between President Truman and his advisers made his preferences dramatically evident. Ambassador Harriman, who had rushed to Washington from Moscow at the news of Roosevelt's death, depicted the Red Army's advance into Germany as a "barbarian invasion of Europe." Harriman joined James Forrestal (then secretary of the navy), Secretary of State Edward R. Stettinius, and Truman's chief of staff Admiral William Leahy in arguing that Poland already proved the Soviets were hostile to the principle of self-determination and the ideal of international cooperation. During these discussions Truman repeatedly expressed his determination to stand up to the Soviets and "make no concessions from American principles or traditions for the fact of winning their favor." The former Roosevelt intimates tried without success to restrain him. Secretary of War Stimson and General George Marshall, the army chief of staff, warned that a showdown would not cause the Soviet Union to abandon its "vital" interests in Eastern Europe, while it might cost the United States the Soviet military assistance deemed essential in prosecuting the final year of the war in the Pacific. Already a minority among Truman's advisers, this old guard was soon to retire (or in several notable cases be driven) from Washington.[51]

Even so Truman could not at once translate his feelings into a consistent policy. He remained constrained as well as distracted by the need to shape a European settlement and by pressure for demobilization and lower taxes. Nevertheless, the sense of alarm in the Truman administration became ever more pronounced as policymakers took up indictments against the Soviet Union that would stand for decades to come. For some Moscow was primarily the source of radical revolutionary doctrine. The men in the Kremlin were, as Bolsheviks had always been, secretive and sinister figures well versed in terror, propaganda, and subversion. They were served by leftist parties abroad made up—so concluded George Marshall in early 1947 just after returning to Washington to serve as secretary of state—of "disloyal, contaminated, or politically immature elements.'' Each Communist, Truman's attorney general J. Howard McGrath warned in 1949 and 1950 in terms redolent of an earlier red scare, ''carries in himself the germs of death for society.''[52]

Others saw Russia as a monstrous tyranny whose command of a massive military machine menaced Western civilization. Stalin was a new Hitler, and the Red Army's advance into Eastern Europe seemed a replay of Germany's march into the Rhineland. The Soviets with their advantageous geopolitical position were beyond doubt bent on world domination, just as Germany in league with Japan had been. With its potent combination of ''ideological zeal and fighting power,'' the Soviet Union seemed a threat to Western Europe comparable, Dean Acheson later recalled, to ''that which Islam had posed centuries before.''[53]

Of the various permutations of these views, Truman's was the most important, for it influenced his choice of advisers and the policies he embraced. A vulnerable, easily angered provincial, Truman assumed his duties reluctantly and with a keen sense of his own inadequacies. With virtually no foreign-affairs experience, he took refuge in a homespun Wilsonianism and the conventional lessons of the past. Wilson's war had in his opinion saved Europe from barbarism, and he was proud of his small contribution as an artillery officer on the western front. He recalled how Wilson's summons to service had left him ''stirred in heart and soul.'' He regretted that Americans had ''turned the clock back'' after the war. A supporter of Franklin Roosevelt's interventionist policy, Truman had as early as 1939 denounced Germany and Italy as well as Russia as adherents of ''a code little short of caveman savagery.'' At the same time he expressed hostility toward Lindbergh and concern that isolationist fevers might again, as in Wilson's day, keep the country from accepting its ''responsibility as a world power.'' Once the United States was in the war he lent his support in the Senate for a new league of nations where the democratic states could cooperate in bringing an end to a bankrupt system of power politics.[54]

Truman took a jaundiced view of the Soviet Union. In December 1941 he had characterized the Soviets as ''untrustworthy as Hitler and Al Capone.'' In a famous exhortation the previous June, just after Germany had invaded the Soviet Union, he had called for a policy of playing the two off against each other and ''that way let them kill as many as possible.'' The Bolshevik Revolution had, in his view, simply replaced one ruthless elite with another, leaving the peace-loving Russian people as oppressed as ever. The czars and noblemen were gone, but Russia remained a ''police government pure and simple'' and a ''hotbed of special privilege.'' For a time after he took over the reins of policy in 1945, Truman was hopeful that tough bargaining might lead to some agreement with Stalin. By early 1946, with Eastern Europe lost and the Soviets apparently threatening elsewhere, Truman had "tired of babying the Soviets." His old antipathies came increasingly to the fore, ruling out diplomacy and compromise. "Only one language do they understand—'How many divisions have you?' " He was now convinced there was "no difference" between the Soviet regime and Hitler's. Each "represents a totalitarian state—a police government." By 1948 he had taken the comparison a step farther. The "Frankenstein dictatorship" in the Kremlin was "worse than any of the others," including (Truman explicitly noted) Hitler's Third Reich.[55]

During his years in the White House Truman made of the lives of great men and the history of great empires a mirror for himself and his generation. He was convinced that the Soviet challenge constituted a recrudescence of that imperial impulse that had always driven oriental despots. Stalin was the heir not only of Marx and Lenin but of Genghis Khan, Tamerlane, Ivan the Terrible, and Peter the Great. Once more the " 'Eastern hordes'," now represented by the Soviets, threatened the forces of peace, Christianity, honor, and morality in the world. The United States, blessed with the "greatest government that was ever conceived by the mind of man," would have to lead the resistance. While the impending conflict, as Truman saw it, bore a resemblance to those great international rivalries that he had read about, it also carried consequences of unprecedented significance. "We are faced with the most terrible responsibility that any nation ever faced. From Darius I's Persia, Alexander's Greece, Hadrian's Rome, Victoria's Britain, no nation or group of nations has had our responsibilities." It was now the task of Americans, who had become great yet had renounced self-aggrandizement, "to save the world from totalitarianism."[56]

Truman's personal task as chief magistrate was, as he himself saw it, to attempt to live up to the lofty example set by those heroes in his republican pantheon: Aristides, Cincinnatus, Cato the Younger, and Washington. Like them, he led in a time of adversity. He too had to struggle against the corrupting forces that had ruined the Greek city-states and the Roman republic. The urgent task at hand was to "mobilize the people who believe in a moral world against the Bolshevik materialists." But American vision, he feared, was being "dimmed by greed, by selfishness, by a thirst for power." He heard disturbing "pacifist talk." Truman saw himself standing with his countrymen at one of those historical junctures where a successful assertion of national will and power would promote liberty abroad while revitalizing the spirit of freedom at home. The consequences of failure were unthinkable.[57]

Between March and June 1947, in response to a leftist insurgency in Greece that the British could no longer contain, the Truman administration finally made a concerted call to arms. The appeal, launched by Truman and seconded by Marshall and Acheson, was every bit as much informed by ideological concerns as Truman's private musings noted above. To his cabinet Truman declared gravely that he faced "a situation more serious than had ever confronted any President." Acheson stunned a gathering of congressional leaders with a warning no less grave that the Kremlin was on the verge of a geopolitical "breakthrough [that] might open three continents to Soviet penetration." As Greece went, so might go South Asia, North Africa, and Western Europe.[58]

When Truman at last asked Congress for aid to Greece as well as Turkey, he also asked Americans to accept the "great responsibilities" that the struggle against Communism imposed on them. Consistent with the geopolitics now in vogue among his national-security advisers, Truman invoked the old Wilsonian collective-security creed. Peace was indivisible, and aggression anywhere endangered the security of the United States. Truman also invoked the lessons of the past. The sacrifices imposed by World War II served as a reminder that peace was not to be had cheaply. But the major point of Truman's address, made explicitly, repeatedly, and emphatically, was that the United States had to enter the lists in behalf of freedom and against totalitarianism. Americans had an obligation to maintain an international environment hospitable to "free institutions, representative government, free elections, guarantees of individual liberty, freedom of speech and religion, and freedom from political oppression." Though available government resources might not be fully equal to the challenge Truman had taken up, it was important to him and his aides to keep in sight this noble and compelling national mission.[59]

The ideological emphasis evident in private musings and public statements was sustained in the major secret national-security papers approved by the president over the following three years. They were couched in the stark and sweeping terms usually reserved for crusades. As early as November 1948 Truman had, in accepting a Kennan-drafted statement, made the ultimate aim of his policy "to reduce the power and influence of the U.S.S.R." to the point where the Soviets would "no longer constitute a threat to the peace, national independence and stability of the world family of nations," as well as to encourage the national life of satellite countries. The last major policy statement prepared before the outbreak of the Korean War was the most emphatically ideological in that series. While it made a ritual bow to the lessons of the past and the strategic imperatives of geopolitics, it put its real faith in a creed that proclaimed "a basic conflict between the idea of freedom under a government of laws, and the idea of slavery under the grim oligarchy of the Kremlin.'' The struggle against the ''new fanatic faith'' of the Communists and their ambitions for world conquest would decide the fate ''not only of this Republic but of civilization itself.'' The authors of NSC 68 promised that a practical demonstration of ''the integrity and vitality of our system'' together with the power purchased by a tripling of defense spending would mean salvation. It would ''frustrate the Soviet design and hasten the decay of the Soviet system.''[60]

★ ★ ★

After five years of gestation a policy geared to greatness and counterrevolution had taken shape. In Europe it quickly proved a success. The Marshall Plan, the largest of the postwar assistance programs, rescued the Continent's war-ravaged economies, while American-backed Christian Democrats drove the large French and Italian Communist parties from power. The North Atlantic Treaty Organization functioned no less effectively as a shield against the Red Army. West Germany, with its valuable manpower and industry, was not subjected to ''pastoralization'' (as punitive wartime plans had intended) but integrated into the alliance. With American support, insurgency was stopped in Greece, and Turkey withstood Soviet pressure. These successes in turn nourished hopes for the ultimate liberation of Eastern Europe.

Elsewhere along the containment line stretching from the Middle East to Northeast Asia, American leaders encountered greater difficulties. Indeed, not only here but throughout the ''Third World'' (in other words, lands unfamiliar to Americans, even those making up the foreign-policy elite) they would find military and political problems ambiguous, complex, intractable, and in the final analysis ill suited to a straightforward policy of containment modeled on the European experience. Rural economies more sorely pinched by poverty than those in Europe, leaders still struggling to end colonial control and give form to their national aspirations, and peoples largely immune to the appeal of American political values left the lands of Asia, Latin America, and Africa in ferment. American cold warriors constantly worried about the disorder these continents were prone to. Unsettled conditions not only made for infirm allies and fickle dependents but, more troubling still, invited Communist subversion or invasion.

Realizing that the solution of these problems was the precondition for the defense of the Third World, Washington came to embrace a policy of development. Development was the younger sibling of containment. While containment focused on the immediate problems of holding the Soviets and their leftist allies at bay, development was intended to provide long-term immunity against the contagion of communism. Like containment, development policy drew inspiration from the long-established ideology. But while containment underlined the obligations of a great nation to defend liberty, development theory drew its inspiration from the old American vision of appropriate or legitimate processes of social change and an abiding sense of superiority over the dark-skinned peoples of the Third World. Social scientists and policymakers often described the goals of development in abstract, neutral catchwords. They spoke of the modernization of traditional societies, nation building, or the stimulation of self-sustaining economic growth in once stagnant economies. In practice, though, these impressive new formulations amounted to little more than a restatement of the old ethnocentric platitudes about uplift and regeneration formerly directed at the Philippines, China, and Mexico.

According to the gospel of development, peoples still laboring under a traditional way of life would acquire modern institutions and outlooks, the best guarantees of stable and free societies. Education would promote rationality in the place of superstition. A common sense of nationhood would emerge as a political system marked by broad participation displaced one flawed by popular passivity or narrow family, tribal, or ethnic loyalties. Sophisticated science and technology would push aside primitive agricultural and handicraft techniques and create new wealth and prosperity. A closed, fragmented, stagnant economy would burgeon under the influence of outside capital and markets. In this process American institutions would provide the models, and American experience would serve as the inspiration. Thanks to American wisdom and generosity and to the marvels of social engineering, the peoples of these new nations would accomplish in years what it had taken the advanced countries decades to achieve.

Development policy was in its infancy during the early stages of the Cold War, and funding was sharply limited by the priority given to European reconstruction. But the essential insight was already present. "The seeds of totalitarian regimes are nurtured by misery and want," Truman noted in his famous March 1947 speech. "They spread and grow in the evil soil of poverty and strife." He later described his aid program, known as Point Four, as "a plan to furnish 'know-how' from our experience in the fabulous development of our own resources."[61]

Development policy entered its golden age in the early 1960s under John F. Kennedy's patronage and the challenge of Soviet-backed wars of national liberation. Virtually all foreign aid was now devoted to this new battleground, and social scientists such as Walt W. Rostow, an MIT academic preoccupied with the supposedly universal stages of economic growth, enlisted in the struggle. They carried to Washington the expertise that would set off "the revolution of modernization" and win the battle for the hearts and minds of the Third World. Communists, "the scavengers of the modernization process," would of course attempt to exploit the strains inherent in "the transitional process." It was up to the United States to perfect the techniques of counterinsurgency and stand ready to apply them in behalf of people struggling against subversion to build "a democratic, open society."

Development theory can be seen as a response to the fourth wave of revolutions Americans had had to confront. Rolling across the face of Latin America, Africa, and Asia, this most recent wave of radicalism and unrest raised for American leaders the specter of Soviet meddling at the same time that it directly challenged American values. Terror, random violence, class warfare, violation of private property—in all these ways revolutions once more broke the venerable rules of appropriate political and social change and again sent American policymakers looking for bulwarks of order. This might mean striking collaborative bargains with dictators who could bring their careening countries under control and provide enlightened direction to people unready to manage their own affairs. Better to support a rightist strongman in a time of unrest than to allow a leftist takeover that would permanently foreclose the prospects for freedom. It might also mean working with colonial powers to win time and hold down the Communist element until the "natives" were ready for independence. Once the doors were closed to the heirs of the Bolshevik Revolution, these new nations could move with greater assurance and security toward the creation of that condition of "ordered liberty" that John Adams and all his heirs had extolled.

Condescending and paternalistic, development theory also carried forward the long-established American views on race. Changing domestic practices and international conditions had, however, made untenable a hierarchy cast in explicitly racial terms. From the 1940s Jim Crow laws had fallen under mounting attack, culminating in the civil-rights movement of the late 1950s and early 1960s. Over that same period a hot war against Nazi supermen and a cold war in the name of freedom and the liberation of oppressed peoples had made racial segregation at home and pejorative references to race in public a serious embarrassment. Moreover, scientists had by then turned their backs on grand racial theories, thereby further undermining the legitimacy of thinking in terms of race. Policymakers, whose impulse to see the world in terms of a hierarchy was ever more at odds with the need for political discretion, found their way out of their bind by recasting the old racial hierarchy into cultural terms supplied by development theorists. No longer did leaders dare broadcast their views on barbarous or backward people, race traits, or skin color. It was instead now the attributes of modernity and tradition that fixed a people's or nation's place on the hierarchy.

Not surprisingly, though, the resulting rankings were strikingly similar to the ones assigned two centuries earlier by race-conscious ancestors. Americans could remain secure in the superiority of their own kind. Anglo-Americans were still on top, followed by the various European peoples. Then came the "Third World." The term, which gained currency in the 1950s and 1960s, defined the battleground between the democratic First World and the Second World of the socialist bloc that had emerged after World War II. The Cold War concern with the Third World as a zone of conflict rested on a sturdy bedrock of American thinking on race. Though the socialist monolith fell apart and the struggle for the political soul of the Third World sputtered on inconclusively, the idea of the Third World as a single entity survived, sustained by the American conviction of its backwardness and the repressed American consciousness of the color of its peoples. Black Africa occupied the lowest rung, just as black ghettos represented the lower reaches of American society. Higher up stood Asians and Latins, still exotic and still difficult to classify with exactitude because of the unstable mixture of attractive and repulsive characteristics assigned to them. An American society where skin color still powerfully defined an individual's place and prospects was unable to transcend the policy implications of long-nurtured assumptions about racial differences. The change in vocabulary had not altered the hierarchy; it had simply made more plausible the denial of any links to an unfashionably racist world view.

The private comments of American leaders from the 1940s to the 1960s suggest that the old stereotypes and condescension did indeed cling to the new hierarchy of development. For example, Franklin Roosevelt believed that "there are many minor children among the peoples of the world who need trustees," foremost among them "the brown people of the East." While he wished to liberate Japanese-held Korea, French Indochina, British India and Malaya, and the Dutch East Indies from colonial chains, he insisted that they would still need several decades of guidance before they would be ready to walk on their own. For Sumner Welles, a Roosevelt intimate in the State Department, liberation for Africans was even farther off, since they "are in the lowest rank of human beings." Through the 1940s the Chinese remained the special friends and dependents of the United States. The Korean War resurrected the equally old notion that Orientals were cruel, frenzied, and inscrutable.[62]

George Kennan, the paragon of foreign-policy expertise, revealed how deeply his "realism" was wedded to a sense of Anglo-Saxon mission when in 1949 he urged Americans to go "forth to see what we can do in order that stability may be given to all of the non-communist world." He saw in the Chinese Communists in 1949 "a grievously misguided and confused people" (though he also somehow concluded that theirs was a "fluid and subtle oriental movement"). He was predictably outraged by the Chinese intervention in the Korean War, "an affront of the greatest magnitude to the United States." The Chinese had become "savage and arrogant." They deserved "a lesson." Kennan's response to a tour through Latin America was equally in keeping with past national attitudes. He was unable to imagine "a more unhappy and hopeless background for the conduct of human life" than he found in those "confused and unhappy societies." Latinos had retreated into "a highly personalized, anarchical make-believe," while their prospects for progress were blocked by an intemperate climate, promiscuous interracial marriage, and the Spanish legacy of "religious fanaticism, frustrated energy, and an addiction to the most merciless cruelty." Arabs were no better. A brief exposure to Iraq in 1944 had Kennan recoiling in distaste from a people he regarded as not only ignorant and dirty but also "inclined to all manner of religious bigotry and fanaticism."[63]

The quintessential racist in the Truman administration may have been the president himself. His early correspondence is replete with racial references. Mexico was "Greaserdom." Slavic peoples were "bohunks." Still lower in his esteem were the "nigger" and the "Chinaman." None, the young Truman observed, belonged in the United States. Service in World War I introduced him to "kike town" (New York), evoked the stereotype of the avaricious Jew, widened his range of reference to include "frogeater" (the French) and "Dago," and stimulated a hatred for Germans. "They have no hearts or no souls," he wrote home in 1918. The next world war introduced "Jap" into his vocabulary and convinced him that they were, as he wrote at Potsdam in 1945, "savages, ruthless, merciless and fanatics." Accustomed to the Southern pattern of race relations that had prevailed in Independence, Missouri, Truman continued to refer to blacks as "nigs" and "niggers" at least as late as 1946. As president he also continued to express impatience with "hyphenates," those Americans of foreign descent who refused to jump into the cultural melting pot. He lavished on the British, whom he saw as the source of American law and as close allies, the most fulsome praise he could manage for any foreigners, noting that "fundamentally . . . our basic ideas are not far apart. . . ."[64]

The Eisenhower administration followed this same general pattern of thinking. Secretary of State John Foster Dulles and Ambassador to the United Nations Henry Cabot Lodge used "non-white" in an off-handedly condescending way to refer to the Third World. C. D. Jackson, an Eisenhower adviser, patron of development theorists, and sometime delegate to the United Nations, denied that he was "a pigmental snob" and then made an observation that proved quite the opposite: "The Western world has somewhat more experience with the operations of war, peace, and parliamentary procedures than the swirling mess of emotionally super-charged Africans and Asiatics and Arabs that outnumber us. . . . " Ike himself regarded the Greeks as "sturdy people," the Indians as "funny people" and not fully trustworthy, the Vietnamese as "backward," and the Chinese as "completely reckless, arrogant, . . . and completely indifferent to human losses." Above them all stood "the English-speaking peoples of the world" with their special duty to "set something of a model for the necessary cooperation among free peoples." Eisenhower retained his sense of solidarity with "those British" even in the midst of the Suez crisis—"they're still my right arm."[65]

This well-worn outlook led to predictable positions on the Third World. The president thought "dependent peoples" should submit to several additional decades of Western tutelage. Otherwise, prematurely free nations would be easily manipulated by Moscow and eventually led into "slavery." Those of their leaders that developed "ambitious pretensions," such as Gamal Abdel Nasser of Egypt, would have to be put back in their place. Dulles was no more ready than Eisenhower to accommodate Nasser ("an extremely dangerous fanatic") and other restive Third World leaders. Dulles' insistence on their patience and good behavior derived from his favorable estimate of Western colonialism. It had arisen not "primarily from mere force" but out of the appeal of Western ideas. Its effects had been benign, and it would prove uniquely "self-liquidating" as "political rule by the West" underwent "a peaceful withering away."[66]

The long-term strategy of development combined with the pressing requirements of containment to shape American policy toward the Third World. In each region cold warriors adjusted their approach to local conditions. Africa evoked the strongest developmental concerns, heavily tinctured in that case with racial prejudice and backed by scant aid. The hallmark of African policy was an anxiety about stability in that "fertile field for communism." Washington recognized privately that repression by European colonial authorities or minority white regimes was likely in the long run to produce just those conditions of instability, race war, and Communist-backed rebellion that policymakers most feared. But they regarded "premature independence for primitive, undeveloped peoples" as even riskier. By the late 1950s all of black Africa except the Portugese colonies, Rhodesia, and South Africa was on the road to independence and liberation from white minority governments, and still Washington stewed over "the premature withdrawal of white men from positions of authority" and the actions of black "political extremists." Though Kennedy went into the White House trailing statements sympathetic to Third World nationalism, he also soon fell prey to anxiety over hasty decolonization, overzealous liberation movements, and incompetent black rulers.[67]

Policymakers who were emphatic defenders of human rights in Soviet-dominated Eastern Europe were strikingly quiescent in Africa. Nowhere was this more true than in South Africa. Though troubled by the apartheid system established in the late 1940s and fearful it might drive "the natives to communism," the Truman administration and its successors learned to appreciate that country as an island of stability and to secure American strategic and economic interests there without letting the issue of self-determination get in the way. American critics of this policy railed in vain. For example, in the wake of the Sharpeville massacre in 1960, in which white police killed sixty-nine black demonstrators and wounded over two hundred, Eisenhower would go no farther than to call apartheid "a touchy thing." The president, who privately argued that segregationists ("not bad people") were only concerned "that their sweet little girls are not required to sit in school alongside some big overgrown Negroes," publicly played Pollyanna. He professed to see in South Africa hopeful signs of peaceful change and "human understanding." The Kennedy administration was similarly averse to challenging apartheid. "We are not the self-elected gendarmes for the political and social problems of other states," Dean Rusk grandly observed without explaining why he was making Africa the exception to the general pattern of American policy.[68]

In fact at the very time Rusk spoke American Congo policy blatantly contradicted him. The end of direct Belgian control had awakened fears in Washington that "precipitate" decolonization might end, as John Foster Dulles put it, in "a captivity far worse than present dependence." The outbreak of civil war, the rape of white nuns, and the mutilation of missionaries evoked old racial phantoms in the American imagination. Policymakers handed down their predictably severe judgments. The Congolese were a "primitive people" responsive only to "simple stimuli," the American ambassador reported. Eisenhower worried about that "restless and militant population in a state of gross ignorance—even by African standards." He did not want "chaos to run wild" and the Communists to step in. As a consequence, Washington backed United Nations intervention to restore order and had the local Central Intelligence Agency (CIA) station mark for assassination Patrice Lumumba, a charismatic nationalist regarded by Ike's aides as a Communist dupe. Nothing changed under Kennedy and Johnson. Even after Lumumba's murder the Congo remained, Kennedy found, "a place where everything falls apart." He and his successor tried to hold it together with pro-American moderates, simultaneously keeping CIA-cultivated rightists in the wings. In an emergency even white mercenaries were helpful in dealing with people still described within the administration as "primitive" and in Congress as "individuals who had hardly jumped out of trees yet."[69]

In Cold War policy toward Latin America, revolutionary concerns prevailed over racial ones. To avert instability Washington made that region the object of a succession of development programs. The Truman administration's Point Four, Eisenhower's campaign to facilitate the flow of foreign capital, and the Alliance for Progress pursued through the Kennedy and Johnson years each in its own way sought to promote the chief goal of policy, defined as early as 1952 as "an orderly political and economic development which will make the Latin American nations resistant to the internal growth of communism and to Soviet political warfare." To combat the success of the Cuban Revolution and its appeal in the region, policymakers in the 1960s raised aid levels. Though Kennedy initially spoke of reform for "desperate peoples," American programs most benefited military strongmen, appreciated in Washington as the steadiest guardians of the status quo.[70]

Whether advocating economic growth, political reform, or authoritarian rule, American leaders consistently assumed their insights were superior to those of Latino authorities. Development, in other words, carried forward the Monroe Doctrine's pretensions to dominance and tutelage. The United States "must not be pushed around by a lot of small American republics who are dependent on us in many ways," Secretary of State Stettinius huffed in 1945. Nor could it rely politically on mass movements in those republics. "The lower class," John Foster Dulles warned, could not be trusted to institute "democracy as we know it." Moreover, Latin "anti-bodies" were too weak to "always repel an intrusion of the Communist virus," observed his assistant secretary of state for inter-American affairs. Dulles' successor as secretary of state, Christian Herter, came away from a meeting with Fidel Castro in April 1959 worried that he was "very much like a child in many ways" and "quite immature regarding problems of government." Lyndon Johnson's chief adviser, fellow Texan Thomas C. Mann, thought a tough line most appropriate. "I know my Latinos. They understand only two things—a buck in the pocket and a kick in the ass." As late as 1969 Nelson Rockefeller, an old hand in the region, argued that "democracy is a very subtle and difficult problem" for most Latins. They were better off under strong governments that could deal with the rampant "forces of anarchy, terror, and subversion."[71]

Where development and authoritarian regimes failed to yield the desired stability in Latin America, Washington did not hesitate to return to those interventionist strategies out of favor since the interwar years. It did not regard intervention as a violation of a neighbor's sovereignty any more now than in the days of the big stick. By viewing communism as an external force and not indigenous to the Americas, policymakers reconciled their counterrevolutionary practice to their commitment to self-determination. Where they saw signs of a dangerous drift to the left—whether indicated by neutralism in foreign affairs, by economic nationalism, by labor unrest, or by land reform—American leaders turned the economic and political screws and, as a last resort, sent in the troops or unleashed the CIA.

Guatemala had the dubious distinction of being the target for the first of these major Cold War interventions in the Americas. By April 1954 Eisenhower had concluded that "the Reds are in control" and were bent on moving into neighboring El Salvador. The State Department, Congress, and the press agreed that Communist penetration in the Arbenz government required action. A CIA-engineered coup proved so successful in eliminating one Communist beachhead in the Americas that it induced policymakers to try their luck on a second beachhead, Cuba's Bay of Pigs, in 1961. Once again the telltale signs of Communist influence had sent the CIA operatives to the drawing boards. Only this time, when Kennedy set their plans in motion, the revolutionaries had learned their own lessons from Guatemala and were ready. The failure was a bitter one to which Kennedy could not be reconciled. "A small band of conspirators has stripped the Cuban people of their freedom" and handed them over "to forces beyond the hemisphere," he told a Miami audience during his last week as president. The shadow of Cuba also hung over Lyndon Johnson when he decided in 1965 to send troops into the Dominican Republic. He would not allow "a band of Communist conspirators" to succeed again in taking control of "a popular democratic revolution."[72]

In East Asia development policy was so closely coupled to containment that the two were virtually inseparable. Victory over Japan had made the dream of the Pacific as an American lake entirely possible; Cold War calculations made it imperative. Truman declared in January 1946 that he wanted nothing less than to "maintain complete control of Japan and the Pacific" and to "rehabilitate" China and Korea so each would have "a strong central government." By 1949 American policymakers had formally set their sights in the region on the "elimination of the preponderant power and influence of the USSR." The achievement of that goal would depend in part on ending poverty and misery. Programs promoting trade, social stability, administrative efficiency, education, road building, and agricultural and industrial development were seen as the key to long-term success here. The immediate need was to help Asian peoples turn back communism, described by Dean Acheson in early 1950 as "the most subtle instrument of Soviet foreign policy that has ever been devised." Extensive American military aid and even the dispatch of American troops would be Washington's response to Soviet aggression by proxy.[73]

The Asian front was the scene of some notable American Cold War successes. Japan, like West Germany, was turned into a Cold War bastion by occupation authorities, who in 1947–48 began to incorporate Japan as the northern anchor in the American chain of bases dominating the maritime fringe of East Asia. By 1951 Japan had become an ally, a stable junior partner in the American Pacific condominium. The Philippines, still an American colony at the war's end, was the scene of the other signal success. Formally granted independence in 1946, the islands became a convenient symbol of the benevolent role Americans believed they had always played in Asia. Yet the economy of the Philippines remained an extension of the American economy; the ruling oligarchy, which had long collaborated with the United States to preserve its own privileges, continued attentive to the preferences of their former overlord; and the American military retained bases needed for the Asian cold war.

South Korea might also be counted a success were it not for the costly "police action" American forces fought there. After occupying the southern half of the peninsula in 1945, American authorities sponsored, as they had in Japan and the Philippines, conservative and safely anti-Communist leaders. Syngman Rhee emerged as America's nominee, though not a particularly cooperative one, to rule the South. By June 1950 he faced not only serious domestic opposition but an invasion launched by Kim Il Sung, his Northern, Soviet-backed rival, and had to be rescued. Troops led by Douglas MacArthur turned back Kim's forces, and then in a massive miscalculation attempted to liberate the North, drawing the Chinese into the conflict. A field commander regarded as an expert on "oriental psychology" had unthinkingly challenged vital Chinese strategic interests, and a secretary of state who could see Korea as nothing to China but "a road to somewhere else" had contributed to the blunder.[74] After prolonged battering, South Korea emerged in 1953 a stable, pro-American garrison state.

The major nemesis of American goals in Asia was a peasantry discontented with the status quo. Even at the sites of American success the agrarian problem had commanded attention. In Japan the remedy was American-promoted land reform; in the Philippines it was an American-sponsored counterinsurgency program against the ill-led Huks; and in Korea it was strong-arm methods by local notables whose power the American occupation had augmented. Only in China and Vietnam, where determined and experienced nationalist elites had tied their programs to the aspirations of the peasantry, did Americans lose control—and suffer two humiliating defeats as a result.

In both countries Washington had found that even generous support for proxies was not enough. Chiang Kai-shek's Nationalists had received in excess of $3 billion after World War II, yet still lost the struggle against Mao's Communists. From the ensuing debacle, the Truman administration salvaged Taiwan, another island base to add to its chain and a refuge where former mainland allies could nurse their ambitions behind an American naval screen. Otherwise, Washington had to settle for a policy of isolating a government Truman called "a bunch of murderers" and Dulles later as secretary of state decried as outlaws beyond the pale of "civilized nations."[75]

In Vietnam the United States began to supply substantial aid to the French in 1950. By the last years of the French colonial struggle Americans were footing three-quarters of the bill. When the French finally negotiated their way out of Indochina in 1954, the Eisenhower administration went looking for another proxy. It found one in Ngo Dinh Diem, a staunchly anti-Communist conservative whose assignment was to build a nation in the southern half of Vietnam. To improve the chances for his success against Ho Chi Minh and those "professional agitators" subservient to Moscow, Washington pumped aid and advice into Diem's fledgling state and erected a protective regional alliance around it. Diem proved no more successful than the French in holding the countryside and perhaps even less cooperative than Rhee in Korea. In 1963 Kennedy's aides gave the signal to the South Vietnamese military to push Diem aside. The generals would prove more subservient but no more effective.[76]

Vietnam inexorably became an American war. Successive administrations had declared the stakes too high to contemplate retreat or admit defeat, so that Americans would have to step in once all the proxies had failed. The Truman team had calculated that the loss of Indochina would imperil neighboring states and set the balance of Southeast Asia "in grave hazard." Eisenhower had reaffirmed the geopolitical stakes by proposing "the 'falling domino' principle," and warned, "When the freedom of a man in Viet-Nam or in China is taken away from him, I think our freedom has lost a little."[77]

The Kennedy and Johnson administrations held to the course earlier marked out because they agreed with its premises and because they were unprepared to absorb in Vietnam a mortal political wound of the sort the loss of China had inflicted on Truman. Already in 1956 Kennedy saw in the Diem regime an opportunity to use American guidance, aid, and capital to create a revolution "far more peaceful, far more democratic, and far more locally controlled" than the Communists could offer. Professing to hear after the Bay of Pigs "the rising din of Communist voices in Asia and Latin America," he decided that Vietnam was a challenge the United States could not afford to neglect. He boosted American forces to 16,000, and when that proved insufficient Johnson expanded the American role in the ground war and launched an air war. Somehow this display of American power and will was expected to seduce the oriental minds in Hanoi into accepting a permanent division of their nation.[78]

Vietnam proved the culmination not only of the American Cold War struggle in Asia but of an old impulse to impose on the world the patterns of an ideological foreign policy. Johnson asked the obvious question in an April 1965 speech on Vietnam. "Why must this Nation hazard its ease, and its interest, and its power for the sake of a people so far away?"[79] The answers were as obvious to him and as familiar to us as the responses of his predecessors had been.

Revolution continued, as it had ever since the 1790s, to summon up visions of a reign of terror, of brutal assassinations, and of an international conspiracy against order and reason. Revolutionary forces operating in an agrarian political economy that Americans did not understand provoked knee-jerk opposition. Moreover, the chance to direct a backward and appreciative people toward a better, "modern" life retained an appeal long inspired by the notion of racial hierarchy. Successfully taught, the lessons of the American experience in development could help uplift inferior folk. Finally, the United States had "voluntarily assume[d] the burden and the glory of advancing mankind's best hopes." Americans dedicated to freedom and "democratic individualism" had to struggle to live up to this historic obligation to rescue oppressed peoples from "governmental despotism" and imperiled peoples from a "foreign yoke." Thereby might this special nation "save the world" from becoming a "vast graveyard of human liberties." The lessons of the past and the axioms of geopolitics taught that any abdication by the United States of its role as defender of freedom meant unleashing aggression abroad, encouraging isolationism at home, and sending dominos toppling down the long containment line.[80]

By 1967 half a million Americans, moved by dreams and fears as old as their nation and yet still as fresh as yesterday, were fighting in Vietnam.

6 The Contemporary Dilemma

Men make their own history, but they don't make it just as they please; they do not make it under circumstances chosen by themselves, but under circumstances directly encountered, given, and transmitted from the past. —Karl Marx (1852)

The social function of science vis-à-vis *ideologies is first to understand them—what they are, how they work, what gives rise to them—and second to criticize them, to force them to come to terms with (but not necessarily to surrender to) reality.*
—Clifford Geertz (1964)

We would do well to accept the young Marx's promptings. In foreign policy as in other spheres of human activity, the past is important to our understanding of the present in a paradoxical fashion. It instructs us in the special ways we are compromised by circumstances not of our own making, and at the same time it equips us to rise above those circumstances. A familiarity with the history of those ideas that led Americans into the thicket of international politics may, as Geertz in turn suggests, prove helpful in getting us through the perils that lie ahead.

The preceding chapters have made the case for the existence of an American foreign-policy ideology. Its origins are inextricably tied up with the emergence of an American nation. Its main features reflected from the start the class and ethnic preferences of those most intimately concerned with questions of foreign policy. Under the sway of that ideology, American policymakers measured the worth of other peoples and nations against a racial hierarchy. They displayed hostility toward revolutions that diverged from the American norm, especially those on the left. Finally, they were convinced that national greatness depended on making the world safe for liberty.

The general direction American policies have taken is inexplicable, perhaps even inconceivable, without taking account of the influence of this constellation of ideas. It was not inevitable that the United States would become dominant in the Americas and the hegemon in Central America and the Caribbean. Some mysterious fate did not decree the ambivalent relationship with China and Japan, which translated into three decades of hostility with one country, followed after a Pacific war by three decades of hostility with the other. Nor was it preordained that the United States would emerge as a crucial player in the European balance of power, twice throwing itself into the bloody wars of that continent and finally seeking to fill the vacuum created by the collapse of empires after 1945. In historical perspective, however, these developments should not seem surprising or accidental. An ideology that had been tested, refined, and woven into the fabric of the national consciousness had helped propel twentieth-century U.S. foreign policy ever deeper into the thicket of international politics and warfare.

The blend of ideas that oriented policymakers to the world should neither be treated in isolation nor be counted as determinative of policy. Cynical opportunism and economic interests can indeed be found as elements in the larger pattern of perception and calculation circumscribed by the ideas emphasized here. Personality, bureaucratic pressures, available national resources, and the international environment must also be given their due as potent influences over the ways ideas are translated into action. But even after all these points are conceded, ideology remains the obvious starting point for explaining both the American outlook and American behavior in world affairs.

Though persistent, this ideology has by no means been static or invulnerable to countervailing pressures. We have already noted that the conception of national greatness took a full century to become fully consolidated and that even afterward, during the first four decades of this century, it invited occasional if unsuccessful attacks. We have also seen the racial hierarchy redefined in the mid-twentieth century in cultural terms, though not fundamentally transformed. At the same time, widespread acceptance of geopolitical codes and the lessons of the past have supplemented as well as reinforced the inherited ideology. (Alone attitudes toward revolution have escaped significant change or challenge.) Collectively the precepts guiding American policy are not precisely the same now as they were nearly two hundred years ago, but the family resemblance is as easy to discern as it would be delusory to ignore.

★ ★ ★

Though no historian can entirely rise above personal prejudice, success at illuminating the past depends in large measure on controlling those prejudices. Where (as here) the subject under scrutiny is a living body of ideas and assumptions, it is also necessary to achieve a degree of intellectual and emotional detachment—in effect, to see ideology as from a distance. But the historian's recital is unavoidably "tainted" by personal experience and convictions. Indeed, the case can be made that the mix of professional detachment and personal commitment is altogether appropriate. The historian is also a citizen and consequently bears a special duty to reflect on the relation of past to present and to indicate forthrightly what practical meaning historical findings have for our present conditions and future prospects as a people. This is no novel doctrine. Kennan and Williams both offer germane and worthy examples of using an understanding of the past in order to address public issues. Readers are not expected to accept unthinkingly the concluding judgments offered here, but they are asked to weigh them carefully.

The key conclusion that I draw from the preceding history can be summarized simply: a powerful foreign-policy ideology has yielded unfortunate consequences that are essential to recognize if we are to make that ideology "come to terms with reality." Vietnam offers a recent, stark, and unsettling illustration of the point. A crusade that may have been foredoomed left 56,000 Americans dead and another quarter of a million wounded; it also absorbed well in excess of a hundred billion dollars.[1] As the war machine ground ahead year after year, it alienated Americans from their leaders and institutions, put hallowed national myths in doubt, and inflicted on the homefront the same casual violence that had become the pattern on that distant battlefield. The prolonged, highly technological Indochina conflict imposed a higher price still on the people who lived in its midst. In Vietnam alone two million individuals may have lost their lives. Bombing of an intensity unprecedented in all the history of organized violence devastated the entire country. In the South the war ravaged a fragile tropical environment with incalculable long-term consequences, visited indiscriminate destruction on the countryside, spawned over six million refugees, and relentlessly tore away at the social fabric. As the war spilled over into Cambodia, it became just as destabilizing there. From Norodom Sihanouk's neutralism to the American-backed military government of Lon Nol, Cambodians stumbled on—into the arms of a sanguinary Khmer Rouge, famine, social collapse, and ultimately Vietnamese occupation.

The Vietnam War raises an obvious question: why did the United States fight so frightfully expensive and destructive a war in a small and distant country where no tangible interests were at stake and where the central justifications for American involvement were, like all matters of theology, untestable and ultimately based on faith? That question and its answers lead to a string of others that take us back to the role of ideology and its capacity, when linked to formidable power, to elicit great sacrifice, incur high costs, and impose great pain. As Americans fled from the ruins of that war, they began to wonder about the mistaken assumptions and broader costs imposed by the reigning foreign-policy ideology.

Ideology has set Americans at odds with the assumptions and practices of traditional power politics. As Walter Lippmann once observed, "The history of diplomacy is the history of relations among rival powers, which did not enjoy political intimacy, and did not respond to appeals to common purposes."[2] Yet Americans have indeed assumed that intimacy and friendship among peoples of the world was the norm and have ascribed evil intentions to those whose exercise of power or pursuit of self-interest ran athwart American expectations. At the heart of this American aversion to traditional forms of great-power rivalry has been a hostility to spheres of influence. Though such spheres were the product of time-honored security calculations, American leaders have with few exceptions condemned them as illegitimate, an affront to the principles of liberty and self-determination.

Ironically, the more actively Americans have devoted themselves to destroying spheres of influence, the farther we have gone toward creating our own. To an incredulous world Americans have time and again explained that our benevolent intentions and selfless treatment of the countries of Central America, the Caribbean, and the Pacific clearly distinguish the extension of American influence from traditional practice. Where others seek to exploit and repress, so the argument goes, Americans seek only to protect and guide.

This American position on spheres of influence—denying them to others while carving them out for ourselves—has from the foreign perspective made the United States seem hypocritical and aggressive rather than enlightened and peace-loving. Not surprisingly, then, that position has been a prime source of international misunderstanding and conflict. The collisions with Japan over Northeast Asia in the 1930s, with the Soviet Union over Eastern Europe at the end of World War II, and with China over North Korea in late 1950 demonstrate dramatically how a principled American rejection of one of the constants of international life has led to redoubled and unexpected resistance on the part of the indicted party.

Ideology has also set the nature and force of revolutionary change beyond the bounds of American comprehension. Revolutions that failed to conform to the standards of America's own moderate, constitutional beginnings inspired hostility and, with increasing frequency, active opposition. Vietnam was part of a pattern going back to the late eighteenth century. That pattern was confirmed in response to the two major twentieth-century revolutions—in Russia and China—and carried forward more recently in Nicaragua, El Salvador, and Iran.

Accommodation to revolution has, if anything, become more difficult in the twentieth century. Peasant economies, where problems of commercialization and land tenure have helped set the stage for the most dramatic social revolutions of recent times, lay well beyond the experience of contemporary Americans. Leaders in Washington responded with development policy, an ethnocentric exercise in fitting a diverse world on the procrustean bed of the American experience. They expected to find a neat, unilinear advance from traditional to modern ways in countries whose course of development in fact bore little if any resemblance to the American pattern. Moreover, the tendency to see a conspiracy by the Soviet Union and international communism behind every outbreak of disorder has intensified the old allergy to revolution. By denying the social roots and historical legitimacy of radical revolutions, the United States arrays itself on the side of an unpopular and often oppressive status quo (as in China), sets itself against the nationalist impulses that have swept much of the world in recent times (as in Vietnam), and exposes itself to feelings of frustration and humiliation after each counterrevolutionary failure (as in Cuba).

Our inability even in the face of failure to modify our rigid, reflexive attitudes toward revolutions has tended to make a bad situation worse. This inflexibility has made Washington unresponsive to overtures from new revolutionary regimes eager to neutralize American hostility and thereby avoid a prolonged and costly confrontation. Confirmed in their suspicions of implacable American hostility, revolutionary leaders have turned to cultivate friends in the anti-American camp. Mao's China, driven deeper into the Soviet embrace following the flat rejection of overtures in 1949, offers a particularly dramatic instance of this commonplace phenomenon that has proven strategically costly for the United States.

Paradoxically, the counterrevolutionary stance taken by the United States must be regarded as a failure even where it has seemingly succeeded. Each American victory has served notice on aspiring revolutionary leaders that their strategies must anticipate and prepare for an American policy of active hostility. Leaders such as Fidel Castro have as a result become more determined, as well as more formidable, foes intent on mobilizing the popular, military, and international support essential to holding at bay the counterrevolutionary forces that the past teaches the United States will sponsor.

Successful campaigns against the left have, moreover, repeatedly created time bombs. Repressive rightist regimes favored by the United States have neglected or exacerbated serious social and economic problems, creating the preconditions for an explosion against the established order and against Americans implicated in the creation and maintenance of that order. Counterrevolutionary victories followed after a time by still-greater defeats has been the story of the American experience in Nicaragua, Cuba, South Vietnam, and Iran. Seemingly cost effective in promoting a semblance of order, collaborative arrangements with the Somoza family for fifty years, Batista for over twenty-five years, Ngo Dinh Diem for nearly a decade, and the Shah in Iran for a quarter century each proved in the end costly beyond imagination. By continuing this practice, Americans will have more of these bills to pay with the names of other countries marked on them.

U.S. foreign-policy ideology has also proven disabling by cutting Americans off from an understanding of, not to mention sympathy for, cultures distant from our own. The sense of national superiority central to that ideology has given rise to stereotypes that diminish other people by exaggerating the seemingly negative aspects of their lives and by constricting the perceived range of their skills, accomplishments, and emotions. By denigrating other cultures as backward or malleable, these stereotypes raise in Americans false expectations that it is an easy enterprise to induce and direct political change and economic development. On encountering obstinacy or resistance, Americans understandably feel frustrated and resentful and in extremity may indulge dehumanizing stereotypes that make possible the resort to forms of coercion or violence otherwise unthinkable. This pattern, first fully apparent in relations with blacks and native Americans, continues to govern American dealings with "Third World" peoples.

The American tendency to see the world as simple and pliable has been reinforced by geopolitics, with its conception of the globe as a chessboard, neatly demarcated and easily controlled by anyone with enough strong pieces and the proper strategy. But the world, complex and slow to change, has resisted our efforts to impose our will and enforce our rules. We have known the bewilderment of the chess master who discovers that in fact no square is like another, that pawns often disturbingly assume a life of their own, and that few contests are neatly two-sided.

The American experience in Vietnam offers examples aplenty of all these unfortunate tendencies inspired by our ideological constructs and reflected in our stereotypes. We dehumanized the Vietnamese by the everyday language applied to them. We called them "gooks" or "slopes" (just as we had earlier derided other unruly peoples as "gu-gus" and "niggers"). Reflecting our diminished sense of their humanity, we made massive and indiscriminate use of firepower and herbicides, killing noncombatants as well as combatants and poisoning the land. At the same time, we promoted a pattern of national development informed by the American experience, taught the Vietnamese how to fight and govern, and when necessary both fought and governed for them. The resulting devastation, dislocation, and subordination was the price the Vietnamese paid for our self-assigned crusade to stop communism, save a people we regarded as backward, and revitalize an outmoded culture.

The paternalism and contempt evident in the Vietnam "adventure" testifies to the continuing influence of a culture-bound, color-conscious world view that still positions nations and peoples in a hierarchy defined at the extremes by civilization and barbarism, modernity and tradition. It renders us sympathetic to forward-looking Israelis, seen largely as European, at loggerheads with swarthy, bearded, polygamous, fanatical Arabs. It supports empathy for civilized white South Africans rather than a black underclass barely removed from their "primitive" tribal origins. We wring our hands over repression of Soviet-dominated Eastern Europe, while the continuing plight of the native peoples of the Americas—of dark skin and peculiar habits—could for all the attention it gets in the United States be a problem on some yet undiscovered planet.[3]

The American refusal to accept the legitimacy of spheres of influence, to tolerate social revolutions, and to respect cultural patterns fundamentally divergent from our own has carried a price tag. One part of the bill must be calculated in terms of the collapse of American reform movements. In the competition for limited national resources and psychic energy, the protagonists of global greatness promising a better ordered, more liberal, and hence more secure world have repeatedly prevailed over their domestic-oriented opponents. Progressivism, whether defined as a political outlook, a national movement, or a political program, was quickly eclipsed once the United States entered World War I. In the late 1930s Mr. New Deal made way for Mr. Win-the-War as a growing preoccupation with international crises sealed the fate of Roosevelt's already floundering reform program. Lyndon Johnson launched his Great Society in 1964 in response to a pent-up demand for change, only to have Vietnam steal the money and erode the public and congressional support needed to keep reform a going concern.

The lesson is clear: by attempting to honor the claims the world ostensibly makes on us, an activist foreign policy diminishes our capacity for domestic renewal. Such a foreign policy diverts us from the public issues raised by rapid technological, economic, and social change. It also devours the funds essential to improving the quality of our lives, whether measured in terms of health, education, environment, or the arts. Currently more than half of the federal budget is committed to international programs and military operations past, present, and future. The pursuit of greatness reflected in those figures severely compromises the stewardship of our domestic affairs and imposes costs in socially inequitable and politically irresponsible ways. To serve their ideological vision policymakers, comfortable in their affluence, have channeled national resources abroad to the detriment of both their less comfortable countrymen and future generations. Foreign policy should not serve as a means of economic redistribution. Nor should policymakers be allowed to minimize the cost by leaving it to future taxpayers to foot the bill. We would do well to heed Thomas Jefferson's injunction that it is "incumbent on every generation to pay its own debts as it goes," a principle, he shrewdly added, which "if acted on, would save one half the wars of the world."[4]

Against our ideological foreign policy we must also count the harm done the established ideals of our political and economic systems. Put in other words, a foreign policy dedicated to liberty may contribute to conditions at home inimical to that very principle. Part of the damage can be measured in terms of the atmosphere of intolerance and repression that has been the domestic by-product of foreign crusades. World War I witnessed a repression of dissenters and persecution of ethnics that persisted into the postwar period. World War II brought an unconstitutional internment of citizens of Japanese descent. The Cold War and the Korean conflict combined to produce a form of anticommunist witch-hunting known as McCarthyism. Vietnam bred a fortress mentality in Richard Nixon's White House and led to the violations of law and abuse of authority associated with the term *Watergate*.

Foreign policy has further undermined liberty at home by its accelerating tendency to concentrate power in what one former booster of a powerful executive concedes has become the "imperial presidency."[5] Through the twentieth century foreign affairs has strengthened the financial resources, expertise, and discretion available to the executive branch. Congress has been overshadowed, the public left in the dark, and a cult of national security has flourished. These trends have undermined constitutional checks and balances, restricted the flow of information, impeded intelligent debate, and diminished the electoral accountability of policymakers—all serious blows to the workings of a democratic political system.

Economic liberty no less than political liberty has suffered erosion. Twentieth-century foreign-policy commitments, and especially the four major wars to which they have given rise, have dramatically increased Washington's role in the economy as taxer, spender, and regulator. Economic power thus centralized has, champions of the market mechanism argue, led to fiscal irresponsibility (most evident in massive budget deficits), to distortion of industrial development, and to slowed economic growth. There is growing evidence that national security programs, by orienting economic activities toward military needs, render the economy overall less productive and competitive. A large defense budget has a strong inflationary bias, at least under the current military procurement system based in practice on a ''cost-plus'' approach. Lacking incentives to hold costs down, military contractors tend to bid up the price of scarce resources, with effects felt throughout the entire economy. Moreover, a compelling case has been made that large defense budgets, with their substantial research-and-development component, skew scientific and engineering funds and talent toward military research and the space program rather than to projects with obvious or immediate civilian application.[6]

These consequences should prove as troubling to strategists as to champions of the marketplace. The claims made on the economy today in the name of national security may constrict, perhaps significantly, the availability of goods and services on which the nation can draw for its defense in the future. This prospect is even more alarming coming as it does in the wake of a dramatic American fall from the commanding economic heights occupied at the end of World War II. As the American share of goods and services as well as currency reserves has declined, strategists have had to accept significantly diminished leverage over the international economy.[7]

Policymakers in the twentieth century have shown a remarkable inability to anticipate the economic and political costs of activism in world affairs. In this respect they have been victims of their own ignorance, wishful thinking, and the inherent difficulty of forecasting, let alone controlling, the complicated effects of foreign policy on domestic affairs. Leaders have also displayed a remarkable insensitivity, some even a studied indifference, once those costs have become apparent. Under the influence of a powerful foreign-policy ideology, they have soldiered on convinced that the momentous principles at stake justified the costs, whatever they might be.

In recent decades the sole striking exception to this pattern of insensitivity has been Dwight D. Eisenhower and his cabinet of millionaires. Prolonged and heavy defense spending, these fiscal conservatives feared, would unbalance the budget and result in either repressive taxation or inflationary deficit spending. Either way economic growth and efficiency would suffer, impairing the economic strength on which long-term security needs depended. Eisenhower shifted defense policy toward a heavy reliance on nonconventional military power (nuclear weapons supplemented by covert operations) in order to reduce defense claims and the attendant strains on the free market.

Unshaken in his views, Eisenhower left office warning against the influence of "an immense military establishment and a large arms industry" nurtured by defense budgets. In this military-industrial complex he saw a potential danger to liberty and the democratic process.[8]

The fiscal prudence of the eight Eisenhower years stands in relief against the profligate practices of Democratic presidents, who otherwise dominated policy during the Cold War years between 1945 and 1968. Harry S. Truman decided in 1950 to triple defense spending.[9] His aides promised that the economic effect would be beneficial. John F. Kennedy's call to "pay any price, bear any burden" announced an end to the gray caution of his Republican predecessor and foreshadowed a major buildup of both conventional and strategic forces. Lyndon B. Johnson mistakenly judged the economy strong enough to support both his "bitch of a war" in Vietnam and his real love, the Great Society program.[10] He lost his love and had to meet the unremitting demands of the war through inflationary deficit spending.

In evaluating the costs of particular foreign policies the public in a democracy serves as the ultimate arbiter. The role of arbiter is, however, one the public is seemingly ill equipped to fill. Polling data has long suggested that the mass public is ignorant of international affairs. An example, easily multiplied many times, underlines the point. After nearly a decade of Strategic Arms Limitation Talks (SALT) between the United States and the Soviet Union and the conclusion of two major agreements as a result of those talks, only 34 percent of Americans polled in late 1978 could correctly identify the two nations involved.[11] The concomitant to this ignorance on major international questions is, the polls reveal, an intolerance of ambiguous policy, an impatience with complicated, long-term solutions to difficult policy problems, and deep divisions over how to handle major commitments that run into serious, unexpected difficulties.

Precisely because of these traits and the suspicion that many Americans are at heart isolationist, policymakers have been reluctant to make the public a genuine partner in policymaking or to risk open and vigorous debate. Dean Acheson revealed the underlying mistrust felt by other post–World War II influentials when he observed in a fit of candor, "If you truly had a democracy and did what the people wanted, you'd go wrong every time."[12] Policymakers have instead preferred to exploit the tendency of the electorate to take at face value official estimates of the world scene and to withhold information likely to excite popular isolationism or diminish the likelihood of getting the national resources essential to realizing their vision of national security.

Policymakers, however, deprive the public of an opportunity to make an early and informed judgment at their own peril. Action undertaken to help a foreign friend or resist a foreign foe usually wins immediate public support and is likely to be sustained so long as steady, tangible progress is made toward some clearly defined and easily understood goal. On the other hand, if an initiative, even one advanced as vital to American interests, leads to unanticipated claims on life and treasure, the public may repudiate the policy and sometimes the policymaker as well. This capacity of the public to subject foreign commitments to a critical if crude and belated evaluation was made dramatically evident by the Korean and Vietnam wars. (The reaction to the seizure of the Philippines and to involvement in World War I could also be used to make the same point.) Both Korea and Vietnam reveal how an apparently solid foreign-policy consensus can quickly turn soft as war costs exceed public tolerance. Antipathy to the Korean War mounted as it dragged on inconclusively for three years, leaving a depressing trail of casualties in its wake. Disenchantment went farther in the case of the longer, more costly Vietnam commitment. Having concluded that its trust had been abused, the public in both cases withdrew its support.

If leaders cling to commitments gone awry, the public stands ready to translate its disaffection into political action that can immobilize policy and drive its architects from office. A crisis of confidence, if prolonged, may destroy the basic consensus on which any durable and coherent foreign policy in a democracy depends. Public opposition may in extreme cases erupt into political demagoguery, bitter recrimination, violent protest, and official repression, straining the legitimacy of the political system. All of these manifestations of public opposition and alienation were evident during the Korean and Vietnam wars as well as earlier in the wake of World War I and the nineteenth-century wars against Spain and Mexico. For example, the corrosive Vietnam War combined with Watergate to eat deeply into trust in the government and into support, especially and most critically among well-informed, influential Americans, for the interventionism associated with previous Cold War policy.[13]

The public, belittled as ignorant and fickle, deserves recognition and respect as a brake against some of the excesses of the reigning American foreign-policy ideology. Though its role makes policymaking messy and fraught with risks, at least for overeager and less than candid leaders, the public has shown a valuable, commonsensical capacity to evaluate policies and to check those gone out of control. This role has become indispensable as Congress has surrendered some of its constitutional powers in peacetime and virtually abandoned them in time of war. This role is also entirely proper in a democracy, for (in the language of one sage political observer) "upon the effects of foreign policy are staked the lives, the fortunes, and the honor of the people, and a free people cannot and should not be asked to fight and bleed, to work and sweat, for ends which they do not hold to be so compelling that they are self-evident.''[14] Policymakers would do well to show greater sensitivity to public opinion, allowing it fuller information and acknowledging the limits of its tolerance rather than attempting to preempt it or hold it at a distance.

★ ★ ★

By the late 1960s a growing recognition of the costs of Cold War policy had set the stage for a period of experimentation. Richard Nixon was waiting in the wings, ruminating on the lessons learned as Eisenhower's understudy in the 1950s and as an avid student of international affairs during his 1960s sojourn in the political wilderness. He had come to accept Eisenhower's view that American power was limited and to believe that the world was more fluid and less threatening than previously assumed. Rather than lead a crusade for universal liberty and an end to communism, this man who had once been a classic cold warrior followed instead a balance-of-power approach that gave highest priority to the search for stability in relations with the Soviet Union and China. Both were to be treated as powers with legitimate international interests, not as ideological threats, embodiments of evil, or revolutionary mutants. The task of diplomacy thus became more manageable—to seek to identify areas of mutual interest where compromise and accommodation were possible.

After his election Nixon selected Henry Kissinger as his chief adviser, thereby reinforcing the impulse to move beyond a bankrupt Cold War policy. Kissinger's heroes were not Wilson and Truman, but Metternich and Bismarck, statesmen who had used their power and prestige to hold their worlds in balance. Speaking the language of realpolitik that he associated with those models of European statecraft, Kissinger quickly established himself as an articulate, like-minded associate with the intellect and energy to flesh out and implement Nixon's policy preferences. He also soon proved that he could be as devious and secretive as his boss in advancing administration objectives.

The most pressing task facing the two was liquidating the Vietnam War, which had ruined Johnson's presidency and could do the same to Nixon's. Nixon and Kissinger sought to arrange a face-saving settlement with Hanoi, an objective Johnson had already reluctantly accepted in his last year in the White House. That settlement finally come in January 1973, over four years— and many deaths—after Nixon had proclaimed the existence of a secret plan to end the war. Arms control, too, appeared at the top of the new administration's agenda. Nixon rejected the illusion, as the Johnson administration had before him, that nuclear superiority meant greater national security. He sought instead to stabilize the nuclear-arms race and assure the United States and the Soviet Union positions of parity. The treaty that emerged from SALT in 1972 represented an important step toward those goals and laid the foundation for an era of détente, with its expanded political, economic, and cultural contacts between the two superpowers. Finally, Nixon determined to talk to Peking, thereby shaking off a mindless anticommunism that had governed American China policy for two decades. Three years of patient diplomatic spadework cleared the way for a dramatic presidential journey in 1972 that sealed the new Sino-American rapprochement and above all secured for the United States an improved strategic position in the global balance of power.

While the Nixon-Kissinger team reined in on the old ideological impulses, their "realist" power calculus had not driven from their minds all sentimental notions of a traditional sort. Indeed Kissinger, despite his European background, appears to have carried to his duties a set of unexamined assumptions about the special role of the United States as the "embodiment of mankind's hopes," as "the bulwark of free peoples everywhere" against the twin evils of aggression and totalitarianism, as an agent of modernization in a tradition-bound "Third World" threatened by international communism, and as a check on the arrogance of wild-eyed revolutionaries.[15]

Nixon and Kissinger's preoccupation with maintaining prestige and credibility, particularly evident as they tried to maneuver out of the Vietnam quagmire, sometimes caused them to resuscitate the stark formulations associated with the Cold War and old-style anticommunism. Nixon himself declared in an often-quoted 1970 defense of his Vietnam policy, "If . . . the world's most powerful nation, the United States of America, acts like a pitiful, helpless giant, the forces of totalitarianism and anarchy will threaten free nations and free institutions throughout the world." Six years later Kissinger embroidered on this timeworn theme: "America cannot be true to its heritage unless it stands with those who strive for freedom and human dignity."[16]

The Nixon administration's attitude toward the Third World also flowed along a well-worn channel, confined by indifference on one side and condescension on the other. Washington continued to see it as a collection of nations that were backward, plagued by turbulence, and led by touchy, stubborn men. They were frustratingly difficult to manage.

In Africa the administration worried that Communists might exploit the issues of colonialism and racial oppression to gain power. Reflecting Nixon's own earlier view that independence was "not necessarily the best thing for

Africa or Africans,'' a secret 1969 National Security Council study declared that "force [applied by nationalist groups] is not an appropriate means to bring about constructive change in southern Africa,'' and it predicted confidently if altogether incorrectly that there was "no likelihood in the foreseeable future that liberation movements could overthrow or seriously threaten'' either Portugese-ruled Angola and Mozambique or white-ruled Rhodesia.[17]

These same biases distorted Washington's vision of other parts of the Third World. North Vietnam's leaders proved incomprehensible and unyielding. Kissinger in an outburst of impatience called them "a bunch of shits. Tawdry, filthy shits." Both Kissinger and Nixon wrote them off as ideological fanatics. Allende's "takeover" in Chile caused considerable heartburning. Nixon, who had already sweepingly dismissed his neighbors to the south as "a bunch of kooks," set covert operations in motion against a popularly elected government. Kissinger meanwhile struggled for a rationale. "I don't see why we have to let a country go Marxist just because its people are irresponsible." American leaders, not Latin American voters, would "set the limits of diversity," he declared.[18]

Nixon's resignation in 1974 left Kissinger, serving now as Gerald Ford's secretary of state, to sustain the partial break from Cold War thinking. To those who urged new sacrifices to save a sinking South Vietnam, he countered that Americans had already made "a monumental effort" in behalf of that nation. He defended détente. The capability of the two superpowers to end life on earth made it essential that they "attempt to transform the cold war into a more cooperative relationship" and not treat their interactions as "tests of manhood."[19] Finally, he played up the strategic and economic advantages that accrued to the United States from the new China ties.

Thereafter, between 1977 and 1981, it fell to Jimmy Carter to maintain the resistance to Cold War assumptions. He would continue the arms-control effort and maintain the opening to China. But his outlook, shaped by his Baptist faith and the values of the small-town South, cast him in the mold of those other two Southern Democrats, Woodrow Wilson and Harry Truman, with whom Carter personally identified, and created a gulf between him and Nixon and Kissinger.

Carter entered the White House committed, as Jefferson had been long before him, to a restrained, just, populist foreign policy, confident that the world was becoming an ever more hospitable place for American values. He perceived "the new reality of a politically awakening world," which in turn called "for a new American foreign policy—a policy based on constant decency in its values and an optimism in our historical vision." His policy would "be designed to serve mankind" and make his countrymen "proud to be Americans." That meant rejecting the resort to secret deals and covert operations that had recently sullied the nation's reputation and championing the cause of human rights. He declared that his commitment to this cause was "absolute"; he would work to shield "the individual from the arbitrary power of the state" without regard, he implied, to national boundaries. Carter hoped this new approach would restore to American policy a popular base of support at home, burnish the tarnished national prestige abroad, and align the United States with the irresistible forces of liberty and progress everywhere.[20]

Carter, it soon became apparent, was unprepared for the foreign-policy heights to which his presidential aspirations had catapulted him. His thinking on the issues before him was shallow and unsystematic as well as conventional. For example, he reflexively blamed revolutionary turmoil in Iran, Central America, and Africa on the legacy of colonialism and meddling by the Soviet Union. He sought stability there by propping up old allies or encouraging the indigenous military. In Iran he tried both tactics, all the while insisting that Washington had not intervened in that country's internal affairs. For a president who along with his advisers still thought in the primitive categories of tradition and modernity, the victors in that revolutionary struggle seemed inexplicably "determined to commit political and economic suicide." Khomeini in particular appalled Carter; he saw no more in that charismatic religious leader than a "crazyman." China, to take another example, excited his imagination the way it might have stirred the missionary enthusiasts who had impressed him as a child. Nothing in his dealings with Deng Xiaoping appears to have given Carter greater pleasure than the thought that he had secured for the Chinese the freedom to worship and read the Bible.[21]

The conflicting advice of Secretary of State Cyrus Vance and National Security Adviser Zbigniew Brzezinski compounded Carter's problem. Vance made the success of the continuing SALT negotiations his top priority, thus appealing to Carter's constructive instincts. On the other side Brzezinski, who carried from his native Poland a deep-seated anti-Soviet animus, pushed the president toward a policy of confrontation and skillfully played on the themes of self-determination and human rights to advance his own crusade against the Kremlin's grand strategy of expansion and its repressive practices at home. Crises in the Horn of Africa and Iran as well as differences over China policy drove a still-deeper wedge between Carter's two advisers and made the presidential straddle ever more difficult to maintain. Attempts to meld contrary points of view further muddied Carter's own outlook, left policy adrift, and stimulated a cry for leadership and a return to the old foreign-policy verities.

The Cold War recommenced in 1979 in a rush of events that made the world seem once more bipolar and hostile and gave a boost to resurgent anticommunism. The Soviet Union, already engaged in an arms buildup, invaded Afghanistan, while its Vietnamese allies were tightening their control over Cambodia. Carter, instructed by Brzezinski in the complexities of the Russian mind (it "tended to respect the strong and had contempt for the weak"), responded by abandoning efforts to get Senate ratification of the SALT II agreement, increasing his own arms budget, and imposing a grain embargo on the Soviets.[22] So much for détente and arms control.

In the midst of all this a string of revolutions stirred old fears of "turbulence" and Communist subversion among backward peoples. Leftist regimes in Angola and Ethiopia invited in Cuban forces, regarded by Washington as Soviet proxies, to help consolidate power. Closer to home, one revolution toppled Somoza in Nicaragua and another threatened to succeed against a no less repressive regime in neighboring El Salvador. Another American-backed strongman fell in Iran. Though free of any Marxist taint, the Iranian Revolution proved in its radical character and nationalist fervor just as offensive and incomprehensible to Americans. The seizure of hostages in the Teheran embassy provided a reminder of the terror any revolution held.[23] These developments led Carter to write finis to noninterventionism and transformed human rights into an anticommunist rallying cry.

The electorate was ready for a clear, forceful, reassuringly familiar articulation of American purpose in the world, and Ronald Reagan was eager to oblige. Both as candidate and as chief executive, Reagan repeatedly celebrated that familiar conception of an American "rendezvous with destiny," sounding like Woodrow Wilson and actually invoking Thomas Paine's vision of a nation great enough "to begin the world over again." Like his ideological forebears, Reagan regarded his own country as exceptional. It had been born out of "the only true revolution in man's history." (All others had "simply exchanged one set of rulers for another.") And it had become an "island of freedom" assigned by "Divine Providence" the role of defender of world peace and liberty. Pitted against a moral, benevolent America was the Soviet Union, "the most aggressive empire the modern world has seen." Reagan time and again characterized the Soviets as evil. They were "the most evil enemy mankind has faced in his long climb from the swamp to the stars," "an evil force that would extinguish the light we've been tending for 6,000 years," or finally "the focus of evil in the modern world." Revealing his Wilsonian intellectual roots, Reagan contended that the Kremlin, like any "autocratic," "centralized," or "totalitarian" government, was bound to be warlike and implacable in its hostility to freedom.[24]

The obvious and politically convenient target of Reagan's restorationism was Jimmy Carter. He had given away the Panama canal, which Reagan claimed was as much American as Texas or Alaska, and had compromised American security by concluding SALT II with the "evil empire." Reagan's real nemesis, however, was Richard Nixon. Reagan had a visceral aversion to détente with the Kremlin and to rapprochement with a Chinese government that "subscribes to an ideology based on a belief in destroying governments like ours" and that had beguiled the United States into a reprehensible sellout of old, freedom-loving allies on Taiwan. To complete his repudiation of the Nixon legacy, Reagan wanted to celebrate, not put behind, the war in Vietnam. He went out of his way to praise it as "a noble cause," a justified attempt "to counter the master plan of the communists for world conquest."[25]

Reagan and his associates called for restoring American power and prestige and summoned the country to confront the Communist adversary with confidence. By rearming massively, applying economic and diplomatic pressure, and intervening vigorously to assist "freedom fighters" around the world, the United States could ultimately bring about the collapse of an unworkable, unstable, and inherently weak Communist system. It could free the peoples of Russia and Eastern Europe, frustrate the plans of professional revolutionaries worldwide, and ultimately "leave Marxism-Leninism on the ash heap of history."[26] This foreign-policy vision of Reagan's, like the visions of the cold warriors before him, was shaped by the lessons of Munich. It was reinforced by a myth, intended to counter the enfeebling post-Vietnam national malaise, of a golden age of American omnipotence in the years immediately after World War II.

As president, Reagan was true to his campaign promises to put behind the shamefully passive, humiliatingly irresolute, and foolishly parsimonious practices of Nixon and Carter. He launched a major arms buildup, pushing federal spending significantly higher. (To the horror of fiscal conservatives, the budget deficit soared as well.) He waged economic warfare against the Soviets by restricting scientific and technological exchange and challenging a clumsy Soviet system to compete with the superior capitalist economy in a high-tech arms race. He sent American expeditionary forces into Lebanon and Grenada, stepped up Carter's counterrevolutionary program in El Salvador, and sought to topple the regime in Nicaragua. To put a stop to misguided public criticism, he sought to keep outsiders from snooping into government business and insiders from talking once out of office. Reporters, whose negativism he blamed for the unpopularity of the Vietnam War, were to be kept away from military operations. Scholars, also agents of discontent and doubt, would find officialdom and the official record less accessible. Only on China policy did Reagan reluctantly give ground—and then only because he came to realize that even Communists could tie down parts of the Red Army far from Western Europe's military frontier.

This reversion to Cold War orthodoxy was due, in part, to the failure of Nixon and Kissinger to institutionalize their innovations in great-power relations. Preferring to play a lone hand, they had held the bureaucracy, Congress, and the informed public at a distance. Such an approach facilitated a diplomacy of maneuver, but it left unchallenged the still-strong anticommunist currents within American politics.

No sooner had the Vietnam War ended than restless cold warriors organized such groups as the Committee on the Present Danger to exploit the opening left by Nixon and Kissinger. Sympathetic scholars and publicists began to praise the American effort in Vietnam and argue that prompt and vigorous use of military power would have brought victory. They prepared alarmist studies of a Soviet arms buildup and of leftist revolutions. These cold warriors wanted above all to rebuild the old consensus and, in the words of Norman Podhoretz, supply the nation with "a surge of self-confident energy." The Atlantic Council's "successor-generation" project, launched in 1981, illustrates the broad and familiar themes struck by this campaign of ideological revitalization. Sounding like a cross between a boy scout and a nineteenth-century empire builder, the Council celebrated "the genius of Western civilization" and insisted that Western civic and religious values (by which it really meant Anglo-American values) represented "a universal aspiration for all of mankind." For the American people "to study and propagate these values is not to nurture chauvinism but to affirm their viability as guides to the fulfillment and satisfaction of all human societies." It warned, "To do less is to court disunity, and the disaster of capitulation to a world order which decries human freedom and dignity."[27]

The return to a Cold War mentality also had its roots in a public longing by the late 1970s for a restored sense of national pride and power and for a reaffirmation of comforting old verities, however simplistic. The prolonged and humiliating hostage episode in Iran hurt like salt rubbed into the still-open Vietnam wound. Americans eager to feel good again happily indulged in nostalgia for an earlier era, supposedly characterized by national omnipotence, clear-cut moral issues, and national unity. Nationwide polls make clear that the public vibrated sympathetically to the strong nationalist chords struck by the Reagan team. Four out of five Americans in mid-1981 believed that the United States had as ever a "special" role to play in the world and over half thought that the "best times" for the nation were yet to come. A willingness to make international commitments was on the rise, rearmament was in vogue, and that old bogey, isolationism, was out of favor by a two-to-one margin.[28] An American public was enjoying the nationalist glow from this rekindled ideological fire and for the moment at least remained tolerant of its costs and dangerous consequences.

★ ★ ★

The dictates of the American foreign-policy ideology have from time to time been challenged, defied, or finessed but not dislodged. Eisenhower's concern with controlling the price of the Cold War, Franklin Roosevelt's idea of a four-power consortium, and Theodore Roosevelt's restrained Asian policy all to some extent ran counter to the fundamental impulses of U.S. foreign policy. None was sustained by the succeeding administration. That foreign-policy ideology is not easily shaken off even today, as its partial influence on the Nixon administration and its resurgence under Carter and Reagan make clear. The power of old ideas has carried Washington back to the Cold War, and the public has cheerfully followed, despite the memory of the costs of intervention in Vietnam, despite the horrible specter of nuclear war, despite budget deficits and erosion of domestic programs.

This resurgence is no aberration. Though it can to some extent be explained in terms of a peculiar concatenation of domestic and international developments, it cannot be understood apart from the powerful grip that the old foreign-policy ideology continues to exercise on the policy elite and the public alike. The attitudes carried forward by successive generations, and still an important part of our intellectual baggage, account for much of the perplexity we face as we try to manage a complex and often recalcitrant world. Critics of a revived Cold War policy, preoccupied with its consequences, have underestimated the power and durability of an ideology with its roots deep in our political culture. To recognize the continuity and vitality of ideology is to take a major step toward confronting the formidable difficulties involved in effecting the policy reforms that those critics have championed.

Much of the power that foreign-policy ideology retains—as well as much of the difficulty reformers will encounter in combatting it—can be traced to the intimate connection between that ideology and American nationalism. Core foreign-policy ideas emerged and gained focus in the context of a prolonged struggle to identify and promote a single, coherent notion of American purpose and character. Viewed in this light those ideas are expressions of a civic religion formulated to hold an ethnically, racially, regionally, and religiously diverse country together.

The particular tenets that came to define the nationalists' faith reveal the hands of its self-appointed high priests. A narrowly based elite, initially white male property holders who could vote and hold office, succeeded in defining American nationality in their own image and in correspondence with their own self-interest. Whites would dominate those with darker skins; the political regime would promote economic growth and secure property; and Anglo values would prevail over divergent ethnic preferences. These dominant propositions drove competing ideas and nonconforming groups to the fringes of national life. Egalitarian values were carefully neutralized, and recurrent red scares intimidated and isolated the left. Nativist movements worked to exclude "undesirable" immigrants, while the public schools proselytized those foreigners who stayed. Indians were moved onto reservations, and blacks were shackled with social restrictions.

With the passage of time, the dominant foreign-policy ideology came to stand in a reciprocal relationship to nationalism. While the core ideas of that policy originally grew out of an ascendant nationalism, the implementation of those ideas as the United States became stronger served, in turn, to validate and further consolidate the preexisting conception of nationhood. Twentieth-century American policy has largely functioned in this latter role. No longer the battleground over which issues of nationality were once fought, American foreign policy in its days of greater global assertion has in the main served to affirm the received definition of nationality, to override divisions at home, and to proclaim American virtue and destiny.

Domestic trends over the last century have accentuated this nationalist function of foreign policy. In contrast to domestic issues, which have an inherent tendency to be divisive, foreign policy has the potential to promote solidarity in the face of a common external problem or danger. As politics at home has become increasingly dominated by the seemingly petty, at times even sordid, squabbling among competing interest groups, foreign affairs has retained a nobility and grandeur appropriate for the expression of national purpose. Consequently, a single-minded foreign policy has provided a symbolic counterweight to a pluralistic domestic political system that, in the exasperated words of one recent president, seems to involve nothing more than "handing out goodies."[29] Moreover, foreign-policy ideas have offered a sense of continuity for a nation apparently in constant flux, a steady set of reference points for nationalists hard pressed to find a solid, unchanging, inspiring core of Americanism at home. Little wonder, then, that the enunciation of a nationalist foreign policy has proven irresistible to leaders wishing to rally the electorate while simultaneously appearing to stand "above politics."

The symbiotic relationship between American foreign-policy ideology and nationalism is not unique. Nor should it be surprising. By asserting broad propositions about man and society, a nation's self-conception provides the intellectual underpinnings—the guiding assumptions and concerns—for foreign policy and may even in crucial respects dictate its terms. By defining what the nation is about and how it relates to the world, it orients thinking, sets conceptual bounds that make some solutions to problems more obvious and appealing than others, and in general reduces the complexities of the international environment to manageable terms. It thus serves as an indispensable safeguard against those two threats to policymaking: immobility and indecision.

The tendency for policy to assimilate nationalist ideas and then to deal with the world in terms of those ideas is by no means a monopoly of Americans. Indeed, it is a commonplace, perhaps even universal, phenomenon in international relations. The parallels between the late nineteenth-century British conception of imperial mission and the American views treated in this volume are so obvious as to need no elaboration. Even states to which the United States is not usually compared have embraced policies shaped by a nationalist outlook on those fundamental concerns about national destiny, racial standing, and revolutionary change that American nationalists also addressed. In Germany National Socialists promoted a conception of special national destiny suffused with preoccupations with racial purity and revolutionary perils. Japanese nationalists pursued a foreign policy in the 1930s guided by their own formulations on these very same, seemingly ubiquitous, concerns.[30]

The impulse to deny our own deeply nationalist ideological outlook and, even more, to fail to see the parallels with other nationalisms can itself be traced to one of the more pronounced features of American nationalism itself: its strong millennial strain. That strain has cast and kept the nation in the role of a redeemer bearing an extraordinary obligation to all humanity. Thomas Paine, in placing within the grasp of Americans the prospect of creating the world anew, and John Adams, in making the United States no ordinary nation but one "destined in future history to form the brightest or the blackest page," gave voice to this view that was to prevail in nationalist thinking.[31]

Americans increasingly understood their redemptive role in active, missionary terms rather than merely passive and exemplary ones. They were saviors with a duty to reach out to enslaved and backward peoples. By the early twentieth century Wilson was not alone in seeing the national duty in terms of creating a just international order, altogether new and morally su-

perior to the corrupt system it would displace. The dream of global renovation, sustained by the time-tested jeremiad and appropriately adorned by
occasional references to Paine, continued to move twentieth-century Americans. Their duty was clear. Mankind groaning in bondage cried for liberation.
The forces of evil were on the march. World peace hung in the balance.
Time for action was short.

A foreign policy whose costs are high yet whose guiding ideas are intertwined with American nationalism confronts us with the contemporary dilemma that the critics have thus far played down. How do we reconcile our
sense of nationhood with an enlightened foreign policy? We are thrust toward
one horn of the dilemma if we take as our first principle that nationalism is
a force for ill, so pernicious in its effects on humanity that a sane policy
must work to shake free of its influence. Thorstein Veblen spoke eloquently
for those who take this first position. "Born in iniquity and conceived in
sin, the spirit of nationalism has never ceased to bend human institutions to
the service of dissension and distress. In its material effects it is altogether
the most sinister as well as the most imbecile of all institutional encumbrances
that have come down out of the old order."[32] A foreign policy no longer
chained to our current tribal misconceptions and vaulting ambition might
well be a better policy. However—and this is the crux of the matter—it
would also be policy without any supporting ideological base. Such a policy
might be prone to intellectual incoherence, and it would certainly be politically vulnerable.

A more positive appraisal of nationalism carries us toward the other horn
of the reformer's dilemma. If we accept the need for a prudent accommodation with nationalism, a force if not for good then at least one so pervasive
that we cannot hope to wrench policy free from its grip, then we may decide
to leave foreign policy and nationalism in their existing symbiotic relationship. But—and here is the difficulty on this other side of the argument—we
shall have to continue to pay a heavy price in our dealings with the world.
We shall have to reconcile ourselves to an open-ended rivalry with the Soviet
Union, ostensibly over the ultimate fate of mankind, an anxious if not un-
comprehending relationship with cultures markedly different from our own,
and a misplaced fear of revolutionary change bordering on paranoia.

There may be a way around the dilemma created by a nationalist foreign
policy that imposes unacceptably high costs yet offers an indispensable element of intellectual coherence and popular appeal. That way may be found
by reversing the preoccupations of the critics discussed in chapter 1. Those
critics advocate a reformed and thereby more restrained policy and downplay
the nationalist roots of policy. In doing so, they treat the symptoms rather

than the disease. This approach may demonstrate good tactical sense, but in the long term it may be self-defeating, for it will leave available a potent source of inspiration and support for the old policy that diehard cold warriors can continue to tap. Why not escape this impasse by reversing the critics' priorities? Why not, in other words, first work out a fresh approach to the nationalist roots of foreign policy and leave policy itself for later attention? Though studded with difficulties, this alternative at least deserves consideration.

Refashioning the nationalist base so that it will support a new, more prudent and restrained American policy would require a twin effort. The less daunting half of that effort would involve cross-cultural education. By exposing Americans to the yawning gap between our own national experience and ideals and those of most of the other inhabitants of the globe, we might curb the arrogant and ethnocentric impulses evident in our long-standing views on international affairs. While it must be conceded that exposure to other cultures might stimulate an ugly intolerance rather than greater empathy or understanding, that risk is easy to accept when the alternative is to acquiesce in the current state of popular ignorance about the world. A more cosmopolitan view might help dampen our nationalist fervor and promote tolerance for ways of life markedly different from our own. An America alive both to the universal quest for community, security, and purpose and to the many different roads others might take in pursuit of these goals might feel more at ease in the world and with itself.[33]

Education thus offers one powerful antidote to the long-prevalent core ideas of U.S. policy. American values, especially the American conception of liberty, do not export as well as we would like to think. It is time Americans made this discovery and accepted the limits of our power to shape other societies, time we pondered the contradiction we have long perpetrated by seeking to impose our conception of self-determination and development on peoples with aspirations quite different from our own. Moreover, a deeper appreciation of the diversity and worth of other cultures should help displace American pretensions to superiority and belief in a cultural hierarchy, whether cast covertly in racial terms or in the blander language of progress and development. Less certain in our superiority, we may more effectively resist the impulse to impose solutions on others or even to assume that solutions are within our grasp. Less often committed to foredoomed enterprises abroad, we shall less often need to vent our frustration and humiliation in scapegoating others, witch-hunting among ourselves, or inventing international conspiracies. Finally, a better understanding of both the conditions that give rise to revolutions and the underlying aspirations revolutions respond to may defuse our fears. Revolutions, we shall discover on closer examination, are invariably complex and often powerful, making it difficult for outsiders either to guide or block them. We try at our own peril.

A more international education might also act as a solvent on those notions that have reinforced foreign-policy ideology in the mid-twentieth century. Geopolitics, development theory, and the "lessons of the past" have, in their separate ways, embodied simplistic assumptions that have accentuated and compounded the defects of the older core ideas. A close examination of the history of international relations will expose the lessons of the past peddled by cold warriors as dubious special pleading. Geopolitics, that other plaything of cold warriors, offers a vision of the world that is conceptually crude and bereft of cultural insights and hence is a dangerous influence on policy. A more aware public may recognize that these two poor nags deserve to be put out to pasture right away, after long years of overwork in the harness of Cold War policy.

If education can serve on one side as a check on the old foreign-policy ideology and its recent accretions, republicanism offers a source of inspiration for the other, more formidable task of creating a base of support for a new orientation in foreign policy. The crucial step here involves resuscitating a strain of republican thinking strong early in American history but since the late nineteenth century fallen into eclipse, ignored or rejected for its insistence on defining American greatness in terms of perfecting liberty at home rather than promoting it abroad.

Central to any new republicanism would have to be the notion that American greatness should be measured against domestic conditions. The question always to ask is how free Americans are and how closely their welfare is attended to. In relation to the world, republicanism places the United States in the role of a model, not a molder. By better arranging our own affairs Americans can serve as an inspiration to others to win and preserve freedom. Not all nations will respond, and among those who do some will lack the resolve or internal circumstances essential to success. Americans cannot be indifferent witnesses to the fate of freedom abroad, but neither can we impose liberty without doing harm to ourselves and without violating the right of others to make their own choices, whether for good or ill.

Any proponent of this new republicanism would have to follow the example of earlier republican critics in their instinctive wariness toward foreign political entanglements. Rivalry with great powers and policing small ones damage domestic life by directing emotional and material resources abroad, and they simultaneously introduce the corrosive forces of militarism, concentrated power, and self-seeking factionalism. Republics, once locked into foreign engagements, inevitably degenerate into empires and lose the liberty that had once been their prize. John Quincy Adams eloquently stressed the limits historical experience set for a republican foreign policy. While proclaiming the cause of freedom and cheering on those who struggled for it, America should not go roaming overseas "in search of monsters to destroy." His warning against the United States violating that rule still deserves a respectful hearing.

> By once enlisting under other banners than her own, were they even the banners of foreign independence, she would involve herself beyond the power of extrication, in all the wars of interest and intrigue, of individual avarice, envy, and ambition, which assume the colors and usurp the standard of freedom. The fundamental maxims of her policy would insensibly change from *liberty to force.* . . . She might become the dictatress of the world. She would be no longer the ruler of her own spirit.[34]

Much in our recent experience bears out the insights of the early republicans and the repeated warnings of their disciples as they fought unsuccessfully against an activist foreign policy. Abroad the United States has assumed a position of imperial dimensions. There is no other adjective to apply to a nation that has come to hold substantial control over the fate of a great number of other nations. As with any empire, our intentions are benevolent; our interests are far-flung and interdependent; and our mechanisms of control are as diverse as the nations that we have brought within our sway. One student of the Roman Empire has written of it thus:

> There was no corner of the known world where some interest was not alleged to be in danger or under actual attack. If the interests were not Roman, they were those of Rome's allies; and if Rome had no allies, then allies would be invented. When it was utterly impossible to contrive such an interest—why, then it was the national honor that had been insulted. . . . Rome was always being attacked by evil-minded neighbors. . . .[35]

It is easy to recognize in this portrait more than a faint resemblance of ourselves.

Americans have long fancied themselves unique on precisely this point, that other, less enlightened nations might embrace the goals and tools of empire, but not the United States. To accept the republican contention that we have evolved into precisely what we thought we were the antithesis of should arm us with a degree of historical perspective. Only thus armed can we hope to reverse the drift from our early national vision and undo the serious self-deception we have, in the process, worked on ourselves.

Pericles, addressing downhearted Athenians in the midst of the Peloponnesian War, observed, "You cannot decline the burdens of empire and still expect to share its honors."[36] Americans still stalking greatness would do well to ponder the converse: with the glories of empire come its costs. Those doleful symptoms of empire anticipated by republicans are evident in the rise of an imperial presidency; the economic distortions, drains, and long-term indebtedness associated with preparing for and fighting our wars; the rise of bureaucratic and industrial fiefdoms resistant to policy change and popular control; the encroachment on civil liberties; and the increase in government secrecy. Though the proponents of ideological assertiveness have insisted on the compatibility of liberty with the "national security policies" they have advocated, the republican critics have proven the better prophets. Our experiment in freedom is indeed at odds with an activist, imperial foreign policy. We may choose to perfect liberty at home at the expense of dominion abroad or pursue dominion at the price of steadily eroding the foundations of liberty at home. We cannot do both.[37]

Republicanism is easy to dismiss as an antique curiosity, too much of a political anachronism to serve as an ideological basis for policy renovation. To be sure, its ideals were eclipsed by the economic and technological forces that spawned powerful large-scale institutions, especially the modern cor-poration and the federal bureaucracy. These institutions will doubtless remain potent forces, and with them the atomizing, depersonalizing, and alienating influences that are inimical to a republican spirit will continue to flourish. Yet republicanism is far from dead. Its themes still sound disparately in American politics.

If republicanism is to sustain a new foreign policy, those themes that retain a residual appeal must be brought together in social and political programs devoted to creating those conditions of rough social equality and political community that republicans of a Jeffersonian persuasion have long linked to liberty. The republican ideal of an informed and public-spirited citizenry possessed of significant influence over both the fate of the republic and their lives can be realized only if popular political participation is rescued from the depths to which it has now fallen, whether measured by the American past or by current voter turnout in other major industrial democracies.[38] Important steps toward that goal might include a renewed stress on the obligations of citizenship, a more open path to high office for those without personal wealth or large campaign chests, and an emphasis on increased government accountability and openness, without which public debate is rendered irrelevant and policymaking is left an elite preserve.

A republican revival would have to diminish the marked inequalities in the United States. Those inequalities are determined—our Horatio Alger ideals to the contrary—not just by luck or hard work and ability but also by the accident of birth. To a wildly disproportionate degree, those who exercise political power as well as enjoy wealth, leisure, good education, and quality health care have parents who were themselves influential, moneyed, leisured, well educated, and healthy.[39] Steps to create greater equality of individual opportunity and welfare are essential to the realization of a new American republic where life's chances, and concomitantly the political process, are not stacked heavily against the poor and powerless (today as in the past disproportionately people of color, women, and children) and in favor of the wealthy and powerful (now as before chiefly white males of "good" background).

A foreign policy informed by republican values would not be a vehicle for the pursuit of national greatness abroad but a buffer against outside shocks and threats to our pursuit of greatness at home. It would have to be guided above all by the recognition that Americans can work toward a just, equitable society only by restraining the impulse toward global reform. A world that is resistant to our ministrations is also infinitely capable of consuming resources desperately needed at home.

Fashioning a new policy will prove a formidable task. It will mean tailoring our list of regional commitments and expensive client states to conform to demonstrable security needs.[40] It will mean accepting the limits of our ability as a nation to transform a world prone to violence, chaos, exploitation, brutality, and oppression. It will mean breaking out of the vicious cycle of suspicion with the Soviet Union and, under the compelling threat of mutual annihilation, finding ground for mutual accommodation. It will mean perhaps above all fashioning a fresh conceptual basis, a new ideology, for American foreign policy that is both acceptable to the public and comprehensible to our allies. It will *not* mean—and this deserves emphasis—the triumph of isolationism, if that term is taken to mean a refusal to take an interest in the workings of the wider world. Even though embarked on a more prudent international course, the United States will still have political friends and foes, will continue as an important player in the global economy, and will remain in the mainstream of the transnational flow of technology, ideas, and people.

Those who embrace this third, republican alternative are launched on an experiment whose success is far from assured and indeed whose consequences, it must in candor be admitted, cannot be entirely or clearly foreseen. Once again we would do well to listen to Pericles, who warned his countrymen as they wavered on the edge of retreat from empire, "to recede is no longer possible. . . . For what you hold is, to speak somewhat plainly, a tyranny; to take it perhaps was wrong, but to let it go is unsafe.''[41] Retreat to safer ground will not be easy. Even a narrowed definition of American policy objectives will leave ample room for disagreement from moment to moment over the course of action that best serves American interests. A fresh approach can supply a general policy orientation biased toward a calculated restraint, but it cannot supply, any more than the old verities could, detailed solutions to a host of ever-present problems. The collision of opinion that is inescapably a part of making policy will be compounded by the need, initially at least, to reappraise inherited commitments. In some cases, unwanted or unjustified responsibilities will have to be balanced against the possible harm extrication may do to the consensus at home or to the countries directly involved.

Perhaps the most troublesome single requirement imposed by a new foreign-policy ideology is that it asks Americans to sustain a dual standard, or double vision, that distinguishes between domestic and foreign affairs. Though it would not force us to renounce liberty as a universal good, it would limit our active promotion of liberty to our own domestic sphere and have us accept as appropriate to some, perhaps even most, other societies organizing principles that diverge from our own norms. Can Americans behave as true believers at home and agnostics before the world? By putting in question the depth of our commitment to liberty for all people, will we weaken the faith in liberty at home and be left feeling diminished and isolated as a nation?

Tampering with American nationalism and even partially challenging the sense of exceptionalism that has inspired it carries real risks. The entire process of readjustment will doubtless prove prolonged and complicated. Each step toward a new, more modest national self-conception will involve a good deal of debate and occasional perplexity. But the proponents of such a course may be buoyed by the knowledge that they will be bringing American goals in closer alignment with American resources, securing a sounder foundation of popular support, and in both these ways contributing signally to the building of a more democratic and humane American society. We may cease to aspire to global mastery but we may gain greater mastery over our own national life.

Essay on the
Historical
Literature

The works cited in the notes and discussed in this essay constitute but a sampling of a foreign relations literature that has grown voluminously over the last several decades. Thanks to a run of new publications, anyone wishing to consult that literature can now turn to a marvellously helpful set of historiographical and bibliographical guides. The three most important contributions all appeared in 1983, making that something of a vintage year. They are Richard D. Burns, ed., *Guide to American Foreign Relations since 1700*; Jerald A. Combs, *American Diplomatic History: Two Centuries of Changing Interpretations*; and Warren I. Cohen, ed., *New Frontiers in American–East Asian Relations: Essays Presented to Dorothy Borg*. Combs can be supplemented by Gerald K. Haines and J. Samuel Walker, eds., *American Foreign Relations: A Historiographical Review* (1981). Cohen brings up to date an especially active subfield first surveyed in Ernest R. May and James C. Thomson, Jr., eds., *American–East Asian Relations: A Survey* (1972). Finally, Alexander DeConde, ed., *Encyclopedia of American Foreign Policy* (3 vols., 1978), deserves mention as a useful introduction to key themes, issues, and concepts.

Chapter 1: Coming to Terms with Ideology

George F. Kennan's *American Diplomacy, 1900–1950* (1951) and William Appleman Williams' *The Tragedy of American Diplomacy* (1959) still today command the interpretive heights of U.S. foreign relations—by default if for no other reason. Asked to recommend a single brief general synthesis, most diplomatic historians would be hard pressed to name an acceptable alternative. Like any work offering a sweeping and boldly drawn perspective on the historical landscape, each has had its admirers and imitators as well as its detractors.

Kennan's principal champion within the historical profession has been

John Lewis Gaddis. His books on the Cold War and his essays (foremost a July 1977 contribution to the journal *Foreign Affairs*) celebrate Kennan's "realistic" insights in the realm of policy. Kennan's impact as a historian, though equally significant and widely recognized, has yet to be carefully scrutinized. A generation of diplomatic historians whose works dominated the 1950s and 1960s borrowed heavily from Kennan and his fellow realist, Hans J. Morgenthau. The successor generation in contrast has on the whole been less taken by "realism." Thomas Paterson's sketch of Kennan in Frank Merli and Theodore Wilson, eds., *The Makers of American Diplomacy* (1974), vol. 2; Jonathan Knight, "George Frost Kennan and the Study of American Foreign Policy," *Western Political Quarterly*, 20 (March 1967); Barton Gellman, *Contending with Kennan: Toward a Philosophy of American Power* (1984), all reflect this latter-day tendency to question Kennan's acumen, clarity, and consistency, whether as policymaker, historian, or political philosopher. Any interested reader would be well advised to give Kennan the last word by turning to *American Diplomacy*, his two-volume memoir (1967, 1972), where his talents as a sensitive observer are well framed, and his critique in *The Cloud of Danger* (1977) and *The Nuclear Delusion* (1982) of the Cold War policy he had earlier helped articulate.

A good deal of general commentary and interpretation has recently flowed from the pen of William Appleman Williams, in particular *The Roots of Modern American Empire* (1969), *History as a Way of Learning* (1973), and *Empire as a Way of Life* (1980). *Tragedy*, however, remains his seminal work. It supplied the intellectual capital on which much of Williams' later efforts would draw as well as the rallying point for a group of like-minded historians, many trained at the University of Wisconsin by Williams or his mentor, Fred Harvey Harrington. This group, which includes Walter La-Feber, Lloyd Gardner, and Robert Freeman Smith, has been variously labeled "New Left revisionists," "new economic determinists," or simply "the Wisconsin school." No more monolithic than the realists, members of this group often share little more than a common belief that economic interests make the world go round and that foreign relations is no exception to the rule.

Mainstream academic historians have by and large been unpersuaded by these propositions and critical of Williams' logic and use of evidence, sometimes intemperately so—as in Robert J. Maddox, *The New Left and the Origins of the Cold War* (1973). The best overall appraisals are Robert Tucker, *The Radical Left and American Foreign Policy* (1971); J. A. Thompson, "William Appleman Williams and the 'American Empire,' " *Journal of American Studies*, 7 (April 1973); and Bradford Perkins, "The Tragedy of American Diplomacy: Twenty-five Years After,'' *Reviews in American History*, 12 (March 1984). Historians on the left, such as Eugene Genovese in ''William Appleman Williams on Marx and America,'' *Studies on the Left*, 6 (Jan.–Feb. 1966), have also been unhappy with Williams, in their case for his lack of rigor in employing Marxist terminology and theoretical constructs.

My own interests in ideology as a way of moving beyond realism and the open-door interpretation have led me at least part way up a mountain of literature shrouded for the most part in a fog of abstraction. Unusually sensible and suggestive from a historian's vantage point are the reflections by Clifford Geertz in ''Ideology as a Cultural System,'' in David E. Apter, ed., *Ideology and Discontent* (1964); Sidney Verba's discussion of ''Comparative Political Culture,'' in Lucian W. Pye and Verba, eds., *Political Culture and Political Development* (1965), especially pp. 512–17; the essay in definition by Willard A. Mullins, ''On the Concept of Ideology in Political Science,'' *American Political Science Review*, 66 (June 1972); Raymond Williams' sophisticated reinterpretation of ''Base and Superstructure in Marxist Cultural Theory'' included in his *Problems in Materialism and Culture* (1980); and T. J. Jackson Lears' thoughtful exploration of ''The Concept of Cultural Hegemony: Problems and Possibilities,'' *American Historical Review*, 90 (June 1985).

The notion of ideology rooted in culture is hardly a new one for historians, as is made clear by Ronald G. Walters, ''Signs of the Times: Clifford Geertz and the Historians,'' *Social Research*, 47 (Autumn 1980), and Robert F. Berkhofer, Jr., ''Clio and the Culture Concept: Some Impressions of a Changing Relationship in American Historiography,'' *Social Science Quarterly*, 53 (Sept. 1972). Robert Kelley's *The Cultural Pattern in American Politics: The First Century* (1979) and his ''Ideology and Political Culture from Jefferson to Nixon,'' *American Historical Review*, 82 (June 1977), are adventuresome applications of the cultural approach to ideology that every diplomatic historian could read with profit.

Any exploration of the nationalist context in which foreign-policy ideology took shape has a large literature on which to draw. Geoff Eley, ''Nationalism and Social History, *Social History*, 6 (Jan. 1981), is an especially helpful attempt to synthesize two classic approaches—one, championed by Hans Kohn and later Elie Kedourie, stressing the development and diffusion of nationalist ideas; the other, pioneered by Karl Deutsch, emphasizing the socioeconomic developments contributing to the rise of national consciousness. Other helpful accounts are John Breuilly, *Nationalism and the State* (1982), especially the chapter on ''The Sources and Forms of Nationalist

Ideology"; Anthony D. Smith, *Theories of Nationalism*, 2d ed. (1983); Smith, *Nationalism in the Twentieth Century* (1979); and K. R. Minogue, *Nationalism* (1967).

Chapter 2: Visions of National Greatness

The Jefferson-Hamilton contest inaugurating the struggle over the future of American foreign policy has attracted a remarkable succession of realist historians, each championing the superior insights of one or the other of the two protagonists. The latest in that line is Jerald Combs in *The Jay Treaty: Political Battleground of the Founding Fathers* (1970). He sides with Hamilton and the Federalists. Cecelia M. Kenyon, "Alexander Hamilton: Rousseau of the Right," *Political Science Quarterly*, 73 (June 1958), and Felix Gilbert's *To the Farewell Address: Ideas of Early American Foreign Policy* (1961) are important earlier works that evaluate the basic principles of early American foreign policymakers in the familiar terms of realism and idealism.

Notable New Left works on this period stress not conflict but a fundamental consensus on the goal of expansion, with Hamilton oriented toward the sea and Jefferson the continent. See for example the essays by William Appleman Williams in *William and Mary Quarterly*, 3d series, vol. 15 (Oct. 1958), and by Walter LaFeber in Williams, ed., *From Colony to Empire* (1972), as well as Richard W. Van Alstyne's general interpretation, *The Rising American Empire* (1960).

Neither interpretive approach deals adequately with the republican assumptions influencing policy. A small army of intellectual historians mobilized by Bernard Bailyn's *The Ideological Origins of the American Revolution* (1967) has devoted itself to pinning down republicanism and exploring the context in which it operated. Robert E. Shalhope proves an excellent guide in his two surveys of the resulting literature in *William and Mary Quarterly*, 3d series, vol. 29 (Jan. 1972) and vol. 39 (April 1982). The most impressive attempts so far to relate republicanism and foreign policy are in Gerald Stourzh, *Alexander Hamilton and the Idea of Republican Government* (1970), chaps. 4 and 5; Drew R. McCoy, *The Elusive Republic: Political Economy in Jeffersonian America* (1980); Lance Banning, *The Jeffersonian Persuasion: Evolution of a Party Ideology* (1978); and Roger H. Brown, *The Republic in Peril: 1812* (1964).

The study of the 1840s, the period of the second major collision over the aims of U.S. foreign policy, was the life work of Frederick Merk. *Mission and Manifest Destiny* (1963), his major study, distinguishes between a benign sense of national mission and the harmful influence of an aggressive expansionism that led the nation momentarily astray, first in 1846 and again in

1899. Merk's argument constitutes in effect an oblique attack on Albert K. Weinberg's massive compendium, *Manifest Destiny* (1935), which remains important for its insistence on treating even the more pugnacious forms of expansionism as genuine, if unfortunate, expressions of American nationalism. Merk also seems to endorse George Kennan's contention that an emotional public is one of the chief threats to a sound U.S. foreign policy. Merk has, not surprisingly, set Polk's critics in a favorable light in his contribution to *Dissent in Three American Wars* (1970).

Merk's treatment of antebellum expansionists should be supplemented by *Empire on the Pacific: A Study in American Continental Expansion* (1955) by Norman Graebner, a realist whose interpretation here incongruously anticipates the New Left; by Charles Sellers' multivolume biography of Polk (1957–   ), which has yet to round out the presidential years; by Robert V. Remini's three-volume biography of Andrew Jackson (1977–84); by David M. Pletcher, *The Diplomacy of Annexation: Texas, Oregon, and the Mexican War* (1973); by Thomas R. Hietala, *Manifest Design: Anxious Aggrandizement in Late Jacksonian America* (1985), a fresh look at the major strands of expansionist thought; and by Robert E. May, *The Southern Dream of a Caribbean Empire, 1854–1861* (1973), on the cooling effect sectional conflict had on expansionist policy. On the opponents of expansion the most recent study is by John H. Schroeder, *Mr. Polk's War: American Opposition and Dissent, 1846–1848* (1973). Nationalist thought for this period is described in broad terms by Fred Somkin, *Unquiet Eagle: Memory and Desire in the Idea of American Freedom, 1815–1860* (1967); Major L. Wilson, *Space, Time and Freedom: The Quest for Nationality and the Irrepressible Conflict, 1815–1861* (1974); and Rush Welter, *The Mind of America, 1820–1860* (1975).

The 1890s have been exhaustively examined, as befits a period long and widely regarded as a watershed. McKinley and his supporters are seen in an unflattering realist perspective in Ernest May, *Imperial Democracy: The Emergence of America as a Great Power* (1961), and Richard Hofstadter, "Manifest Destiny and the Philippines," in his *The Paranoid Style in American Politics* (1966). Though not usually associated with the realist school, Hofstadter in this well-known essay (published in its original form in 1952) does put opportunistic politicians and an emotional public at the center of the historical stage. Walter LaFeber, *The New Empire: An Interpretation of American Expansion, 1860–1898* (1963), and to a lesser extent David Healy, *US Expansionism: The Imperialist Urge in the 1890s* (1970), represent the revisionist perspective. These last two authors credit expansionists with more insight and adroitness than do their realist detractors. LaFeber can be read as an elaboration of Williams' argument in *The Tragedy of American Diplomacy* and as a rebuttal to Julius W. Pratt, *Expansionists of 1898: The Acquisition of Hawaii and the Spanish Islands* (1936), itself an assault on an economic interpretation. Robert L. Beisner's *From the Old Diplomacy to the New, 1865–1900*, 2d rev. ed. (1986), is a helpful and accessible introduction to the scholarly controversies over this era.

McKinley's critics lost the policy debate but not the interest of historians. Fred Harvey Harrington's early sketch of "The Anti-Imperialist Movement in the United States, 1898–1900," *Mississippi Valley Historical Review*, 22 (Sept. 1935), remains a serviceable introduction. It has, however, been greatly amplified by a flurry of research prompted by a search for a usable past inspired by the Vietnam War. Robert L. Beisner, *Twelve Against Empire: The Anti-Imperialists, 1898–1900* (1968), was the first (and still is the most engaging) account in the resulting string of publications. Other items include Frank Freidel's essay in *Dissent in Three American Wars* (1970); E. Berkeley Tompkins, *Anti-Imperialism in the United States: The Great Debate, 1890–1920* (1970); Daniel B. Schirmer, *Republic or Empire: American Resistance to the Philippine War* (1972); Richard E. Welch, Jr., *Response to Imperialism: The United States and the Philippine-American War, 1899–1902* (1979); and Thomas J. Osborne, *"Empire Can Wait": American Opposition to Hawaiian Annexation, 1893–1898* (1981). John W. Rollins, "The Anti-Imperialists and Twentieth Century American Foreign Policy," *Studies on the Left*, 3 (1962), is noteworthy as an early example of the tendency on the part of New Left historians to look for a consensus on expansion in the 1890s and to minimize the importance of the contemporary debate over Hawaii and the Philippines.

Chapter 3: The Hierarchy of Race

Perhaps no topic in recent decades has engrossed historians of the United States more than race and ethnicity. The phenomenon has been broken down and examined from a dizzying variety of perspectives. The most useful overview for the purposes of this study is Ruth Miller Elson's *Guardians of Tradition: American Schoolbooks of the Nineteenth Century* (1964), based on a thousand of the most popular texts used in the first eight years of schooling. While it does not reveal what the common man thought about race, this work does indicate what he was told at a formative age to believe— and to recite as an aid to memory. Other broad studies include Thomas F. Gossett, *Race: The History of an Idea in America* (1963); Gary B. Nash and Richard Weiss, eds., *The Great Fear: Race in the American Mind* (1970); George Sinkler, *The Racial Attitudes of American Presidents from Abraham*

Lincoln to Theodore Roosevelt (1971); Rubin F. Weston, *Racism in U.S. Imperialism: The Influence of Racial Assumptions on American Foreign Policy, 1893–1946* (1972); Ronald T. Takaki, *Iron Cages: Race and Culture in Nineteenth-Century America* (1979); and Robert W. Rydell, *All the World's a Fair: Visions of Empire at American International Expositions, 1876–1916* (1984). Stimulating general discussions that help set the American case in perspective are to be found in David B. Davis, *The Problem of Slavery in Western Culture* (1966), chaps. 2 and 15; Pierre van den Berghe, *Race and Racism: A Comparative Perspective* (1967); and Dante A. Puzzo, "Racism and the Western Tradition," *Journal of the History of Ideas*, 25 (Oct.–Dec. 1964).

Blacks and Indians, the two peoples of color drawn most deeply into American life and mythology, have attracted attention commensurate with their prominence. Good starting points for understanding how thinking on race became a central strand in the fabric of national life are Winthrop D. Jordan, *White Over Black: American Attitudes Toward the Negro, 1550–1812* (1968); George M. Fredrickson, *The Black Image in the White Mind: The Debate on Afro-American Character and Destiny, 1817–1914* (1971); and Michael McCarthy, *Dark Continent: Africa as Seen by Americans* (1983). The woeful tale of the Indian's abasement can be followed through Henry F. Dobyns, *Native American Historical Demography: A Critical Bibliography* (1976); Roy Harvey Pearce, *The Savages of America: A Study of the Indian and the Idea of Civilization* (1953, rev. ed. 1965); Francis Jennings, *The Invasion of America: Indians, Colonialism, and the Cant of Conquest* (1975); Reginald Horsman, *Expansion and American Indian Policy, 1783–1812* (1967); Horsman, "American Indian Policy and the Origins of Manifest Destiny," *University of Birmingham Historical Journal*, vol. 11, no. 2 (1968); Bernard W. Sheehan, *Seeds of Extinction: Jeffersonian Philanthropy and the American Indian* (1973); Robert V. Remini, *Andrew Jackson and the Course of American Empire, 1767–1821* (1977); Remini, *Andrew Jackson and the Course of American Freedom, 1822–1832* (1981), chap. 15; Remini, *Andrew Jackson and the Course of American Democracy, 1833–1845* (1984), chap. 20; Ralph K. Andrist, *The Long Death: The Last Days of the Plains Indians* (1964); and Robert M. Utley, *The Indian Frontier of the American West, 1846–1890* (1984). Robert K. Berkhofer, Jr., *The White Man's Indian: Images of the American Indian from Columbus to the Present* (1978), and Brian W. Dippie, *The Vanishing American: White Attitudes and U.S. Indian Policy* (1982), are two recent entries in a growing literature on perceptions of native Americans.

The place of the Latino in American thinking can be established with some help from Arthur P. Whitaker, *The United States and the Independence of Latin America, 1800–1830* (1941); David J. Weber, " 'Scarce more than apes.' Historical Roots of Anglo American Stereotypes of Mexicans in the Border Region," in Weber, ed., *New Spain's Far Northern Frontier: Essays on Spain in the American West, 1540–1821* (1979); Raymund A. Paredes, "The Origins of Anti-Mexican Sentiment in the United States," in Ricardo Romo and Paredes, eds., *New Directions in Chicano Scholarship* (1978); Paredes, "The Mexican Image in American Travel Literature, 1831–1869," *New Mexico Historical Review*, 52 (Jan. 1977); Arnoldo De León, *They Called Them Greasers: Anglo Attitudes toward Mexicans in Texas, 1821–1900* (1983); Robert W. Johannsen, *To the Halls of the Montezumas: The Mexican War in the American Imagination* (1985); and Gerald F. Linderman, *The Mirror of War: American Society and the Spanish-American War* (1974), particularly chap. 5, which deals with images of Cubans and the Spanish.

The images and policies evoked by East Asian immigrants have been studied systematically and in depth. See in particular Stuart C. Miller, *The Unwelcome Immigrant: The American Image of the Chinese, 1785–1882* (1969); Michael H. Hunt, *The Making of a Special Relationship: The United States and China to 1914* (1983); and Roger Daniels, *The Politics of Prejudice: The Anti-Japanese Movement in California and the Struggle for Japanese Exclusion* (1962).

Anglo-Saxonism and the racial ideas that dominated the battles over territorial acquisitions in the 1890s have been treated in Reginald Horsman, *Race and Manifest Destiny: The Origins of American Racial Anglo-Saxonism* (1981); Stuart Anderson, *Race and Rapprochement: Anglo-Saxonism and Anglo-American Relations, 1895–1904* (1981); Stuart C. Miller, *"Benevolent Assimilation": The American Conquest of the Philippines, 1899–1903* (1982); James P. Shenton, "Imperialism and Racism," in Donald Sheehan and Harold C. Syrett, eds., *Essays in American Historiography* (1960); and Christopher Lasch, "The Anti-Imperialists, the Philippines and the Inequality of Man," *Journal of Southern History*, 24 (Aug. 1958). These should be supplemented by the items cited above that deal with the 1890s debate over liberty and national greatness.

Chapter 4: The Perils of Revolution

The American response to revolution is the subject of a remarkably motley collection of literature. An impressive portion of it dates back forty or more years; another substantial body appeared in a surge during the 1970s. Some of the still-relevant works deal primarily with attitudes, others emphasize policy, and yet others combine both elements in various proportions.

Works dealing with the earliest American reaction to revolution illustrate this diversity in vintage and approach. Charles D. Hazen, *Contemporary American Opinion of the French Revolution* (1897), a venerable study unabashedly neo-Federalist in tone, draws on the writings of the political elite, whereas Gary B. Nash's more recent "The American Clergy and the French Revolution," *William and Mary Quarterly*, 3d series, vol. 22 (July 1965), uses sermons as a barometer of opinion. Similarly, Charles C. Griffin's *The United States and the Disruption of the Spanish Empire, 1810–1822* (1937) and Arthur P. Whitaker's *The United States and the Independence of Latin America, 1800–1830* (1941), both political narratives based on periodicals, congressional records, and the writings of special-interest groups, contrast with Winthrop D. Jordan's *White Over Black: American Attitudes Toward the Negro, 1550–1812*, chap. 10, a 1968 study of the anxiety evoked by the rise of the Haitian republic.

Much of the seminal work on the United States and the mid-nineteenth century revolutions appeared in the 1920s and 1930s, when shockwaves from the recent plunge into European war and diplomacy sent historians off on a search for the roots of this unprecedented American entanglement in Old World affairs. The best of that earlier generation of scholarship are Edward Mead Earle, "American Interest in the Greek Cause, 1821–1827," *American Historical Review*, 33 (Oct. 1927); John G. Gazley, *American Opinion of German Unification, 1848–1871* (1926), a massive compilation covering turmoil not just in Germany but in France and Hungary as well; Eugene N. Curtis, "American Opinion of the French Nineteenth-Century Revolutions," *American Historical Review*, 29 (Jan. 1924); Elizabeth Brett White, *American Opinion of France: From Lafayette to Poincaré* (1927); and Howard R. Marraro, *American Opinion of the Unification of Italy, 1846–1861* (1932). The work on France should be supplemented by George L. Cherry, "American Metropolitan Press Reaction to the Paris Commune of 1871," *Mid-America*, 32 (Jan. 1950). Paul Constantine Pappas, *The United States and the Greek War for Independence, 1821–1828* (1985), is a slim new synthesis that confirms the main lines of earlier accounts.

Merle Curti deserves special mention as the author of two interpretive articles important to an understanding of this second revolutionary era— " 'Young America,' " *American Historical Review*, 32 (1926), and "The Impact of the Revolutions of 1848 on American Thought," *Proceedings of the American Philosophical Society*, 93 (June 1949). Curti's treatment of the Hungarian Revolution in " 'Young America' " and in a traditional diplomatic study published in 1926 in *Smith College Studies in History*, vol. 11, has been largely superseded by Donald S. Spencer, *Louis Kossuth and Young*

America: A Study of Sectionalism and Foreign Policy, 1848–1852 (1977), with its "realist" interpretive slant.

The literature on the early twentieth-century revolutions is on the whole of recent origin, though it reveals no less than the rest of the literature a wide variation in its handling of public opinion and policy. New Left historians have shown a special interest in what they interpret as a consciously and vigorously counterrevolutionary American stance. William Appleman Williams, *America Confronts a Revolutionary World: 1776–1976* (1976), a collection of his essays that develops themes familiar from his other work, comes closest to a general account. Special studies of this era with a New Left cast include Jerry Israel, *Progressivism and the Open Door: America and China, 1905–1921* (1971); N. Gordon Levin, Jr., *Woodrow Wilson and World Politics: America's Response to War and Revolution* (1968); Lloyd C. Gardner, *Wilson and Revolutions: 1913–1921* (1976); and Gardner's full-scale study, *Safe for Democracy: The Anglo-American Response to Revolution, 1913–1923* (1984).

The New Left literature should be read alongside Link's multivolume biography of Wilson (1947–   ) and James Reed's *The Missionary Mind and American East Asian Policy, 1911–1915* (1983), chap. 4. On Russia, useful studies include Arthur W. Thompson and Robert A. Hart, *The Uncertain Crusade: America and the Russian Revolution of 1905* (1970), supplemented by Filia Holtzman, "A Mission That Failed: Gor'kij in America," *Slavic and East European Journal*, 6 (Fall 1962); Peter G. Filene, *Americans and the Soviet Experiment, 1917–1933* (1967), chaps. 1 and 2; John Lewis Gaddis, *Russia, the Soviet Union, and the United States* (1978), chap. 3; and Robert K. Murray, *Red Scare: A Study of National Hysteria, 1919–1920* (1955). Eugene P. Trani, "Woodrow Wilson and the Decision to Intervene in Russia: A Reconsideration," *Journal of Modern History*, 48 (Sept. 1976), is a judicious and well-documented introduction to a long-running historical controversy.

Chapter 5: Ideology in Twentieth-Century Foreign Policy

Historians of twentieth-century foreign relations, a prolific lot, have provided considerable grist for the mill of any student of ideas. Some have traveled the path cleared by Kennan and Williams—and hence make somewhat predictable interpretive points. Others have gone their own way in examining particular policymakers or problems, putting forward results that are often fresh and helpful in establishing links to older intellectual patterns.

Students of the Roosevelt-Wilson era have led the way in the search for the intellectual roots of a foreign policy that virtually all see as related in some way to a special progressive temper or mentality. The most important of these works are N. Gordon Levin, Jr.'s study (noted above) and William E. Leuchtenburg's "Progressivism and Imperialism: The Progressive Movement and American Foreign Policy, 1898–1916," *Mississippi Valley Historical Review*, 39 (Dec. 1952). Leuchtenburg's essay gave rise to an academic cottage industry devoted to testing its claims on the domestic roots of policy and to wrestling with those two supremely slippery concepts juxtaposed in the article's title. Joseph M. Siracusa, "Progressivism, Imperialism, and the Leuchtenburg Thesis, 1952–1974," *Australian Journal of Politics and History*, 20 (Dec. 1974), is a useful guide to the ensuing discussion.

The period between the two world wars, long treated as a barren era of "isolationism," is undergoing substantial revision at the hands of corporatist historians influenced to one degree or another by Williams. Books by Michael J. Hogan (1977), Burton I. Kaufman (1974), Melvyn P. Leffler (1979), Carl P. Parrini (1969), and Joan Hoff Wilson (1971) have demonstrated how powerful interest groups, corporations and banks not least among them, worked with Washington to sustain the United States at a considerably higher level of international involvement than previously allowed by realist morality plays. This new approach is sympathetically showcased by Thomas J. McCormick, "Drift or Mastery? A Corporatist Synthesis for American Diplomatic History," *Reviews in American History*, 10 (Dec. 1982), while John Braeman offers a critical look in "The New Left and American Foreign Policy during the Age of Normalcy: A Reexamination," *Business History Review*, 62 (Spring 1983).

The argument for continuity is further strengthened by those biographies dealing with the social background and basic values of the leading interwar personalities—Henry Cabot Lodge (William C. Widenor [1980]); Charles Evans Hughes (Merlo J. Pusey [1951]); Frank B. Kellogg (L. Ethan Ellis [1962]); Calvin Coolidge (Donald R. McCoy [1967]); Herbert Hoover (Joan Hoff Wilson [1975]); Henry L. Stimson (Elting E. Morison [1960]); and Franklin D. Roosevelt (Robert Dallek [1979] and Robert A. Divine [1969]). Special studies that add to the case for ideological continuity are Douglas Little, "Antibolshevism and American Foreign Policy, 1919–1939," *American Quarterly*, 35 (Fall 1983); Hugh De Santis, *The Diplomacy of Silence: The American Foreign Service, the Soviet Union, and the Cold War, 1933–1947* (1981); Mark L. Chadwin, *The Hawks of World War II* (1968); and Robert A. Divine, *Second Chance: The Triumph of Internationalism in America during World War II* (1967). Philip H. Burch, Jr., *Elites in American History* (1980–81), vols. 2–3; G. William Domhoff, *Who Rules America?*

(1967); and Robert D. Schulzinger, *The Wise Men of Foreign Affairs: The History of the Council on Foreign Relations* (1984), are equally useful in highlighting elite predominance in foreign affairs not only during the interwar period but also well beyond.

Those who sought to check an activist policy are treated in biographies of William E. Borah (Robert J. Maddox [1969]), Charles A. Lindbergh (Wayne S. Cole [1974]), and Gerald P. Nye (Cole [1962]). These accounts should be supplemented by John Milton Cooper, Jr., *The Vanity of Power: American Isolationism and the First World War, 1914–1917* (1969); Alexander DeConde, "The South and Isolationism," *Journal of Southern History*, 24 (1958); Thomas N. Guinsburg, *The Pursuit of Isolationism in the United States Senate from Versailles to Pearl Harbor* (1982); Manfred Jonas, *Isolationism in America, 1935–1941* (1966); Cole, *America First: The Battle against Intervention, 1940–1941* (1953); Robert Griffith, "Old Progressives and the Cold War," *Journal of American History*, 66 (Sept. 1979); and Justus D. Doenecke, *Not to the Swift: The Old Isolationists in the Cold War Era* (1979).

Historians struggling to make sense of a cold war still in progress have published prodigiously over the last several decades (as will quickly become evident to anyone who consults the relevant chapters in Burns, *Guide to American Foreign Relations since 1700*). What follows here can only be a selection of some of the signal contributions to our understanding of guiding foreign-policy ideas.

Containment, easily the most studied and controverted policy conception, is set in a realist framework in John Lewis Gaddis' careful *Strategies of Containment: A Critical Appraisal of Postwar American National Security Policy* (1982). Gabriel Kolko's *The Politics of War: The World and United States Foreign Policy, 1943–1945* (1968) and Joyce and Gabriel Kolko's *The Limits of Power: The World and United States Foreign Policy, 1945– 1954* (1972), both audacious in scope, treat containment in New Left terms.

Other influential ideas closely associated with containment receive their due in Ernest R. May, *"Lessons" of the Past: The Use and Misuse of History in American Foreign Policy* (1973); Les K. Adler and Thomas G. Paterson, "Red Fascism: The Merger of Nazi Germany and Soviet Russia in the American Image of Totalitarianism, 1930's–1950's," *American Historical Review*, 75 (April 1970); and Daniel M. Smith, "Authoritarianism and American Policy Makers in Two World Wars," *Pacific Historical Review*, 43 (Aug. 1974). Geopolitics awaits a thorough treatment, though for a preliminary look see Joseph S. Roucek, "The Development of Political Geography and Geopolitics in the United States," *Australian Journal of Politics and History*, 3 (May 1958); Geoffrey J. Martin, *The Life and Thought of Isaiah Bowman* (1980); and Alan Henrikson, "The Map as an 'Idea': The Role of Cartographic Imagery during the Second World War," *American Cartographer*, 2 (April 1975).

The obvious starting point for understanding development as a theory and as a policy is Robert A. Packenham, *Liberal America and the Third World: Political Development Ideas in Foreign Aid and Social Science* (1973). It should be supplemented by Robert A. Nisbet, *Social Change and History: Aspects of the Western Theory of Development* (1969); Joseph R. Gusfield, "Tradition and Modernity: Misplaced Polarities in the Study of Social Change," *American Journal of Sociology*, 72 (Jan. 1967); Dean C. Tipps, "Modernization Theory and the Comparative Study of Societies: A Critical Perspective," *Comparative Studies in Society and History*, 15 (1973); and Aidan Foster-Carter, "From Rostow to Gunder Frank: Conflicting Paradigms in the Analysis of Underdevelopment," *World Development*, 4 (March 1976).

Chapter 6: The Contemporary Dilemma

A storm has been brewing in the last decade over the basic direction of American foreign policy, sending observers of all stripes scurrying to their typewriters. The search for the lessons of Vietnam offers a handy barometer by which to gauge the nature, intensity, and direction of the storm. Although attempts to draw lessons were underway even before the war ended, the first full dress examination did not appear until 1976. That was *The Vietnam Legacy: The War, American Society and the Future of American Foreign Policy*, edited by Anthony Lake and sponsored by the Council on Foreign Relations. It was followed the next year by W. Scott Thompson and Donaldson D. Frizzell, eds., *The Lessons of Vietnam*. The reaction against the early, predominantly disillusioned view of the Vietnam experience is evident in Guenter Lewy, *America in Vietnam* (1978), and Harry G. Summers, Jr., *On Strategy: A Critical Analysis of the Vietnam War* (1982). The most recent efforts to sort matters out are in Harrison E. Salisbury, ed., *Vietnam Reconsidered: Lessons from a War* (1984); Gabriel Kolko, *Anatomy of a War: Vietnam, the United States, and the Modern Historical Experience* (1985); Loren Baritz, *Backfire: A History of How American Culture Led Us into Vietnam and Made Us Fight the Way We Did* (1985); and John Hellman, *American Myth and the Legacy of Vietnam* (1986).

Deserving a place alongside the Vietnam literature is the wide-ranging and perceptive work by reformist critics of American policy. Prominent among them are Richard J. Barnet, Melvin Gurtov, Richard E. Feinberg, Robert A. Packenham, Earl C. Ravenal, David P. Calleo, I. M. Destler, Leslie Gelb, and Anthony Lake. (Their work is cited in the notes for chapter 1.)

Custodians of policy through the recent stormy period have been quick to justify themselves once out of office. The Nixon and Kissinger memoirs (1978 and 1979–82 respectively) were soon followed by those of Ford (1979), Carter (1982), Vance (1983), and Brzezinski (1983). Haig (1984) has already provided the first glimpses into the Reagan presidency, and no doubt others liberated by the end of the first term will want to tell their tales too. These memoirs, whatever their inherent dangers as exercises in concealment and special pleading, will remain essential, along with the policymakers' public statements, until a fuller historical record becomes available.

The problems of recent policy derive in large measure from the collapse of the Cold War consensus and misperception of revolutionary change. The former is well handled by John E. Mueller, *War, Presidents and Public Opinion* (1973), which examines Vietnam and Korea, and Ole R. Holsti and James N. Rosenau, *American Leadership in World Affairs: Vietnam and the Breakdown of Consensus* (1984). There is a large literature on the latter topic. I have found particularly instructive Bruce Cumings, "American Policy and Korean Liberation," in Frank Baldwin, ed., *Without Parallel: The American-Korean Relationship Since 1945* (1974); James Peck, "The Roots of Rhetoric: The Professional Ideology of America's China Watchers," in Ed Friedman and Mark Selden, eds., *America's Asia* (1971); David McLean, "American Nationalism, the China Myth, and the Truman Doctrine: The Question of Accommodation with Peking, 1949–50," *Diplomatic History*, 10 (Winter 1986); Jeffrey Race, *War Comes to Long An: Revolutionary Conflict in a Vietnamese Province* (1972); Richard H. Immerman, *The CIA in Guatemala: The Foreign Policy of Intervention* (1982); Richard E. Welch, Jr., *Response to Revolution: The United States and the Cuban Revolution, 1959–1961* (1985); Walter LaFeber, *Inevitable Revolutions: The United States in Central America* (1983); and Barry Rubin, *Paved with Good Intentions: The American Experience and Iran* (1980).

Notes

Preface

1. Gordon Craig, "Political and Diplomatic History," in Felix Gilbert and Stephen R. Graubard, eds., *Historical Studies Today* (New York, 1972), p. 362.
2. Michael H. Hunt, *The Making of a Special Relationship: The United States and China to 1914* (New York, 1983), p. 302. Dorothy Borg has made this same point somewhat more straightforwardly: "The motives underlying our policy in Eastern Asia may more often than not have been the same as those which formed the basis of our policies toward the rest of the world." Borg, *American Policy and the Chinese Revolution, 1925–1928*, 2d ed. (New York, 1968), p. xiv.

Chapter 1: Coming to Terms with Ideology

Epigraph. Walter Lippmann, *U.S. Foreign Policy: Shield of the Republic* (Boston, 1943), p. 138; and Henry Kissinger, *The White House Years* (Boston, 1979), p. 54.

1. Graham T. Allison, "Cool It: The Foreign Policy of Young America," *Foreign Policy*, no. 1 (Winter 1970–71), p. 144; Michael Roskin, "From Pearl Harbor to Vietnam: Shifting Generational Paradigms," *Political Science Quarterly*, 89 (Fall 1974): 563.
2. Richard J. Barnet, *Intervention and Revolution: America's Confrontation with Insurgent Movements Around the World* (New York, 1968), which he subsequently supplemented with a more urgent but less compelling attack, *Roots of War: The Men and Institutions Behind U.S. Foreign Policy* (New York, 1972), and more recently with *Real Security: Restoring American Power in a Dangerous Decade* (New York, 1981).
3. Melvin Gurtov, *The United States Against the Third World: Antinationalism and Intervention* (New York, 1974); Richard E. Feinberg, *The Intemperate Zone: The Third World Challenge to U.S. Foreign Policy* (New York, 1983); Robert A. Packenham, *Liberal America and the Third World: Political Development Ideas in Foreign Aid and Social Science* (Princeton, 1973).
4. Earl C. Ravenal, *Never Again: Learning from America's Foreign Policy Failures* (Philadelphia, 1978); Ravenal, *Strategic Disengagement and World Peace: Toward a Noninterventionist American Policy* (San Francisco, 1979); David P. Calleo, *The Imperious Economy* (Cambridge, Mass., 1982). See also the indictment of an increasingly erratic, ideological, and partisan policy process presented by insiders I. M. Destler, Leslie Gelb, and Anthony Lake in *Our Own Worst Enemy: The Unmaking of American Foreign Policy* (New York, 1984).
5. Ravenal, *Never Again*, p. 15.
6. The earlier works by Barnet, Gurtov, and Packenham embody roughly the same set of insights and weaknesses evident in Ravenal and Feinberg. See Barnet, *Intervention*, p. 78; Gurtov, *The United States*, pp. 2–9, 204, 213; Packenham, *Liberal America*, especially chaps. 3 and 4 and pp. 350, 357.

7. Ravenal, *Never Again*, pp. 51, 108, 129, 137; Ravenal, *Strategic Disengagement*, p. 5.
8. Feinberg, *The Intemperate Zone*, pp. 25, 191–92, 234, 257.
9. Chicago, 1951.
10. Kennan, *American Diplomacy*, pp. 22, 36; Kennan, *Memoirs* (Boston, 1967, 1972), 2:71–73.
11. Kennan, *American Diplomacy*, p. 79; Kennan, *Memoirs*, 2:322.
12. Kennan, *Memoirs*, 1:69, 246, 261, 511, 549, 551, 2:171–72, 252. Kennan joined Cold War liberals in campaigning for an "end of ideology." This movement, whose inception coincided roughly with Kennan's 1950 Chicago lectures, gathered momentum in the United States and Western Europe through the decade. Prominent social scientists associated with the Congress for Cultural Freedom—Edward Shils, Daniel Bell, Seymour Martin Lipset, and Raymond Aron, among others—sought to popularize the notion that ideology was an encumbrance that complex modern societies, faced with essentially technical problems, could not afford. Job L. Dittberner, *The End of Ideology and American Social Thought* (Ann Arbor, Mich., 1979), is a helpful introduction.
13. Kennan's views on the tendency of democracy to distort foreign policy were of long standing. He had observed in frustration in 1944, "Our actions in the field of foreign affairs are the convulsive reactions of politicians to an internal political life dominated by vocal minorities." Four years later, looking out from his State Department office on the American scene, he flatly pronounced, "Great democracies are apparently incapable of dealing with the subtleties and contradictions of power relationships." The rise of McCarthyism and the "who lost China?" controversy were soon—at the very time he was writing *American Diplomacy*—to strengthen his concern with the disruptive impact of democracy on foreign policy. Kennan, *American Diplomacy*, pp. 36, 56; Kennan, *Memoirs*, 1:185, 239, 351, 495, 2:221–23, 319–21, 323.
14. Kennan, *Memoirs*, 1:53–54, 2:87. Walter Lippmann anticipated Kennan's views on the problems of public opinion in the early 1910s, developed his position in books published in 1922 and 1925, and restated it in a widely read 1943 study. There is, however, no evidence of personal contact between Kennan and Lippmann, though the former was surely familiar with the latter's regular newspaper column. Ronald Steel, *Walter Lippmann and the American Century* (Boston, 1980), pp. 43, 180–83, 211–13; Lippmann, *U.S. Foreign Policy*.
15. Kennan, *Memoirs*, 2:86. Kennan, a complex and even paradoxical figure, is more of a Christian moralist than any reader of that realist treatise, *American Diplomacy*, would guess. It is, however, less the complex person than the influential book that is of concern here. Chapter 5 below emphasizes the ideological dimension of Kennan's moralism.
16. Clifford Geertz, "Ideology as a Cultural System," in David E. Apter, ed., *Ideology and Discontent* (London, 1964), p. 52.
17. The 1959 edition of *The Tragedy of American Diplomacy*, published in Cleveland, is the basis for the comments that follow. Substantially revised editions appeared in 1962 and 1972. Joseph M. Siracusa, *New Left Diplomatic Historians and Histories: The American Revisionists* (Port Washington, N.Y., 1973), pp. 24–26, offers a sketch of Williams' background.
18. Williams, *Tragedy*, p. 16.
19. *Ibid.*, pp. 34, 43, 118.
20. *Ibid.*, p. 200.
21. Charles Beard, the most outstanding of a previous generation of progressive historians and a fierce opponent of Franklin Roosevelt's foreign policy, was one of Williams' heroes. In 1956 and 1957 Williams had praised Beard for stressing economic conflict and the ties between economic interests and the political process. Williams was also impressed by Beard's moral concern with preserving democracy at home against the machinations of

policymakers intent on promoting narrow economic interest abroad. Williams' essays on Beard appear in *History as a Way of Learning* (New York, 1973).

22. Williams, *Tragedy*, p. 210. Only in subsequent works did Williams suggest what fundamental structural changes he had in mind. The United States would have to set aside the dominant capitalist ethos beneficial only to a "class-conscious industrial gentry." Only then would Americans cease to stand in a predatory and hostile relationship to the world and be able to set to building at home a democratic socialism where community might again flourish as it had in a precapitalist age. Williams, *History as a Way of Learning*, p. 17.

23. Williams, *Tragedy*, pp. 13–15, 53–59 (for references to noneconomic ideas); Williams, *History as a Way of Learning*, p. 9.

24. Clifford Geertz, "Thick Description: Toward an Interpretive Theory of Culture," in his *The Interpretation of Cultures* (New York, 1973), p. 12.

25. Eric H. Erikson, *Young Man Luther* (New York, 1958), p. 22.

26. Geoff Eley, "Nationalism and Social History," *Social History*, 6 (Jan. 1981): 92, 104.

Chapter 2: Visions of National Greatness

Epigraph. Those portions of "Common Sense" from which this and the quotes that follow in the text are drawn appear in Philip S. Foner, ed., *Complete Writings of Thomas Paine* (New York, 1945), 1:19, 23, 44, 45. On Paine's early years and authorship of "Common Sense," see David Freeman Hawke, *Paine* (New York, 1974), chaps. 1–3, and Eric Foner, *Tom Paine and Revolutionary America* (New York, 1976), introduction and chaps. 1–3.

1. Foner, *Complete Writings of Thomas Paine*, 2:1480.

2. Jefferson to Bellini, 30 Sept. 1785, in Julian P. Boyd, ed., *The Papers of Thomas Jefferson* (Princeton, 1950–), 8:568; Jefferson, *Notes on Virginia*, in Andrew A. Lipscomb and Albert E. Bergh, eds., *The Writings of Thomas Jefferson* (Washington, 1903–07), 2:241. More than one historian has noted the paradox that Jefferson, the champion of liberty, held slaves and that the yeomanry he idealized often drew on slave labor.

3. Lipscomb and Bergh, *Writings of Thomas Jefferson*, 2:241, 242.

4. Jefferson, Dec. 1793 report on commerce, in Lipscomb and Bergh, *Writings of Thomas Jefferson*, 3:277, 281.

5. Adams quoted in John C. Miller, *Alexander Hamilton: Portrait in Paradox* (New York, 1959), p. 523. Jacob E. Cooke, *Alexander Hamilton* (New York, 1982), is especially penetrating on personality and motive.

6. Hamilton, "The Federalist No. 6," Nov. 1787, in Harold C. Syrett, ed., *The Papers of Alexander Hamilton* (New York, 1961–79), 4:310, 316.

7. Hamilton, "The Federalist No. 11," Nov. 1787, in *ibid.*, 4:342, 345–46; Jerald A. Combs, *The Jay Treaty: Political Battleground of the Founding Fathers* (Berkeley, Calif., 1970), p. 35.

8. Madison quoted in Drew R. McCoy, "Republicanism and American Foreign Policy: James Madison and the Political Economy of Commercial Discrimination, 1789 to 1794," *William and Mary Quarterly*, 3d series, vol. 31 (Oct. 1974), p. 635n.

9. Jefferson quoted in Merrill D. Peterson, *Thomas Jefferson and the New Nation* (New York, 1970), pp. 64–65; Foner, *Complete Writings of Thomas Paine*, 2:722; doggerel quoted in Donald H. Stewart, *The Opposition Press of the Federalist Period* (Albany, N.Y., 1969), p. 220.

10. Jefferson to Madison, 21 Sept. 1795, in Lipscomb and Bergh, *Writings of Thomas Jefferson*, 9:309; Syrett, *Papers of Alexander Hamilton*, 18:480, 495, 496.

11. Quotes in this and the following paragraph come from Washington to Hamilton, 29 July 1795, in Syrett, *Papers of Alexander Hamilton*, 18:525; "Farewell Address," in John C.

Fitzpatrick, ed., *The Writings of George Washington* (Washington, 1938–44), 35:214–38.

12. Adams quoted in Cooke, *Alexander Hamilton*, p. 195.

13. Jefferson to Thomas Lomax, 12 March 1799, in Lipscomb and Bergh, *Writings of Thomas Jefferson*, 10:24; Jefferson, inaugural address, 4 March 1801, in James D. Richardson, ed., *A Compilation of the Messages and Papers of the Presidents, 1789–1897* (Washington, 1896–1900), 1:323.

14. Alexander DeConde, *This Affair of Louisiana* (New York, 1976), is the latest account of Jefferson's signal foreign-policy achievement.

15. Jefferson to A. Stewart, 25 Jan. 1786, in Lipscomb and Bergh, *Writings of Thomas Jefferson*, 5:260.

16. John L. O'Sullivan, "Annexation," *Democratic Review*, 17 (July–Aug. 1845): 9.

17. Quote from Robert V. Remini, *Andrew Jackson and the Course of American Democracy, 1833–1845* (New York, 1984), p. 418.

18. O'Sullivan, "The Great Nation of Futurity," *Democratic Review*, 6 (Nov. 1839): 427; speech by Rep. Frederick P. Stanton (Democrat, Tennessee), 16 Jan. 1846, in Norman A. Graebner, ed., *Manifest Destiny* (Indianapolis, 1968), p. 94.

19. Speeches by Rep. Chesselden Ellis (Democrat, New York), 25 Jan. 1845, Sen. Lewis Cass (Democrat, Michigan), 10 Feb. 1847, and Sen. Sidney Breese (Democrat, Illinois), 14 Feb. 1848, all in Graebner, *Manifest Destiny*, pp. 73, 158, 218.

20. Walter LaFeber, ed., *John Quincy Adams and American Continental Empire* (Chicago, 1965), pp. 37, 130; Madison quoted in Albert K. Weinberg, *Manifest Destiny* (Baltimore, 1935), p. 228.

21. Breese speech of 14 Feb. 1848, in Graebner, *Manifest Destiny*, p. 218.

22. Corwin speech of 11 Feb. 1847, in Graebner, *Manifest Destiny*, pp. 165, 166.

23. Greeley in *New York Tribune*, 12 May 1846 and 26 Feb. 1848, quoted in Frederick Merk, "Dissent in the Mexican War," in Samuel Eliot Morison et al., *Dissent in Three American Wars* (Cambridge, Mass., 1970), p. 44, and in John H. Schroeder, *Mr. Polk's War: American Opposition and Dissent, 1846–1848* (Madison, Wis., 1973), p. 159; speech by Sen. John C. Calhoun (Democrat, South Carolina), 4 Jan. 1848, in Graebner, *Manifest Destiny*, p. 227; Calhoun speech of 9 Feb. 1847, quoted in Schroeder, *Mr. Polk's War*, p. 70; Albert Gallatin, *Peace with Mexico* (New York, 1847), excerpted in Graebner, *Manifest Destiny*, p. 192.

24. Graebner, *Manifest Destiny*, p. 234; Schroeder, *Mr. Polk's War*, pp. 75–76.

25. Polk quoted in Thomas R. Hietala, *Manifest Design: Anxious Aggrandizement in Late Jacksonian America* (Ithaca, N.Y., 1985), p. 122.

26. George E. Baker, ed., *The Works of William H. Seward* (Boston, 1884–89), 4:165.

27. *Chicago Tribune* quoted in Donald M. Dozer, "Anti-Expansionism during the Johnson Administration," *Pacific Historical Review*, 12 (Sept. 1943): 256.

28. Strong, *Our Country* (New York, 1885), pp. 1, 178; Alfred Thayer Mahan, "The United States Looking Outward" (Aug. 1890), in his *The Interest of America in Sea Power* (Boston, 1897), p. 18; Henry Cabot Lodge, "Our Blundering Foreign Policy," *Forum*, 19 (March 1895): 16, 17. Strong, Mahan, and Lodge, stock figures in accounts of this era, have been the subject of debate over whether their rhetoric signifies colonial or imperial ambitions and whether they had any significant influence over policy. For a recent skeptical treatment, see James A. Field, Jr., "American Imperialism: The Worst Chapter in Almost Any Book," *American Historical Review*, 83 (June 1978): 647–50. The brief treatment here is not meant to join the controversies over specific motivation and practical impact but rather to link all three public voices to an old and well-established nationalist intellectual tradition on which they drew for the terms of their discourse.

29. McKinley quoted in Robert C. Hilderbrand, *Power and the People: Executive Management of Public Opinion in Foreign Affairs, 1897–1921* (Chapel Hill, N.C., 1981), p. 40, and

in Ernest May, *Imperial Democracy: The Emergence of America as a Great Power* (New York, 1961), p. 251; McKinley speech of 16 Feb. 1899, in *Speeches and Addresses of William McKinley from March 1, 1897 to May 30, 1900* (New York, 1900), pp. 186–87, 192.

30. Speech by Sen. Albert Beveridge, 9 Jan. 1900, in *Congressional Record*, vol. 33, 56th Cong., 1st sess., p. 704; Beveridge, "The March of the Flag," in his *The Meaning of the Times* (Indianapolis, 1908), p. 47.

31. Schurz and Cleveland quoted in Fred Harvey Harrington, "The Anti-Imperialist Movement in the United States, 1898–1900," *Mississippi Valley Historical Review*, 22 (Sept. 1935): 212, 213; Sumner, "The Conquest of the United States by Spain," *Yale Law Journal*, 8 (Jan. 1899): 192–93.

32. Merrill D. Peterson, *The Jeffersonian Image in the American Mind* (New York, 1960), p. 270; Beveridge, "The March of the Flag," pp. 49–50; Walter L. Williams, "United States Indian Policy and the Debate over Philippine Annexation," *Journal of American History*, 66 (March 1980): 811–14, 818–22.

33. On these adverse socioeconomic trends, see Rowland Berthoff, "Independence and Attachment, Virtue and Interest: From Republican Citizen to Free Entrepreneur, 1787–1837," in Richard L. Bush et al., *Uprooted Americans* (Boston, 1979); Berthoff and John M. Murrin, "Feudalism, Communalism, and the Yeoman Freeholder: The American Revolution Considered as a Social Accident," in Stephen G. Kurtz and James H. Hutson, eds., *Essays on the American Revolution* (Chapel Hill, N.C., 1973); Stephan Thernstrom, "Urbanization, Migration, and Social Mobility in Late Nineteenth-Century America," in Barton J. Bernstein, ed., *Towards a New Past* (New York, 1968); and Robert F. Gallman, "Trends in the Size Distribution of Wealth in the Nineteenth Century," in Lee Soltow, ed., *Six Papers on the Size Distribution of Wealth and Income* (New York, 1969).

Chapter 3: The Hierarchy of Race

Epigraph. "Observations on the Increase of Mankind," in Leonard W. Labaree and William B. Willcox, eds., *The Papers of Benjamin Franklin* (New Haven, Conn., 1959–   ), 4:234.

1. The following discussion is drawn from *ibid.* On Indians, see 2:411, 4:119, 121, 481–83, 5:458, 6:487, 9:62, 10:296, 342, 402, 408, 409, 11:55. On blacks, see 4:229, 10:396, 11:76, 17:37–44, 19:112–13, 187–88, 269, 20:155–56, 296, 314, 21:151, 22:97, 196, 200, 519. On Germans, see 4:120–21, 234, 483–85, 5:158–60, 20:528. Paul Conner, *Poor Richard's Politicks: Benjamin Franklin and His New American Order* (New York, 1965), pp. 69–87, contains a good discussion of Franklin and race. Gerald Stourzh, *Benjamin Franklin and American Foreign Policy*, 2d ed. (Chicago, 1969), is essential on his expansionist vision. For a definition of racism as the term is used here, see Pierre L. van den Berghe, *Race and Racism: A Comparative Perspective* (New York, 1967), p. 11.

2. Labaree and Wilcox, *The Papers of Benjamin Franklin*, 4:231.

3. Quoted in Alden T. Vaughn, "From White Man to Redskin: Changing Anglo-American Perceptions of the American Indian," *American Historical Review*, 87 (Oct. 1982): 920. Winthrop D. Jordan, *White Over Black: American Attitudes Toward the Negro, 1550–1812* (Chapel Hill, N.C., 1968), explores the origins of this color-sensitive moral outlook. The persistence of the outlook is evident in the claims of a Texas paper in 1865 that "white was the emblem of light, religious purity, innocence, faith, joy and life," while black "expressed the earth, darkness, mourning, wickedness, negation, death, and was appropriate to the Prince of Darkness." *Southern Intelligencer* quoted in Arnoldo De León, *They Called Them Greasers: Anglo Attitudes toward Mexicans in Texas, 1821–1900* (Austin, Tex., 1983), p. 20.

4. Illustrations: fig. 1 from A. von Steinwehr and D. G. Brinton, *An Intermediate Geography* (Cincinnati, 1877), p. 13; and fig. 2 from Arnold Guyot, *Physical Geography* (New York, 1873), p. 114.

5. Ruth Miller Elson, *Guardians of Tradition: American Schoolbooks of the Nineteenth Century* (Lincoln, Nebr., 1964), pp. 87–88,97.

6. Albert K. Weinberg, *Manifest Destiny: A Study of Nationalist Expansionism in American History* (Baltimore, 1935), p. 83.

7. Jackson, annual message to Congress, 6 Dec. 1830, in James D. Richardson, ed., *A Compilation of the Messages and Papers of the Presidents, 1789–1897* (Washington, 1896–1900), 2:522.

8. Sherman letter of Sept. 1868, quoted in Ralph K. Andrist, *The Long Death: The Last Days of the Plains Indians* (New York, 1964), p. 154.

9. Elson, *Guardians of Tradition*. p. 81.

10. Illustrations: fig. 3 from *ibid.*, following p. 74; and fig. 4 from Robert K. Berkhofer, Jr., *The White Man's Indian: Images of the American Indian from Columbus to the Present* (New York, 1978), following p. 138 (original in Library of Congress Prints and Photographs Collection).

11. Elson, *Guardians of Tradition*, p. 154.

12. John J. Ingalls, *America's War for Humanity* (New York, 1898), excerpted in Charles Gibson, ed., *The Black Legend: Anti-Spanish Attitudes in the Old World and the New* (New York, 1971), p. 177; Lodge and Proctor quoted in Gerald F. Linderman, *The Mirror of War: American Society and the Spanish-American War* (Ann Arbor, Mich., 1974), pp. 45, 123.

13. Randolph and Jefferson quoted in Arthur P. Whitaker, *The United States and the Independence of Latin America, 1800–1830* (Baltimore, 1941), pp. 183, 188; Adams in his *Memoirs* (Philadelphia, 1874–77), 5:325.

14. Stephen Austin quoted in David J. Weber, " 'Scarce more than apes.' Historical Roots of Anglo American Stereotypes of Mexicans in the Border Region," in Weber, ed., *New Spain's Far Northern Frontier* (Albuquerque, N. Mex., 1979), p. 298; Walker and Buchanan quoted in Reginald Horsman, *Race and Manifest Destiny: The Origins of American Racial Anglo-Saxonism* (Cambridge, Mass., 1981), pp. 215, 217.

15. Thomas Corwin and Walt Whitman quoted in Norman A. Graebner, ed., *Manifest Destiny* (Indianapolis, 1968), pp. 162, 208; *New York Evening Post* quoted in Julius Pratt, "The Ideology of American Expansion," in Avery Craven, ed., *Essays in Honor of William E. Dodd* (Chicago, 1935), p. 344; John H. Schroeder, *Mr. Polk's War: American Opposition and Dissent, 1846–1848* (Madison, Wis., 1973), pp. 76, 129.

16. Quotes from Horsman, *Race and Manifest Destiny*, p. 233, and Robert E. May, *The Southern Dream of a Caribbean Empire, 1854–1861* (Baton Rouge, La., 1973), p. 7.

17. Leonard Wood quoted in Linderman, *The Mirror of War*, p. 138.

18. Elson, *Guardians of Tradition*, p. 161. The Spanish foe rose in American estimation as the Cubans fell. Spanish troops had fought bravely, and their leaders had proven chivalrous in battle and cooperative in defeat.

19. Illustrations: fig. 5 from William Murrell, *A History of American Graphic Humor* (New York, 1933), 1:191; fig. 6 from *Harper's Weekly*, 35 (7 Nov. 1891): 882 (drawing by Burt Wilder; from Collection of Rare Books, Duke University Library); fig. 7 from *Judge*, 35 (9 July 1898), cover (drawing by Grant Hamilton); fig. 8 from John J. Johnson, *Latin America in Caricature* (Austin, Tex., 1980), p. 81 (drawing by C. Jay Taylor originally in *Puck*, 3 June 1896); fig. 9 from Johnson, *Latin America in Caricature*, p. 89 (in *Chicago Record-Herald*, 1901); fig. 10 from Johnson, *Latin America in Caricature*, p. 127 (in *Chicago InterOcean*, 1905).

20. Elson, *Guardians of Tradition*, p. 162.

21. Michael H. Hunt, *The Making of a Special Relationship: The United States and China to 1914* (New York, 1983), p. 35.

22. California's anti-Chinese memorial to Congress (1877), in Cheng-Tsu Wu, *"Chink!"* A

Documentary History of Anti-Chinese Prejudice in America (New York, 1972), p. 115; Elson, *Guardians of Tradition*, p. 164.

23. Hunt, *The Making of a Special Relationship*, pp. 92, 93.

24. Illustrations: fig. 11 from *San Francisco Illustrated Wasp*, 1 (8 Dec. 1877): 1 (from the collection of the California State Library); fig. 12 from Morton Keller, *The Art and Politics of Thomas Nast* (New York, 1968), #65 following p. 111 (originally in *Harper's Weekly*, 7 Aug. 1869); fig. 13 from Richard Van Alstyne, *The United States and East Asia* (New York, 1973), p. 77 (ascribed to *Life*, 1900); fig. 14 from *Harper's Weekly*, 44 (28 July 1900), cover (drawing by William A. Rogers; in the Collection of Rare Books, Duke University Library); fig. 15 from *Literary Digest*, 32 (10 March 1906): 357 (drawing by Fred Morgan originally in *Philadelphia Inquirer*).

25. Roger Daniels, *The Politics of Prejudice: The Anti-Japanese Movement in California and the Struggle for Japanese Exclusion* (Berkeley, Calif., 1962), pp. 28, 47.

26. Elson, *Guardians of Tradition*, p. 122; Horace Bushnell oration of 1837, quoted in Horsman, *Race and Manifest Destiny*, p. 209.

27. Beveridge speech of 17 Sept. 1898 entitled "The March of the Flag," in his *The Meaning of the Times* (Indianapolis, 1908), p. 47.

28. See Michael McCarthy, *Dark Continent: Africa as Seen by Americans* (Westport, Conn., 1983), chaps. 6–7 on late nineteenth- and early twentieth-century missionary testimony, travel accounts, children's literature, and school texts. The quoted phrase is McCarthy's from p. xvi.

29. Robert Seager II and Doris D. Maguire, eds., *Letters and Papers of Alfred Thayer Mahan* (Annapolis, Md., 1975), 1:593, 2:84, 92, 167, 529, 557–58, 569, 605, 620, 627, 693; Seager, *Alfred Thayer Mahan: The Man and His Letters* (Annapolis, Md., 1977), pp. 29, 37, 96, 142, 464–65.

30. Beveridge speech of 9 Jan. 1900, in *Congressional Record*, vol. 33, 56th Cong., 1st sess., p. 708; McKinley speech of 16 Feb. 1899, in *Speeches and Addresses of William McKinley from March 1, 1897 to May 30, 1900* (New York, 1900), p. 193; Taft quoted in Stuart C. Miller, *"Benevolent Assimilation": The American Conquest of the Philippines, 1899–1903* (New Haven, Conn., 1982), p. 134.

31. Illustrations: fig. 16 from *Literary Digest*, 17 (16 July 1898): 67 (drawing by Charles Nelan originally in *New York World*, 1898); fig. 17 from *Judge*, 39 (11 Aug. 1900), cover (drawing by Victor Gilliam; in the General Research Division, New York Public Library, Astor, Lenox and Tilden Foundations); fig. 18 from Johnson, *Latin America in Caricature*, p. 217 (drawing by William A. Rogers originally in *Harper's Weekly*, 27 Aug. 1898); fig. 19 from National Archives and Records Service (photo no. 111–RB–1169); fig. 20 from *Bee*, 1 (25 May 1898): 8 (drawing by J. Campbell Cory; in the General Research Division, New York Public Library, Astor, Lenox and Tilden Foundations); fig. 21 from *Literary Digest*, 22 (30 March 1901): 372 (drawing by R. C. Bowman originally in *Minneapolis Tribune*); fig. 22 from Johnson, *Latin America in Caricature*, p. 131 (drawing by Thomas May originally in *Detroit Journal*, 1907; reprinted by permission of *Detroit News*, a division of Evening News Association, copyright 1907); fig. 23 from *Literary Digest*, 18 (18 Feb. 1899): 180 (drawing by Thomas May originally in *Detroit Journal*).

Chapter 4: The Perils of Revolution

Epigraph. Charles Francis Adams, ed., *The Works of John Adams* (Boston, 1850–56), 10:397; and Andrew A. Lipscomb and Albert E. Bergh, eds., *Writings of Thomas Jefferson* (Washington, 1903–07), 15:491.

1. Lester J. Cappon, ed., *The Adams-Jefferson Letters* (Chapel Hill, N.C., 1959), pp. 358, 391. My treatment here of Adam's and Jefferson's views has particularly benefited from a reading of John R. Howe, Jr., *The Changing Political Thought of John Adams* (Princeton,

1966); Joyce Appleby, "The New Republican Synthesis and the Changing Political Ideas of John Adams," *American Quarterly*, 25 (Dec. 1973); Peter Shaw, *The Character of John Adams* (Chapel Hill, N.C., 1976); Robert R. Palmer, "The Dubious Democrat: Thomas Jefferson in Bourbon France," *Political Science Quarterly*, 72 (Sept. 1957); and Lawrence S. Kaplan, *Jefferson and France: An Essay on Politics and Political Ideas* (New Haven, Conn., 1967). Merrill D. Peterson, *Adams and Jefferson: A Revolutionary Dialogue* (Athens, Ga., 1976), is a deftly drawn portrait of a fascinating relationship.

2. Clinton Rossiter, "The Legacy of John Adams," *Yale Review*, new series, 46 (June 1957): 532.

3. Known collectively as "Discourses on Davila," these essays were written in response to the initial stages of the revolution in France and the continuing process of political consolidation in the United States. The quotes that follow can be found in order of appearance in C. F. Adams, *The Works of John Adams*, 6: 279, 280, 396, 252.

4. *Ibid.*, 4:358.

5. *Ibid.*, 4:57, 7:151, 9:567–68.

6. Julian P. Boyd, ed., *The Papers of Thomas Jefferson* (Princeton, 1950–   ), 16:293.

7. *Ibid.*, 11:93; Lipscomb and Bergh, *The Writings of Thomas Jefferson*, 10:341–42.

8. Cappon, *The Adams-Jefferson Letters*, p. 347; C. F. Adams, *The Works of John Adams*, 10:155.

9. C. F. Adams, *The Works of John Adams*, 10:283; Cappon, *The Adams-Jefferson Letters*, pp. 574–75, 596–97.

10. Lipscomb and Bergh, *The Writings of Thomas Jefferson*, 14:246.

11. Boyd, *The Papers of Thomas Jefferson*, 11:485–86; C. F. Adams, *The Works of John Adams*, 10:397.

12. Boyd, *The Papers of Thomas Jefferson*, 15:326; Lipscomb and Bergh, *The Writings of Thomas Jefferson*, 9:9.

13. Harold C. Syrett, ed., *The Papers of Alexander Hamilton* (New York, 1961–79), 15:670–71; John C. Fitzpatrick, ed., *The Writings of George Washington* (Washington, 1931–44), 30:497–98, 31:324–25, 32:54; Gouverneur Morris quoted in Charles D. Hazen, *Contemporary American Opinion of the French Revolution* (Baltimore, Md., 1897), pp. 57–58, 110.

14. C. F. Adams, *The Works of John Adams*, 9:570; Charles Francis Adams, ed., *Letters of John Adams, Addressed to His Wife* (Boston, 1841), 2:120.

15. Paul L. Ford, ed., *The Writings of Thomas Jefferson*, (New York, 1892–99), 8:179; Lipscomb and Bergh, *The Writings of Thomas Jefferson*, 13:36, 130, 14:247, 15:129–30, 19:163.

16. Lipscomb and Bergh, *The Writings of Thomas Jefferson*, 6:373, 9:164–65.

17. Winthrop D. Jordan, *White Over Black: American Attitudes Toward the Negro, 1500–1812* (Chapel Hill, N.C., 1968), p. 385.

18. Ford, *The Writings of Thomas Jefferson*, 9:435; Lipscomb and Bergh, *The Writings of Thomas Jefferson*, 13:43, 15:117. See by way of comparison C. F. Adams, *The Works of John Adams*, 10:144.

19. Charles C. Griffin, *The United States and the Disruption of the Spanish Empire, 1810–1822* (New York, 1937), p. 250; James F. Hopkins and Mary W. M. Hargreaves, eds., *The Papers of Henry Clay* (Lexington, Ky., 1959–   ), 2:517; Arnoldo De León, *They Called Them Greasers: Anglo Attitudes toward Mexicans in Texas, 1821–1900* (Austin, Tex., 1983), p. 3.

20. Rush Welter, *The Mind of America, 1820–1860* (New York, 1975), pp. 3, 60; James A. Field, Jr., *America and the Mediterranean World, 1776–1882* (Princeton, 1969), p. 122.

21. Edward Mead Earle, "American Interest in the Greek Cause, 1821–1827," *American*

Historical Review, 33 (Oct. 1927): 28–29; Cappon, *The Adams-Jefferson Letters*, p. 602. The United States did not extend diplomatic recognition to Greece until 1837.

22. Jerzy Jan Lerski, *A Polish Chapter in Jacksonian America: The United States and the Polish Exiles of 1831* (Madison, Wis., 1958), p. 37.
23. Elizabeth Brett White, *American Opinion of France: From Lafayette to Poincaré* (New York, 1927), p. 87.
24. *Ibid.*, p. 131.
25. *Ibid.*, p. 209; George L. Cherry, "American Metropolitan Press Reaction to the Paris Commune of 1871," *Mid-America*, 32 (Jan. 1950): 4, 5.
26. Cherry, "American Metropolitan Press Reaction," p. 7.
27. Michael H. Hunt, *The Making of a Special Relationship: The United States and China to 1914* (New York, 1983), p. 293.
28. *Ibid.*, p. 218.
29. American control extended to three-quarters of Mexico's mining enterprise, more than one-half of her oil production, and cattle ranches and sugar plantations totaling one-seventh of her land area.
30. Arthur S. Link, *Wilson: The New Freedom* (Princeton, 1956), pp. 360, 379; Link, *Wilson: The Struggle for Neutrality* (Princeton, 1960), p. 239; Arthur S. Link et al., eds., *The Papers of Woodrow Wilson* (Princeton, 1966–   ), 29:521–22.
31. Link, *Wilson: The New Freedom*, p. 350; Robert E. Quirk, *An Affair of Honor: Woodrow Wilson and the Occupation of Vera Cruz* (Lexington, Ky., 1962), p. 77.
32. *Los Angeles Times* quoted in Link, *Wilson: Confusions and Crises, 1915–1916* (Princeton, 1964), p. 202.
33. Marc Raeff, "An American View of the Decembrist Revolt," *Journal of Modern History*, 25 (Sept. 1953): 290, 292; John Lewis Gaddis, *Russia, the Soviet Union, and the United States* (New York, 1978), pp. 12, 13.
34. Arthur W. Thompson and Robert A. Hart, *The Uncertain Crusade: America and the Russian Revolution of 1905* (Amherst, Mass., 1970), p. 30.
35. Elting E. Morison et al., eds., *The Letters of Theodore Roosevelt* (Cambridge, Mass., 1951–54), 5:22, 101, 178–79, 345.
36. *Macon Telegraph* quoted in Meno Lovenstein, *American Opinion of Soviet Russia* (Washington, 1941), p. 42.
37. *Ibid.*, p. 33; Leonid I. Strakhovsky, *American Opinion about Russia, 1917–1920* (Toronto, 1961), pp. 40, 52.
38. Link, *The Papers of Woodrow Wilson*, 41:524.
39. Eugene P. Trani, "Woodrow Wilson and the Decision to Intervene in Russia: A Reconsideration," *Journal of Modern History*, 48 (Sept. 1976): 460.
40. Ray Stannard Baker and William E. Dodd, eds., *The Public Papers of Woodrow Wilson* (New York, 1925–27), 6:85.
41. Gaddis, *Russia, the Soviet Union, and the United States*, p. 106; Lovenstein, *American Opinion of Soviet Russia*, pp. 48–49.
42. Lovenstein, *American Opinion of Soviet Russia*, p. 39; Strakhovsky, *American Opinion about Russia*, p. 95; Gaddis, *Russia, the Soviet Union, and the United States*, pp. 105, 106.
43. Peter G. Filene, *Americans and the Soviet Experiment, 1917–1933* (Cambridge, Mass., 1967), p. 59. Theda Skocpol's account of the forces at work in three major revolutions, *States and Social Revolutions: A Comparative Analysis of France, Russia, and China* (New York, 1979), highlights the shallow and procrustean nature of American understanding.
44. Illustrations: fig. 24 from William Murrell, *A History of American Graphic Humor* (New

York, 1933), 1:47; fig. 25 from Morton Keller, *The Art and Politics of Thomas Nast* (New York, 1968), #74 following p. 111 (originally in *Harper's Weekly*, 7 Feb. 1874); fig. 26 from Robert K. Murray, *Red Scare: A Study in National Hysteria, 1919–1920* (Minneapolis, Minn., 1955), p. 34 (drawing by Rehse originally in *New York World*); fig. 27 from *Literary Digest*, 67 (25 Dec. 1920): 17 (drawing by Gale originally in *Los Angeles Times*, Dec. 1920; copyright 1920, *Los Angeles Times*; reprinted by permission); fig. 28 from *Literary Digest*, 63 (25 Oct. 1919): 12 (drawing by Morgan originally in *Philadelphia Inquirer*, 1919; reprinted by permission of *Philadelphia Inquirer*).

45. Gaddis, *Russia, the Soviet Union, and the United States*, pp. 105–06; Baker and Dodd, *The Public Papers of Woodrow Wilson*, 5:301.

46. Lansing quoted in Lloyd C. Gardner, *Wilson and Revolutions: 1913–1921* (Philadelphia, 1976), p. 22.

47. The following generalizations on the role of the elite were suggested by a reading of Donald R. Mathews, *The Social Background of Political Decision-Makers* (Garden City, N.Y., 1954), pp. 23–33; Ernest R. May, *American Imperialism: A Speculative Essay* (New York, 1968), chap. 2; Kenneth Prewitt and Alan Stone, *The Ruling Elites: Elite Theory, Power, and American Democracy* (New York, 1973), chap. 6; Edward Pessen, "Social Structure and Politics in American History," *American Historical Review*, 87 (Dec. 1982); and Ruth Miller Elson, *Guardians of Tradition: American Schoolbooks of the Nineteenth Century* (Lincoln, Nebr. 1964), pp. 136–43, 280–81, 340–41.

48. Alexis de Tocqueville, *Democracy in America*, edited and abridged by Richard D. Heffner (New York, 1956), p. 267.

Chapter 5: Ideology in Twentieth-Century Foreign Policy

Epigraph. Walter C. Sellar and Robert J. Yeatman, *1066 and All That* (New York, 1931), p. vii.

1. For the era of "dollar diplomacy," that strange interlude between Roosevelt and Wilson, foreign-policy ideology receded in importance. Neither President William Howard Taft nor his secretary of state Philander C. Knox had given foreign affairs serious thought before coming into office, and their four years there did little to deepen or clarify their views. The result was a policy that was intellectually muddled, procedurally ad hoc and ill coordinated, and rendered incoherent by a shifting set of rationales. The influence of the familiar core ideas are, to be sure, evident in the Taft administration's professed belief in the exceptional role of the American nation; in its tutelary ambitions in Latin America, the Philippines, and China; and in its tense reaction to revolutionary change in China and Mexico. Mixed in with these conventional concerns, however, was a keen interest in securing and protecting export markets, a heavy reliance on capital investment as a tool of policy, a guarded trial at cooperating with the other major powers in Chinese affairs (while eschewing any involvement in European political affairs), and an indifference to strategic calculations that shocked Roosevelt.

2. Lo Hui-min, ed., *The Correspondence of G. E. Morrison* (Cambridge, U.K., 1976–78), 1:285.

3. Roosevelt quoted in Howard K. Beale, *Theodore Roosevelt and the Rise of America to World Power* (Baltimore, 1956), p. 40.

4. Hermann Hagedorn, ed., *The Works of Theodore Roosevelt* (New York, 1923–26), 15:286, 338–39; Thomas G. Dyer, *Theodore Roosevelt and the Idea of Race* (Baton Rouge, La., 1980), pp. 49, 52, 149.

5. Dyer, *Theodore Roosevelt*, pp. 30, 54, 100, 109; Stuart C. Miller, *"Benevolent Assimilation": The American Conquest of the Philippines, 1899–1903* (New Haven, Conn., 1982), p. 251; Walter L. Williams, "United States Indian Policy and the Debate over Philippine Annexation," *Journal of American History*, 66 (March 1980): 816, 826.

6. Edmund Morris, *The Rise of Theodore Roosevelt* (New York, 1979), chaps. 1–5, sensitively evokes the young TR's family and social milieu.

7. Roosevelt speech of 10 April 1899, in his *The Strenuous Life* (New York, 1900), pp. 6, 7.

8. Arthur S. Link et al., eds., *The Papers of Woodrow Wilson* (Princeton, 1966–   ), 11:66.

9. *Ibid.*, 11:93, 12:19, 216, 14:433, 15:149.

10. *Ibid.*, 11:440, 12:18, 14:433, 18:104.

11. *Ibid.*, 18:93, 23:435.

12. *Ibid.*, 1:518, 8:317.

13. John M. Mulder, *Woodrow Wilson: The Years of Preparation* (Princeton, 1978), pp. 69, 137, 153, 175. Arthur S. Link, *Wilson: The Road to the White House* (Princeton, 1947), chap. 1, and Harley Notter, *The Origins of the Foreign Policy of Woodrow Wilson* (Baltimore, 1937), Part I, are particularly suggestive on this multifaceted Anglophilia.

14. Link, *The Papers of Woodrow Wilson*, 6:172, 22:159.

15. Richard Olney (May 1898) quoted in Ernest R. May, *American Imperialism: A Speculative Essay* (New York, 1968), p. 184.

16. Henry F. Pringle, *Theodore Roosevelt*, rev. ed. (New York, 1956), pp. 219, 220; Roosevelt annual message to Congress, 6 Dec. 1904, in Hagedorn, *The Works of Theodore Roosevelt*, 15:257.

17. Roosevelt speech of 13 May 1903, in his *California Addresses* (San Francisco, 1903), p. 98.

18. Elting E. Morison et al., eds., *The Letters of Theodore Roosevelt* (Cambridge, Mass., 1951–54), 4:768, 770, 5:762.

19. Charles S. Campbell, Jr., *Anglo-American Understanding, 1898–1903* (Baltimore, 1957), and Bradford Perkins, *The Great Rapprochement: England and the United States, 1895–1914* (New York, 1968), develop these points in depth.

20. Link, *The Papers of Woodrow Wilson*, 36:67; John W. Coogan, *The End of Neutrality: The United States, Britain, and Maritime Rights, 1899–1915* (Ithaca, N.Y., 1981), chap. 11.

21. Link, *The Papers of Woodrow Wilson*, 41:527.

22. Ray Stannard Baker and William E. Dodd, eds., *The Public Papers of Woodrow Wilson: War and Peace* (New York, 1927), 2:305.

23. George Norris speech of 4 April 1917, in *Congressional Record*, 65th Cong., 1st sess., vol. 55, pt. 1, p. 214.

24. Albert J. Beveridge, "The Pitfalls of a 'League of Nations,' " *North American Review*, 209 (March 1919): 314; John Braeman, *Albert J. Beveridge: American Nationalist* (Chicago, 1971), p. 260.

25. George Gallup, *The Gallup Poll: Public Opinion, 1935–1971* (New York, 1972), 1:54. The polls cited in this section provide only a rough gauge of national sentiment because the polling techniques then in use were crude.

26. A striking number of leading twentieth-century policymakers issued from the less affluent households of ministers where any deficiency in social contacts and wealth was offset by a dedication to hard work and good works. Foremost among this group would be Woodrow Wilson, Charles Evans Hughes, Dean Acheson, the Dulles brothers, and Dean Rusk.

27. Lodge quoted in Lloyd E. Ambrosius, "Wilson, the Republicans, and French Security after World War I," *Journal of American History*, 59 (Sept. 1972): 344.

28. Henry Cabot Lodge speech of 12 Aug. 1919, in *Congressional Record*, 66th Cong., 1st sess., vol. 58, pt. 4, pp. 3783, 3784.

29. Hoover and Berle quoted in Walter LaFeber, *Inevitable Revolutions: The United States in Central America* (New York, 1983), pp. 63, 81.

30. Howard H. Quint and Robert H. Ferrell, eds., *The Talkative President: The Off-the-Record Press Conferences of Calvin Coolidge* (Amherst, Mass., 1964), p. 257.
31. Douglas Little, "Antibolshevism and American Foreign Policy, 1919–1939: The Diplomacy of Self-Delusion," *American Quarterly*, 35 (Fall 1983): 381, 383.
32. See Allen Woll's treatment of Hispanics and Richard A. Oehling on Asians, in Randall M. Miller, ed., *The Kaleidoscopic Lens: How Hollywood Views Ethnic Groups* (Englewood, N.J., 1980), and Sue Fawn Chung, "From Fu Manchu, Evil Genius, to James Lee Wong, Popular Hero: A Study of the Chinese-American in Popular Periodical Fiction from 1920 to 1940," *Journal of Popular Culture*, 10 (Winter 1976).
33. Quotes from Samuel L. Baily, *The United States and the Development of South America* (New York, 1976), p. 35 (FDR); Robert Dallek, *Franklin Roosevelt and American Foreign Policy, 1932–1945* (New York, 1979), p. 61 (FDR); John A. Garraty, *Henry Cabot Lodge* (New York, 1952), p. 374; Henry L. Stimson, letter to *New York Times*, 7 Oct. 1937, p. 12.
34. Illustrations: fig. 29 from John J. Johnson, *Latin America in Caricature* (Austin, Tex., 1980), p. 145 (drawing by King originally in *Chicago Tribune*, 1915; copyright 1915, Chicago Tribune Company, all rights reserved, used with permission); fig. 30 from Johnson, *Latin America in Caricature*, p. 103 (drawing by Sykes originally in *Philadelphia Evening Public Ledger*, 1923; reprinted by permission of *Philadelphia Inquirer*); fig. 31 from David F. Long, *The Outward View: An Illustrated History of United States Foreign Relations* (Chicago, 1963), p. 303 (drawing by Page originally in Louisville *Courier Journal*; reprinted by permission of *Courier-Journal*); fig. 32 from Foreign Policy Association, *A Cartoon History of United States Foreign Policy, 1776–1976* (New York, 1975), p. 69 (drawing by Hugh Hutton originally in *Philadelphia Inquirer*, 18 July 1937; reprinted by permission of *Philadelphia Inquirer*).
35. Stimson quoted in Christopher Thorne, *The Limits of Foreign Policy: The West, the League and the Far Eastern Crisis of 1931–1933* (New York, 1973), pp. 56, 57, 195; U.S. Department of State, *Foreign Relations of the United States: Japan, 1931–1941*, 2:227 (Hull), 771 (FDR); FDR quoted in Daniel M. Smith, "Authoritarianism and American Policy Makers in Two World Wars," *Pacific Historical Review*, 43 (Aug. 1974): 314, 316. The wartime decision to intern all residents of the United States of Japanese descent (whether citizens or not), the unusually brutal treatment of Japanese soldiers, and the Tokyo war crimes trial indictment of Japan's leaders for "moral blindness" and "mental deficiency" all had their roots in the same racial views that had informed prewar American policy.
36. At the same time and by the same margin Americans indicated they were willing to accept war with Japan. Gallup, *The Gallup Poll*, 1:304, 306, 307.
37. Roosevelt did not act until 1944, when he finally created a government board with limited power to aid Jewish refugees. David S. Wyman, *The Abandonment of the Jews: America and the Holocaust, 1941–1945* (New York, 1984), pp. 5–15, 285–87, 311–27.
38. Robert A. Divine, *Roosevelt and World War II* (Baltimore, 1969), p. 9; Edgar B. Nixon, ed., *Franklin D. Roosevelt and Foreign Affairs* (Cambridge, Mass., 1969), 3:520 (speech of 1 Dec. 1936).
39. Samuel I. Rosenman, comp., *The Public Papers and Addresses of Franklin D. Roosevelt* (New York, 1938–50), 6:410 (speech of 5 Oct. 1937).
40. Charles A. Lindbergh, *The Wartime Journals of Charles A. Lindbergh* (New York, 1970), pp. 110, 401; Lindbergh, "Aviation, Geography, and Race," *Reader's Digest*, 35 (Nov. 1939): 64, 66–67; Wayne S. Cole, *Charles A. Lindbergh and the Battle against American Intervention in World War II* (New York, 1974), p. 97.
41. Lindbergh, "Aviation," 66; Cole, *Charles A. Lindbergh*, p. 38.
42. Lindbergh's Madison Square Garden speech (23 May 1941), in *Vital Speeches*, 7 (1 June 1941): 483; Cole, *Charles A. Lindbergh*, p. 91.

43. Cole, *Charles A. Lindbergh*, p. 9; Lindbergh, *The Wartime Journals*, pp. 379, 404.

44. Cole, *Charles A. Lindbergh*, pp. 128, 130; Rosenman, *The Public Papers and Addresses of Franklin D. Roosevelt*, 9:638 (speech of 29 Dec. 1940).

45. Rosenman, *The Public Papers and Addresses of Franklin D. Roosevelt*, 10:522, 528 (speech of 9 Dec. 1941).

46. *Public Papers of the Presidents of the United States: Harry S. Truman, 1947*, p. 324 (speech of 4 July 1947); Walter Millis, ed., *The Forrestal Diaries* (New York, 1951), p. 400.

47. Dean Rusk news conference of 4 May 1961, in *Department of State Bulletin*, 44 (22 May 1961): 763; Lyndon Johnson speech of 20 April 1964, in *Public Papers of the Presidents of the United States: Lyndon B. Johnson, 1963–1964*, 1:494.

48. U.S. Department of State, *Foreign Relations of the United States, 1946*, 6:698, 699, 701, 706–08.

49. "X" [George Kennan], "The Sources of Soviet Conduct," *Foreign Affairs*, 25 (July 1947): 576.

50. *Ibid.*, 580–82.

51. U.S. Department of State, *Foreign Relations of the United States, 1945*, 5:232, 253.

52. Marshall quoted in Lawrence S. Wittner, *American Intervention in Greece, 1943–1949* (New York, 1983), pp. 46–47; McGrath quoted in Athan Theoharis, "The Politics of Scholarship: Liberalism, Anti-Communism, and McCarthyism," in Robert Griffiths and Theoharis, eds., *The Spector: Original Essays on the Cold War and the Origins of McCarthyism* (New York, 1974), p. 279.

53. Dean Acheson, *Present at the Creation: My Years in the State Department* (New York, 1969), p. 490.

54. Robert H. Ferrell, ed., *The Autobiography of Harry S. Truman* (Boulder, Colo., 1980), p. 41; Ferrell, ed., *Off the Record: The Private Papers of Harry S. Truman* (New York, 1980), p. 98; Ferrell, ed., *Dear Bess: The Letters from Harry to Bess Truman, 1910–1959* (New York, 1983), pp. 419, 474; Wilson D. Miscamble, "The Evolution of an Internationalist: Harry S. Truman and American Foreign Policy," *Australian Journal of Politics and History*, 23 (Aug. 1977), 270, 271. For Truman commentary on Wilson that appeared between 1952 and 1962, see Ferrell, *Off the Record*, pp. 238, 307, 387, 388, 404, and Harry S. Truman, *Mr. Citizen* (New York, 1960), pp. 217–18.

55. Ferrell, *Dear Bess*, p. 471; Truman quoted in *New York Times*, 24 June 1941, p. 7; Ferrell, *Off the Record*, pp. 44, 56–57; Monte M. Poen, ed., *Strictly Personal and Confidential: The Letters Harry Truman Never Mailed* (Boston, 1982), pp. 40, 41; Margaret Truman, *Harry S. Truman* (New York, 1973), pp. 323, 360.

56. Poen, *Strictly Personal*, p. 145; Ferrell, *Off the Record*, pp. 101–02, 118, 218–19; Millis, *Forrestal Diaries*, p. 281; J. Garry Clifford, "President Truman and Peter the Great's Will," *Diplomatic History*, 4 (Fall 1980).

57. Ferrell, *Dear Bess*, p. 551; Ferrell, *Off the Record*, pp. 99, 101–02.

58. Joseph M. Jones, *The Fifteen Weeks* (New York, 1955), pp. 141, 167, 247–48, 269–86; Acheson, *Present at the Creation*, p. 293.

59. *Public Papers of the Presidents of the United States: Harry S. Truman, 1947*, pp. 178, 180 (Truman doctrine speech of 12 March 1947).

60. NSC 20/4 of 23 Nov. 1948, in U.S. Department of State, *Foreign Relations of the United States, 1948*, 1:667; NSC 68 of 7 April 1950, in *ibid., 1950*, 1:237, 239, 242, 244. Truman at once accepted the fervent policy premises articulated by his aides in NSC 68; the outbreak of the Korean War a few months later enabled him to put their spending recommendations into effect.

61. Quotes in this and the next paragraph come from *Public Papers of the Presidents of the United States: Harry S. Truman, 1947*, p. 180; Ferrell, *The Autobiography of Harry S.*

Truman, p. 102; W. W. Rostow speech (Spring 1961), in T. N. Greene, ed., *The Guerilla—and How to Fight Him* (New York, 1962), pp. 55, 56.

62. Robert J. McMahon, *Colonialism and Cold War: The United States and the Struggle for Indonesian Independence, 1945–49* (Ithaca, N.Y., 1981), p. 61 (FDR); Christopher Thorne, *Allies of a Kind: The United States, Britain, and the War Against Japan, 1941–1945* (New York, 1978), p. 594 (FDR); Wm. Roger Louis, *Imperialism at Bay: The United States and the Decolonization of the British Empire, 1941–1945* (New York, 1978), p. 170 (Welles).

63. John Lewis Gaddis, *Strategies of Containment* (New York, 1982), pp. 36, 43, 47n; David McLean, "American Nationalism, the China Myth, and the Truman Doctrine: The Question of Accommodation with Peking, 1949–50," *Diplomatic History*, 10 (Winter 1986): 41; U.S. Department of State, *Foreign Relations of the United States, 1950*, 2:600–02, 618, 7:1385; George F. Kennan, *Memoirs* (Boston, 1967, 1972), 1:184.

64. Ferrell, *Dear Bess*, pp. 34, 39, 52, 158, 242, 254, 293, 298, 341, 366, 416, 417, 464, 471, 520, 527, 565; Ferrell, *Off the Record*, pp. 45, 55, 140, 165.

65. Warren I. Cohen, *Dean Rusk* (Totowa, N.J., 1980), p. 83; LaFeber, *Inevitable Revolutions*, p. 14; Blanche Wiesen Cook, *The Declassified Eisenhower: A Divided Legacy* (Garden City, N.Y., 1981), p. 366n; Robert H. Ferrell, ed., *The Diary of James C. Hagerty: Eisenhower in Mid-Course, 1954–1955* (Bloomington, Ind., 1983), pp. 35, 210; Ferrell, ed., *The Eisenhower Diaries* (New York, 1981), pp. 232, 296; Donald Neff, *Warriors at Suez: Eisenhower Takes America into the Middle East* (New York, 1981), p. 387.

66. Ferrell, *The Eisenhower Diaries*, p. 223; Neff, *Warriors at Suez*, pp. 293, 301; John Foster Dulles, *War or Peace* (New York, 1950), pp. 74–75, 87.

67. Thomas J. Noer, "Truman, Eisenhower, and South Africa: The 'Middle Road' and Apartheid," *Journal of Ethnic Studies*, 11 (Spring 1983): 85, 99.

68. *Ibid.*, 83, 96; Cook, *The Declassified Eisenhower*, p. 173; Richard D. Mahoney, *JFK: Ordeal in Africa* (New York, 1983), p. 242.

69. Melvin Gurtov, *The United States Against the Third World: Antinationalism and Intervention* (New York, 1974), pp. 44, 51; Mahoney, *JFK*, pp. 51, 109, 118, 143.

70. Richard H. Immerman, *The CIA in Guatemala: The Foreign Policy of Intervention* (Austin, Tex., 1982), p. 11; Gurtov, *The United States Against the Third World*, p. 89.

71. Baily, *The United States and the Development of South America*, pp. 58, 118–19, 215–16; LaFeber, *Inevitable Revolutions*, p. 137; Immerman, *The CIA in Guatemala*, p. 132; Richard E. Welch, Jr., *Response to Revolution: The United States and the Cuban Revolution, 1959–1961* (Chapel Hill, N.C., 1985), p. 35.

72. Ferrell, *The Diary of James C. Hagerty*, p. 48; *Public Papers of the Presidents of the United States: John F. Kennedy, 1963*, p. 876 (18 Nov. 1963); *ibid.: Lyndon B. Johnson, 1965*, 1:471 (2 May 1965).

73. Ferrell, *Off the Record*, p. 80; NSC 48/2 of 30 Dec. 1949, in U.S. Department of State, *Foreign Relations of the United States, 1949*, 7:1215; NSC 48/4 of 4 May 1951, in *ibid., 1951*, 6:34–35; Dean Acheson, National Press Club speech of 12 Jan. 1950, in *Department of State Bulletin*, 22 (23 Jan. 1950): 114.

74. Acheson, *Present at the Creation*, p. 603.

75. Ferrell, *Off the Record*, pp. 217–18; Dulles speech of 28 June 1957, in *Department of State Bulletin*, 37 (15 July 1957): 94.

76. *The Pentagon Papers: The Defense Department History of United States Decisionmaking on Vietnam*, Senator Gravel ed. (Boston, 1971–72), 1:594.

77. *Ibid.*, 1:362, 597, 606.

78. John F. Kennedy, *The Strategy of Peace* (New York, 1960), p. 64; *Public Papers of the Presidents of the United States: John F. Kennedy, 1961*, p. 306.

79. Lyndon Johnson, Johns Hopkins speech of 7 April 1965, in *Public Papers of the Presidents of the United States: Lyndon B. Johnson, 1965*, 1:394.

80. Kennedy, *The Strategy of Peace*, p. 8; Dean Acheson letter of 30 July 1949, in U.S. Department of State, *United States Relations with China with Special Reference to the Period 1944–1949* (Washington, 1949), p. xvi; Dulles quoted in Ronald W. Pruessen, *John Foster Dulles: The Road to Power* (New York, 1982), p. 292; John Foster Dulles, "A Policy of Boldness," *Life*, 32 (19 May 1952): 148.

Chapter 6: The Contemporary Dilemma

Epigraph. Karl Marx, "The Eighteenth Brumaire of Louis Bonaparte," in Lewis S. Feuer, ed., *Marx and Engels: Basic Writings on Politics and Philosophy* (Garden City, N.Y., 1959), p. 320; and Clifford Geertz, "Ideology as a Cultural System," in David E. Apter, ed., *Ideology and Discontent* (London, 1964), p. 72.

1. Robert W. Stevens, *Vain Hopes, Grim Realities: The Economic Consequences of the Vietnam War* (New York, 1976), preface and chapter 14, sets outlays directly related to the war between 1950 and 1974 in the $128–172 billion range and estimates veterans' benefits of about $233 billion.

2. Walter Lippmann, *The Cold War: A Study in U.S. Foreign Policy* (New York, 1972), p. 50.

3. Gallup polls asking for approval ratings of various countries, attitudes toward marriage between whites and nonwhites, and even the nationality of the most beautiful women provide evidence for the hardihood of the old racial hierarchy from the late 1930s down to the beginning of the 1980s. See George H. Gallup, *The Gallup Poll: Public Opinion, 1935–1971* (New York, 1972), 1:54, 126, 167, 2:1464–65, 3:2168, 2304; Gallup, *The Gallup Poll: Public Opinion, 1972–1977* (Wilmington, Del., 1978), 1:39–40, 128–29; Gallup, *The Gallup Poll: Public Opinion, 1978* (Wilmington, Del., 1979), p. 218; Gallup, *The Gallup Poll: Public Opinion, 1980* (Wilmington, Del., 1981), pp. 47–49.

4. Paul L. Ford, ed., *The Writings of Thomas Jefferson* (New York, 1892–99), 10:175 (letter of 26 Dec. 1820). While this study was in progress, defense spending grew to $228 billion (27.1 percent of the fiscal 1984 federal budget) and interest on the national debt to $111 billion (13.2 percent). At the same time, means-tested programs targeted primarily at the 35 million Americans below the poverty line took successive cuts that brought assistance down to $62 billion (7.4 percent of the 1984 budget). These cuts occurred even as the poor increased from 11.7 percent of the population in 1979 to 15.2 percent in 1984. *Christian Science Monitor*, 23 January 1985, pp. 3, 5.

5. The phrase is Arthur M. Schlesinger, Jr.'s. His *The Imperial Presidency* (Boston, 1973), especially chaps. 3–8, traces the drift away from the constitutional scheme of checks and balances.

6. A recent report by the Council of Economic Priorities, reflecting the views of the critics of current arms programs, examined the economic performance of thirteen industrial countries over the last two decades. The report concluded that military spending acted as a drag on gross domestic product growth, capital formation essential to investment, and productivity increases. Of the thirteen countries studied, the United States (which spent the highest percentage of gross domestic product on defense) ranked at or near the bottom in all three performance categories. This starving of productive investments and innovative enterprise has in turn had harmful consequences for the competitiveness of American products on the world market. *Christian Science Monitor*, 5 March 1982, p. 4. See also *ibid.*, 11 Sept. 1984, p. 3; Lloyd J. Dumas, "Military Spending and Economic Decay," in Dumas, ed., *The Political Economy of Arms Reduction* (Boulder, Colo., 1982); and Zvi Griliches, "Returns to Research and Development Expenditures in the Private Sector," in John W. Kendrick and Beatrice N. Vaccara, eds., *New Developments in Productivity*

Measurement and Analysis (Chicago, 1980), pp. 445–46, and comment by Edwin Mansfield, p. 456.

7. This relative decline was to a degree inevitable as the other major industrial states rebuilt their economies after World War II and regained their competitive position in international markets. But the decline has continued. It is reflected in a chronic international trade deficit, evident since 1972 and especially serious since 1977. The deficit, which stood at $25.5 billion in 1980, grew by 1985 to $148.5 billion. U.S. Department of Commerce, Bureau of the Census, *Statistical Abstract of the United States, 1985* (Washington, 1984), pp. 801–02; *Christian Science Monitor*, 31 Jan. 1986, p. 6.

8. NSC 162/2 of 30 Oct. 1953, in *The Pentagon Papers: The Defense Department History of United States Decisionmaking on Vietnam*, Senator Gravel ed. (Boston, 1971–72), 1:412–29; Eisenhower's "Farewell Address" of 17 Jan. 1961, in *Public Papers of the Presidents of the United States: Dwight D. Eisenhower, 1960–61*, pp. 1038–39.

9. The Truman administration's 1950 decision increased defense spending from 5 percent of gross national product to 13.5 percent. Eisenhower brought that figure down to the 9 percent range and held it there. Samuel P. Huntington, *The Common Defense: Strategic Programs in National Politics* (New York, 1961), pp. 282–83.

10. Doris Kearns, *Lyndon Johnson and the American Dream* (New York, 1976), p. 251.

11. David W. Moore, "The Public Is Uncertain," *Foreign Policy*, no. 35 (Summer 1979), pp. 70–71.

12. Dean Acheson quoted in Walter LaFeber, "American Policy-makers, Public Opinion, and the Outbreak of the Cold War, 1945–50," in Yōnosuke Nagai and Akira Iriye, eds., *The Origins of the Cold War in Asia* (New York, 1977), p. 60.

13. William Watts and Lloyd A. Free, "Nationalism, Not Isolationism," *Foreign Policy*, no. 24 (Fall 1976), pp. 16–24; John E. Reilly, "The American Mood: A Foreign Policy of Self-Interest," *ibid.*, no. 34 (Spring 1979), p. 76.

14. Walter Lippmann, *U.S. Foreign Policy: Shield of the Republic* (Boston, 1943), p. 86.

15. Henry Kissinger, *The White House Years* (Boston, 1979), pp. 54–70, 229, 677, 1014, 1063–64. The odd mix of European realpolitik and American missionary faith that characterized Kissinger's foreign policy views owes much to his deeply unsettling experience as a man between two cultures. Antisemitism had shattered the security of his childhood world and driven him with his family from Germany. The mature Kissinger's admiration for Metternich and Bismarck was an expression of his abiding preoccupation with the fragility of the political order and the wish to master the subterranean forces of chaos and the irrational that had earlier afflicted him. At the same time Kissinger's need for acceptance in and identification with his adopted country led him to embrace the dominant foreign-policy ideology.

16. Nixon speech of 30 April 1970, in *Public Papers of the Presidents of the United States: Richard Nixon, 1970*, p. 409; Kissinger speech of 22 July 1976, in *Department of State Bulletin*, 75 (Aug. 1976): 217.

17. Richard D. Mahoney, *JFK: Ordeal in Africa* (New York, 1983), pp. 237–38; Mohamed A. El-Khawas and Barry Cohen, *The Kissinger Study on Southern Africa* (Nottingham, U.K., 1975), pp. 60, 94.

18. Richard Nixon, *The Memoirs of Richard Nixon* (New York, 1978), pp. 733, 736; Walter LaFeber, *Inevitable Revolutions: The United States in Central America* (New York, 1983), p. 197; Roger Morris, *Uncertain Greatness: Henry Kissinger and American Foreign Policy* (New York, 1977), pp. 240–41.

19. Kissinger interview by Pierre Salinger, 12 April 1975, in *Department of State Bulletin*, 72 (12 May 1975): 609.

20. Jimmy Carter, inaugural address and speech at Notre Dame University, 20 Jan. and 22

May 1977, in *Public Papers of the Presidents of the United States: Jimmy Carter, 1977*, pp. 2, 957, 958, 962.

21. Jimmy Carter, *Keeping Faith: Memoirs of a President* (New York, 1982), pp. 48 and 207 (on China), 234 and 256 (on revolution), 4, 9, 440, 443, 445, 453, 458, and 459 (on Iran).

22. Zbigniew Brzezinski, *Power and Principle: Memoirs of the National Security Adviser, 1977–1981* (New York, 1983), p. 436.

23. Nikki R. Keddie, "Iranian Revolutions in Comparative Perspective," *American Historical Review*, 88 (June 1983), and Barry Rubin, *Paved with Good Intentions: The American Experience and Iran* (New York, 1980), identify some of the long-simmering discontents that brought the Shah down and eluded the intellectual grasp of culture-bound American policymakers.

24. Ronald Reagan, *A Time for Choosing: The Speeches of Ronald Reagan, 1961–1982* (Chicago, 1983), pp. 38 (30 March 1961), 56, 57 (27 Oct. 1964), 148 (7 Dec. 1973), 233–34 (17 July 1980); Reagan speech of 8 March 1983, in *New York Times*, 9 March 1983, p. A18; Reagan speech of 27 May 1981, in *Public Papers of the Presidents of the United States: Ronald Reagan, 1981*, p. 464; Reagan address to Congress of 27 April 1983, in *Department of State Bulletin*, 83 (June 1983): 4; Ronald Reagan, *Ronald Reagan Talks to America* (Old Greenwich, Conn., 1983), p. 123 (speech of 11 Nov. 1968). Reagan aides have echoed these views. Secretary of State Alexander Haig proclaimed that the United States carried a "historic role in defense of freedom, wherever it may be," while at the same time serving as a model on "how to combine freedom and development, political stability and economic progress." Haig's successor, George Shultz, declared no less grandly that "the yearning for freedom is the most powerful political force all across the planet" and sets the Soviets "swimming against the tide of history." Haig speech of 24 April 1981, in *New York Times*, 25 April 1981, p. 4; Shultz speech of 23 Sept. 1985, reported in *Christian Science Monitor*, 24 Sept. 1985, pp. 3, 5.

25. Robert Dallek, *Ronald Reagan: The Politics of Symbolism* (Cambridge, Mass., 1984), p. 58; Reagan interviews in *Time*, 117 (5 Jan. 1981): 32, and in Charles D. Hobbs, *Ronald Reagan's Call to Action* (Nashville, Tenn., 1976), p. 42.

26. Reagan, *A Time for Choosing*, p. 335 (speech of 8 June 1982).

27. Norman Podhoretz, *The Present Danger* (New York, 1980), p. 22; Atlantic Council, *The Teaching of Values and the Successor Generation* (Washington, 1983), pp. 14, 18, 23.

28. *Christian Science Monitor*, 9 June 1981, p. 3, and 19 January 1982, p. 4; Bruce Russett and Donald R. Deluca, " 'Don't Tread on Me': Public Opinion and Foreign Policy in the Eighties," *Political Science Quarterly*, 96 (Fall 1981).

29. Carter quoted in Brzezinski, *Power and Principle*, p. 522.

30. The observations in this paragraph are intended as an invitation to consider foreign-policy ideology in comparative terms. Good jumping-off points are A. P. Thornton, *The Imperial Idea and Its Enemies: A Study in British Power* (London, 1959); Eberhard Jäckel, *Hitler's Weltanschauung: A Blueprint for Power*, trans. Herbert Arnold (Middletown, Conn., 1972); George L. Mosse, *The Crisis of German Ideology: Intellectual Origins of the Third Reich* (New York, 1964); and William Taubman, *Stalin's American Policy: From Entente to Détente to Cold War* (New York, 1982).

31. Charles Francis Adams, ed., *The Works of John Adams* (Boston, 1850–56), 10:417–18. Anthony D. Smith, *Theories of Nationalism*, 2d ed. (London, 1983), pp. xxv–xxviii, makes the case—contrary to my own position here and that of Ernest Lee Tuveson, *Redeemer Nation: The Idea of America's Millennial Role* (Chicago, 1968), and of Sacvan Bercovitch, *The American Jeremiad* (Madison, Wis., 1978)—that nationalism and millennialism can be related only incidentally.

32. Thorstein Veblen, *Absentee Ownership and Business Enterprise in Recent Times* (New York, 1923), pp. 38–39. Elie Kedourie, *Nationalism* (London, 1960), provides a powerful elaboration of Veblen's indictment.

33. Serious and systematic academic study of foreign cultures developed haltingly in the United States in the 1920s and 1930s and more vigorously since the 1950s, but specialists have, so Robert A. McCaughey contends in his critical *International Studies and Academic Enterprise: A Chapter in the Enclosure of American Learning* (New York, 1984), failed to reach the broader public.

34. John Quincy Adams, address of 4 July 1821, in Walter LaFeber, ed., *John Quincy Adams and American Continental Empire* (Chicago, 1965), pp. 44–46.

35. Joseph Shumpeter, *Imperialism and Social Classes*, trans. Heinz Norden (Cleveland, 1955), p. 51.

36. Thucydides, *The Peloponnesian War*, ii.7.63.

37. To these already apparent costs must be added another that is only potential yet chilling—nuclear war and the possible obliteration of humankind. Here is a hazard made ever greater by the proliferation of nuclear-armed states, the dizzying multiplication of warheads, and the development of ever more complex, hair-trigger systems. We may push the odds against us still higher by persisting in our ideological claims that have contributed to the international insecurity and conflict feeding the nuclear-arms race.

38. Walter Dean Burnham, *The Current Crisis in American Politics* (New York, 1982), pp. 29, 51–52, 152–59, 161n.

39. Jonathan H. Turner and Charles E. Starnes, *Inequality: Privilege and Poverty in America* (Pacific Palisades, Calif., 1976), pp. 19, 22–23, 36, 43, 51; Kenneth Prewitt and Alan Stone, *The Ruling Elites: Elite Theory, Power, and American Democracy* (New York, 1973), chap. 6. Alan S. Blinder, "The Level and Distribution of Economic Well-Being," in Martin Feldstein, ed., *The American Economy in Transition* (Chicago, 1980), pp. 415–79, and Jeffrey G. Williamson and Peter H. Lindert, *American Inequality: A Macroeconomic History* (New York, 1980), highlight some of the complexities involved in calculating, not to mention explaining or correcting, income and wealth inequalities in the United States.

40. Earl C. Ravenal has argued that retrenchment of regional commitments offers the greatest potential for savings. Europe, which will claim $129 billion in the projected 1985 defense budget, can and should do more to defend itself against conventional attack. The defense of Middle East oil, estimated by Ravenal at $47 billion, is another candidate for cuts, since those outlays exceed the possible cost if that oil, constituting less than 2.5 percent of total U.S. energy needs, were to be lost. Still further cuts might be made on the $47 billion allocated to Asia. Ravenal has estimated on the basis of the 1985 budget that $154 billion in savings could be effected chiefly through scaling back our forward defense in these areas. Ravenal, "The Case for a Withdrawal of Our Forces," *New York Times Magazine*, 6 March 1983; Ravenal, "On Scaling Down Defense Ambitions, *New York Times*, 16 Feb. 1984, p. A27.

41. Thucydides, *The Peloponnesian War*, ii.7.63.

Index

Acheson, Dean, 151, 223*n*26; on Soviet Union, 156, 158; and East Asia, 168; on public opinion, 180

Adams, Charles Francis, 33

Adams, John: and Alexander Hamilton, 23, 27; and revolution, 92–101 passim, 123, 220*n*3; on millennial role, 191

Adams, John Quincy: and Latin America, 31, 59, 101; on foreign-policy limits, 195

Addams, Jane, 39

Africa: late nineteenth-century view on, 79; in Cold War policy, 162, 164–66, 183–84

Aguinaldo, Emilio: images of, 84–85

Allende, Salvador, 184

Alliance for Progress, 166

Almond, Gabriel, 12

America First, 147, 150

American Diplomacy, 1900–1950 (Kennan): discussion of, 5–8

American Progress (painting by Gast), 57

American Revolution: as a model, 95, 96, 102, 116, 130, 186

Anglo-Saxonism, 140; in nineteenth and early twentieth centuries, 77–80, 127, 129–30, 133, 134; and World War II interventionists, 149–50; and Cold War, 162, 163, 164, 188

Angola, 184, 186

Anti-Imperialist League, 39

Antisemitism: in late nineteenth century, 79; and response to Holocaust, 145

Arabs, 177; recent view on, 163

Aron, Raymond, 214*n*12

Atlantic Charter, 147

Atlantic Council: and ideological revitalization, 188

Barnet, Richard, 2

Batista, Fulgencio, 139, 176

Beard, Charles, 214*n*21

Bell, Daniel, 214*n*12

Benton, Thomas Hart, 33

Berle, Adolf A., Jr.: on revolution, 138

Beveridge, Albert J.: and overseas expansion, 38, 40–41, 78, 81; and Wilson policy, 135

"Black legend," 101; described, 58; cartoons on, 65–66; and Kennan, 163

Blacks, view on: in eighteenth and nineteenth centuries, 46, 47, 48, 51, 81; in cartoons, 63, 68, 82–84, 86–89, 118, 141; in twentieth century, 127, 130, 163

Bolshevism, fear of: provoked by Russian Revolution, 113–16; cartoons on, 120–22; in interwar period, 134, 138–39, 148; after World War II, 155–56. *See also* Soviet Union

Borah, William E.: and interventionism, 136

Borg, Dorothy: on East Asian policy, 213*n*2

Boston Courier: on revolution in France, 104

Bourne, Randolph: and World War I, 135

Breese, Sidney, 106

Britain, 43; eighteenth-century view on, 19–20, 22–23, 25, 94; nineteenth-century view on, 78; twentieth-century view on, 133–34, 148; and foreign-policy ideology, 191. *See also* Anglo-Saxonism

Bryan, William Jennings, 39; and overseas expansion, 41; in cartoon, 83; and World War I, 134

Brzezinski, Zbigniew: as Carter adviser, 185–86

Buchanan, James: on Mexicans, 60; on Russia, 111

Bundy brothers, 151

Burke, Edmund, 130

Calhoun, John C., 33; on Mexican War, 34

Calleo, David, 2

Cambodia, 173, 186

tion in World War II, 149–50; and costs of foreign policy, 178, 179

El Salvador, 186, 187

Erikson, Eric H.: on ideology, 14

Ethiopia, 186

Ethnicity: and response to revolution, 105, 106, 123; and twentieth-century policy, 123, 136, 147–48; and origins of twentieth-century policy elite, 137

Europe: policy toward, 21–27, 28, 133–35, 138, 159; response to nineteenth-century revolutions in, 102–06. *See also specific countries*

Everett, Edward: on revolution, 102–03

"Farewell Address" (Washington), 26

Federalist party: on Jacobinism, 26, 98–99

Feinberg, Richard, 2, 3

Ford, Gerald, 184

Foreign Affairs, 154

Forrestal, James, 155; on aggression, 152

Fourteen Points, 134

France, view on: in eighteenth and nineteenth centuries, 23, 80, 98–99; revolution in, 95, 97–100, 104–05, 112, 130; illustrated, 118–19; in interwar period, 137

Franco, Francisco, 139

Franklin, Benjamin, 19; and territorial expansion, 46–47; and race, 46–48

Free Soil party, 35; and revolution, 106

Gallatin, Albert: and Mexican War, 34

Gast, John: painting by, 57

Geertz, Clifford: on ideology, 8, 12, 171

Gender as a theme in race thinking: illustrated, 49, 56–57, 66–67, 84, 142; discussed, 59–61, 62, 140

Geopolitics: described, 152–53; critique of, 176, 194

Georgia, governor of: on Indian treaties, 53

Germany: Franklin on, 46, 47–48; nineteenth- and twentieth-century view on, 78–79, 80, 133–34, 148, 156, 163; and Cold War policy, 159; foreign-policy ideology of, 191

Giddings, Joshua R., 33

Gómez, Máximo: in cartoon, 84

Good Earth, The (motion picture), 140

Gorki, Maxim: visit to New York, 112

Gramsci, Antonio, 12

"Great-cycle theory": described, 151–52; critique of, 194

Great Society, 177, 180

Greece, 139, 164; reaction to independence

struggle of, 102–03, 221*n*21; and Cold War policy, 157–58, 159

Greeley, Horace: on Mexican War, 34

Grenada, 187

Guatemala: intervention in, 167

Gurtov, Melvin, 2

Haig, Alexander: on national greatness, 229*n*24

Haiti: view on, 59, 100, 127; in cartoons, 63, 141

Hamilton, Alexander: views of, 23–24, 25–26, 98; policy of, 24–25; influence on Adams and Jefferson administrations, 27–28

Harding, Warren G., 136, 138

Harriman, Averell, 151; and Soviet Union, 155

Harrison, Benjamin, 39; on Chinese immigration, 70

Hawaii: debate over annexation of, 80–81; in cartoon, 84

Herter, Christian: on Castro, 166

Historians: treatment of U.S. policy, xiii, 4–11; as policy critics, 173

Hoar, George F., 39

Ho Chi Minh, 169

Holocaust: response to, 145, 224*n*37

Hoover, Herbert: on Russian Revolution, 138

House, Edward, 133

Houston, Sam, 29

Howells, William Dean, 39

Huerta, Victoriana, 109

Hughes, Charles Evans, 137, 223*n*36; policy of, 138

Huks, 169

Hull, Cordell: and Japan, 140, 145

Hungary: reaction to nineteenth-century revolution in, 104

Ickes, Harold L.: on Lindbergh, 150

Ideology: defined, xi; and U.S. case, xii–xiii, 125, 171–72; costs in U.S. case, 177–79, 228*n*7; in comparative perspective, 191; and policy reform, 197–98; 1950s critics of, 214*n*12

"Imperial presidency": rise of, 178, 181

India, 164

Indians (native Americans): view on, 46, 47, 53–55, 58, 127, 130–31; population decline of, 52–53; policy toward, 53–55; in illustrations, 56–57

Industrial Workers of the World, 112

Infantilization as a theme in race thinking: dis-

59, 160, 165, 167–69, 225n60; and defense spending, 180
Truman Doctrine, 157–58
Turkey, 158, 159
Twain, Mark (pseud. of William Langhorne Clemens), 39

United Mine Workers, 112

Van Buren, Martin, 33
Vance, Cyrus: as secretary of state, 185
Veblen, Thorstein: on nationalism, 192
Verba, Sidney, 12
Vietnam, 186; view on, 162, 164, 184
Vietnam War, 175; postwar reactions to, 1, 187, 188; origins of, 169–70; costs of, 173, 227n1; and foreign-policy ideology, 176–77; public support for, 181; termination of, 182, 183, 184
Villa, Pancho, 110

Walker, Robert J.: on Mexicans, 60
Washington, George, 21; and Jay treaty, 26; view of French Revolution, 98–99
Watergate, 178, 181

Webster, Daniel, 33
Welles, Sumner: on Africans, 162
West (region): view of East Asian immigrants, 70, 77
Whig party: and Mexican War, 32–33, 34, 35; and revolution, 105
Wilhelm II (German kaiser), 133
Williams, William Appleman, 173; treatment of U.S. policy, 8–11, 214n21, 215n22
Wilson, Woodrow, 126, 156, 191, 223n26; view on revolution, 108–10, 113–14, 115, 123, 129–30; view on national greatness, 128–29, 134; view on race, 130–31; policy of, 132, 133–35; compared with F. Roosevelt, 146
Wood, Leonard: in cartoon, 87
World War I, 181; and Wilson policy, 133–35; costs of, 136; political repression during, 178
World War II, 177, 178, 189; debate over intervention in, 145–50; policy during, 155

XYZ affair, 27, 99; cartoon on, 118

Yeatman, Robert J.: on history, 125
"Young America," 106
Yuan Shikai, 108